Powell's Jewish Philanthropy (NoDJ)

OP/5.98 **NDJ** (H)

Judaica & Jewish Studies 103965

JEWISH PHILANTHROPY

PATTERSON SMITH REPRINT SERIES IN
CRIMINOLOGY, LAW ENFORCEMENT, AND SOCIAL PROBLEMS

A listing of publications in the SERIES *will be found at rear of volume*

Publication No. 86: Patterson Smith Reprint Series in
Criminology, Law Enforcement, and Social Problems

JEWISH PHILANTHROPY
AN EXPOSITION OF PRINCIPLES AND METHODS OF JEWISH SOCIAL SERVICE IN THE UNITED STATES

BY

BORIS D. BOGEN

With a New Introduction by
HARRY L. LURIE
*Formerly Executive Director,
Council of Jewish Federations and Welfare Funds, Inc.*

Montclair, New Jersey
PATTERSON SMITH
1969

Copyright 1917 by The Macmillan Company
Reprinted 1969 by special arrangement with The Macmillan Company
Patterson Smith Publishing Corporation
Montclair, New Jersey

New material copyright ©1969 by
Patterson Smith Publishing Corporation

SBN 87585-086-3

Library of Congress Catalog Card Number: 69-16225

TO MAX SENIOR

INTRODUCTION
TO THE REPRINT EDITION

Students of the history of social work and practicing social workers alike will find this comprehensive report on Jewish charities at the beginning of the twentieth century valuable as a record of the past and as illumination for the welfare theories and practices of today. (They will also discover how persistent have been the negative attitudes toward the poor and how prevalent the unfilled hopes of concerned individuals for the abolition of poverty.) Indeed, the pathfinding efforts described in this book are the base against which we must measure our current welfare programs.

The beginning of this century was a period of optimism. America was a land of opportunity and "Americanization" of the immigrants would soon enable them to participate in the growing prosperity. All problems, or nearly all problems, would be solved if welfare efforts could be increased and directed in accordance with "scientific principles." Aided by advances in medical science and the cooperation of the well-to-do, goodwill and day-by-day effort would remove all obstacles. Drastic reform was unnecessary. Such was the mood of the times before the great Depression and the dislocations of two World Wars cast doubts on a future utopia.

Since that naive period there have been changes both in welfare procedures and in the composition of the population groups being served. Responsibility for relief of the poor has been shifted (as Bogen advocated) from the shoulders of voluntary agencies to local, state, and federal governments (although dissatisfaction with these programs on the part of the givers as well as the recipients has not diminished). Also, public assistance provisions have been supplemented by the Social Security programs, undoubtedly the outstanding advance in this field. Many of the Jewish immigrants originally received relief from Jewish charities. However, their native-born descendants, benefiting from high upward economic and social mobility, no longer require assistance. Their places on the relief rolls — now principally sustained by public funds — have been taken by Negroes from the South and Puerto Ricans.

In 1917 relief administrators were beset by fears on the one hand that "excessive" (i.e., adequate) relief would demoralize the poor and spread "pauperism" and on the other that inadequate assistance (called "inefficient relief" by Bogen) would "spell suffering, degradation and further wreckage of humanity." The fear of reasonably adequate relief persists today in the minds of many people, including some in Congress and the state legislature. Fears about the effects of *inadequacy* seem less prevalent, however: disclosures of the existence of malnutrition, starvation, and high infant mortality among the poor are either rejected out of hand or quickly forgotten, and announced goals of abolishing poverty receive half-hearted acquiescence, half measures, and inadequate funds.

The desire on the part of today's established middle class to remove or improve what is now called the "culture of poverty" bears a strong resemblance to the "educational" and "Americanization" programs with which Bogen was concerned. Feelings of moral superiority toward the poor are no less prevalent now than before. The early settlement houses and to a somewhat lesser extent the Charity Organization Societies wanted to impose their own cultural pattern on immigrants they considered alien and uncouth. The presence of these immigrants (mostly from eastern Europe) as members of their own ethnic group was felt to lower the hard-won status of the earlier Jewish immigrants (mostly from central Europe). We hear today similar depreciating judgments about the low culture of our newer urban migrants, judgments reflected in policies of avoidance and de facto segregation. In time the settlement houses became more tolerant of the ways of the immigrants and in fact appreciative of the valuable culture that many brought with them. Settlement workers also came to realize how some of their former attitudes had helped widen the gap between successive generations of immigrant families.

At the turn of the century, condescending attitudes and superiority feelings on the part of the givers of service aroused wide resentment and led to immigrant self-organization. Where acceptance and appreciation of the immigrant culture appeared, improved relations and accommodation of the new with the old ideas followed. But there were underlying difficulties: the newcomers were proletarians — some were radicals or socialists — and the financial supporters of the settlements were employers whose politics and philosophy were conservative. In some settlements administrative changes were made to resist the new ideas, and restrictions were placed on lecture and discussion programs. Writing about the largest of the East Side settlements (where he himself had learned English

INTRODUCTION

as an immigrant), Bogen says that in 1908 it "had lost its direct contact with the great issues affecting the East Side, and since then did not play the same role as it had in the social movements of the New York Ghetto." Over the years the Jewish settlements have been replaced by community and synagogue centers and Young Men's Hebrew Associations, which are operated by leaders from among their largely middle-class membership.

In our metropolitan centers today the rise of resentment of some blacks toward white participation in agencies devoted to Negro needs, the slogan "Black Power," and the activities of the Black Panther and other extremist movements are manifestations parallel to the Jewish immigrant reactions described in this book. Bogen had a clear insight into the political and cultural as well as the economic strivings of his generation of Jewish immigrants. Although the present problems of our urban poor are considerably complicated by racial factors, there is much to learn from the experiences of these earlier generations of disadvantaged.

The recency with which an immigrant has entered a new and strange country has been recognized as the basic reason for his generally submarginal income. Also involved, however, are the lack of jobs, seasonal unemployment, low wages, exploitation of laborers, poor housing, overcrowding, and poor health, including the prevalence of tuberculosis. Bogen is aware that the long-term effects of these conditions can outlast the immigrant's arrival, causing a breakdown of family life leading to desertion and juvenile and adult delinquency. These are recognized as problems to be faced, but attempts at their solution — then as now — left much to be desired.

A major difference between the relief practices of the voluntary agencies of that period and the public welfare programs of today lies in the greater availability of funds and broader policies of eligibility in our present public programs. The voluntary agencies with their meager resources could not, even had they wanted to, accept full responsibility for poor relief. The majority of those in need subsisted as best they could on mutual aid, the charity of friends and relatives, and on other informal sources. The result was widespread poverty and deprivation.

Striking similarities in attitudes toward the poor, however, have remained with us over the years, as the federally sponsored and subsidized Aid to Dependent Children program (ADC) illustrates. Then as now the only laudable way for a husband to leave a dependent wife and children was through death. Assistance to widows could be granted without raising moral scruples about the dangers of pauperization. Even so, some charity workers thought that it might be better for the widows to place their children in orphanages and day nurseries and remain self-supporting. Some Charity Organization Society leaders opposed public mother's aid programs on the basis of their general negative attitude toward public outdoor relief. Bogen was in favor of public relief which would enable mothers to remain at home and care for their children, and he supported the enactment of state provisions for assistance.

Illegitimacy was not a large problem among Jews and was met by placing for adoption children of unmarried parents. The desertion of children and mothers by legally married fathers, on the other hand, was a problem that continued to grow. Since the husbands often had to leave their families in Europe to try to get jobs and save the money necessary to bring over their wives and children, there were prolonged separations frequently resulting in desertion by the husbands after the families' arrival in this country. The agencies that were called upon for family assistance expressed harsh attitudes toward the offending husbands. Existing laws on desertion were neither stringent nor enforceable across state boundaries. Believing that "the main way of checking desertion, if not eradicating it entirely, is proper laws together with a strict prosecution of the deserter," the social agencies induced the states to make family desertion a felony rather than a misdemeanor, thus facilitating arrest and prosecution. The nationally circulated Yiddish newspapers printed photographs and descriptions to help in the location of the errant husbands.

Assistance to the deserted family was inadequate. Sometimes, indeed, it was entirely withheld in the hope of arousing the husband's parental feelings and stimulating his return. Frequently funds were given only when a wife was willing to obtain a warrant of arrest for the deserter. Children of deserted wives were placed in orphanages when the relief given proved inadequate or was withheld entirely.

While the needs arising from illegitimacy and desertion of fathers have today been more broadly assumed by the ADC program, similar harsh attitudes surround its administration and are reflected in the reactions of legislators and parts of the public. In some states attempts are even made to find ways of withholding assistance from children who have been deserted by their married or unmarried fathers.

Against the obvious shortcomings of the charitable work of Bogen's era which have come down to our present day, should be set the many significant contributions to theory and practice made at that time which are reflected in the desirable practices and policies of contemporary social welfare programs:

> The beginning of home care services to supplement treatment of tuberculosis in sanitaria.
>
> The development of family budgets based on standards of living and measured costs to determine the amount of assistance required.
>
> Individualization of treatment, which led to the development of social case work and family counseling.
>
> Recognition that insufficiency of income of employable individuals may be due to a variety of social as well as personal factors, such as lack of trade training, lack of available jobs, sweatshop wages, and labor exploitation; and efforts to find ways of remedying these conditions through labor legislation and special educational and industrial programs.
>
> Establishment of agencies and services for vocational training, job placement, and special workshops; and the providing of capital for small self-employment ventures.

Recognition that large-scale unemployment conditions could be met only by sizable work-relief and public-works programs.

Utilization of the federation method (established in Boston in 1895 and in Cincinnati in 1896) for central fund-raising and joint planning among the various social agencies.

Recognition of the shortcomings of well-meaning volunteer efforts to deal with complex family problems and relationships.

The beginning of placement of dependent children in family foster homes subsidized by the agencies. (The competition between the rival exponents of institutional and foster-home care was acute in the early 1900's.)

Jewish Philanthropy is based on a course of lectures that Bogen gave annually over a six-year period as an early venture in developing formal education for paid social workers. It grew out of Bogen's own experience as an immigrant from Russia and as a teacher in trade, technical, and agricultural schools. As the superintendent of the Cincinnati Federation of Jewish Charities, Bogen was responsible for the financing and the administration of the various charitable and educational programs of that community. The experience he brought to the writing of this book was supplemented by that of other pioneering executives in Jewish social services.

This formative period saw the introduction of paid social workers into a field which was growing conscious of the need to base social work on professional training. The pressure of a vastly increasing number of relief applicants had forced the volunteer workers reluctantly to turn over their tasks to paid agents. The volunteers, however, continued to direct the policies and general administration and to retain responsibility for securing funds.

The paid social workers, influenced by Jane Addams and the developing professionalization of social work in America, often found their role a precarious one, caught between the needs of the poor and neglected and the conservative attitudes of agency trustees perennially short of funds. A frequent cause for friction between the social worker and his organization, Bogen wrote, was "the difference of opinion as to methods and tendencies of the work itself. . . . Notwithstanding the growing demand for social workers, each and everyone of them is in constant fear of losing his position. . . . To lose a position is a great deal easier than to get another one."

In view of such conditions it is a tribute to these early pioneers that they advanced and maintained their social welfare objectives, which frequently ran counter to (and often were anathema to) the basic views of many important contributors and agency trustees. Today social workers are in a more sheltered situation as a result of protective unions, civil service and professional associations, and shortages of personnel. They can (and do) take forthright stands on controversial social issues.

— HARRY L. LURIE

New York
March, 1969

PREFACE

This book is an attempt to meet the demand on the part of those who are engaged or are interested in Jewish social service, for a statement of the principles evolved through the experience of the last two decades in various philanthropic efforts of the Jews of this country. It is primarily a compilation of the different ideas expressed by the leaders of the movements on various occasions, as well as a presentation of the actual practical experiences that were met in the different lines of philanthropic activity. It is intended to serve as a text-book for beginners, and as a ready résumé for those who are already engaged in the field.

No claim for scientific treatment of the subjects is made, but it is hoped that as a first attempt in this direction it may serve as an impetus toward clarifying the indefinite views in vogue at present among Jewish social workers of the country and help beginners to orient themselves in the perplexing problems of Jewish social service.

The book is practically a revision of a course of lectures on Jewish philanthropy given for the last 6 years at the Hebrew Union College of Cincinnati, Ohio. The leading Jewish social workers of the country should be given credit for their co-operation in reading the manuscript and making emendations and corrections without which this book would lose considerable part of its value. Special thanks are due, and are hereby tendered to Dr. Lee K. Frankel, Morris Waldman, Louis Levin, David Bressler, Dr. Ludwig Bernstein, Jacob Billikopf, Rabbi David Philipson, Rabbi Stephen S. Wise, Adolph S. Oko, and A. S. Freidus for suggestions and criticism, to Dr. Kaufman Kohler for aid in preparing Chapter III, and to Mr. Julius Rosenwald, through whose generosity this publication became possible. I desire to acknowledge my indebtedness to Iskander Hourwich who revised and prepared the manuscript for publication.

BORIS D. BOGEN.

CINCINNATI, *October* 1, 1916.

TABLE OF CONTENTS

INTRODUCTION

CHAPTER I

PAGE

THE EXTENT AND SCOPE OF JEWISH PHILANTHROPY.......... 1
   A. The Problem of Modern Philanthropy.................. 1
   B. Reasons for Philanthropic Agencies Specifically Jewish: Sectarianism. Promise of the Jews—Never to Become a Burden on the General Community. Immigration. The Specific Problem....................................... 1
   C. The Extent of Jewish Philanthropy.................... 7
      Questions.. 9

CHAPTER II

DEPENDENCY AMONG JEWS................................. 10
   A. Basic Principles and Specific Causes.................. 10
   B. Temporary Dependency Due to Immigration........... 10
   C. Chronic Dependency of Recent Origin: Resistance Power. Formation of Permanent Slum Conditions. The Necessity for Jewish Agencies.................................. 12
      Questions.. 15

CHAPTER III

CHARITY AMONG THE JEWS................................. 16
   A. Charity Based on Justice............................ 16
   B. Systematic Relief................................... 18
   C. Principles of Relief................................. 21
   D. Jewish Charity in the Middle Ages................... 23
   E. Charitable Societies................................. 26
      Questions.. 26

CHAPTER IV

	PAGE
NATIONAL ORGANIZATIONS.................................	27

A. The Baron De Hirsch Fund: Baron Maurice De Hirsch. The Jewish Colonization Association. Formation of the Baron De Hirsch Fund. The Agricultural and Industrial Aid Society... 27
B. The National Conference of Jewish Charities: Membership 31
C. The Independent Order of B'nai B'rith.................. 33
D. National Institutions for the Care of Consumptives...... 34
E. National Farm School................................. 35
F. The Council of Jewish Women......................... 35
G. The Hebrew Sheltering and Immigrant Aid Society of America.. 35
H. The Educational League.............................. 35
I. The National Jewish Immigration Council.............. 36
J. The National Union of Jewish Sheltering Societies....... 36
K. The American Jewish Committee...................... 36
L. The Joint Distribution Committee..................... 37
Questions.. 37

CHAPTER V

METHODS OF FUND RAISING FOR JEWISH PHILANTHROPIC AGENCIES.. 38
A. Direct Begging....................................... 38
B. The Pushka Method.................................. 39
C. Charity Taxes.. 40
D. Endowments... 41
E. Charity Socials....................................... 42
F. The Federation Idea: Federation Experiences. Advantages of Federation... 43
G. The Subscription Method............................. 49
H. Efficiency Tests for Raising Funds..................... 49
I. Methods of Getting Subscriptions: The Card Catalogue. Circulars. Personal Solicitation. Arguments. Special Help. After Numbers. Special Donations. The Spirit of Rivalry... 50

CONTENTS

	PAGE
J. State and Municipal Subventions	53
K. Outside Contributions	54
L. Collections by Mail	54
M. Publicity: Reports. Pocket Editions. The Daily Press. Moving Pictures	54
N. Emergency Funds	56
Questions	58

CHAPTER VI

TRANSIENTS	59
A. The Stranger in the Past	59
B. The Modern Conception	60
C. The Passing-On Policy	61
D. The Transportation Rules	62
E. Extension of the Transportation Rules	63
F. Special Decisions	64
G. New Transportation Rules Adopted, 1916	68
H. Violations of the Transportation Rules by Outside Agencies	70
I. Hachnosis Orchim	71
J. Professionals	73
K. Temporary Dependent Transients	75
L. Sick and Defective	77
M. The Tramp	79
Questions	82

CHAPTER VII

THE IMMIGRATION PROBLEM	83
A. Early Jewish Immigration to the United States	84
B. Beginnings of Jewish Charity in the United States	85
C. Early Immigration	87
D. Immigration of 1848	88
E. Polish Immigration	89
F. Russian Immigration	89
G. Immigration Funds	91
H. Federal Legislation	91
I. First Aid to the Immigrant	92
J. The Exodus from Russia and Roumania	93

CONTENTS

	PAGE
K. Additional Legislation	96
L. The Immigration Law of 1907	98
M. The Economic Status of the Jewish Immigrant	101
N. Protection of the Immigrant at the Port of Entry	102
O. The Anti-Restriction Movement: The Immigration Commission of 1907. The Jewish Issue Before the Commission. The Burnett-Dillingham Bill	107
P. The Galveston Movement	111
Questions	111

CHAPTER VIII

DISTRIBUTION	113
A. The Industrial Removal Office	113
B. Co-operation	114
C. Local Agencies	115
D. Classification	115
E. Methods	117
F. Reception of New-Comers	120
G. Relation to Relief Agencies	120
H. Results of the Industrial Removal Office Work	121
I. The Galveston Movement	122
Questions	123

CHAPTER IX

THE BACK TO THE SOIL MOVEMENT	125
A. Early Attempts	125
B. The Agricultural and Industrial Aid Society	127
C. The Extent of Jewish Farming	128
D. Recent Efforts	129
E. Woodbine	130
F. The Industrial Settlement	131
G. Self-Government	132
H. The Baron De Hirsch Agricultural School	133
I. The National Farm School	134
J. General Suggestions	135
Questions	137

CHAPTER X

	PAGE
RESIDENT-DEPENDENTS	138
A. The Sick	138
B. School Hygiene	143
C. Defectives	144
D. Hospitals	145
E. Tuberculosis: Home Treatment. After-Care of Consumptives. The Cincinnati Method	148
F. Insanity	155
G. Convalescents	156
H. Chronic Invalids	157
Questions	157

CHAPTER XI

DEPENDENT WOMEN AND CHILDREN	159
A. Congregate Systems	160
B. The Placing-Out System	160
C. The Cottage System	164
D. Self-Government	164
E. State Subventions	165
F. Orthodox Tendencies	165
G. Child-Caring Methods	167
H. After-Care of Orphans	169
I. Day Nurseries	169
J. Family Desertion: Family Desertion as a Problem. Causes of Desertion. Promoting Legislation. Publicity as an Aid. Study of Desertion in New York. The National Desertion Bureau. Methods of Treatment	171
Questions	179

CHAPTER XII

INSUFFICIENCY OF INCOME	181
A. Causes of Insufficiency of Income: Inefficiency of the Breadwinner. Training in Trades. Self-Respect Fund. Employment Agencies	181
B. Establishment in Business	187

CONTENTS

	PAGE
C. Self-Support Funds	190
D. Temporary Dependency	192
Questions	195

CHAPTER XIII

STANDARDS OF RELIEF 196
  A. Different Standards 199
  B. Individual Standards 202
  C. Existing Standards of Living 203
  D. Standards of Relief 208
  Questions 209

CHAPTER XIV

EDUCATIONAL AND SOCIAL ORGANIZATIONS 211
  A. The Rise of Jewish Social Organizations: Young Men's Hebrew Associations. Religious Educational Agencies. The Bureau of Education of the Jewish Community of New York City 211
  B. Sabbath Schools: Radical National Schools. Religious Instruction and Social Service Agencies. Religious Services 219
  Questions 225

CHAPTER XV

THE EDUCATION OF IMMIGRANTS 226
  A. The Palace of Immigrants 227
  B. Americanization 228
  C. Ghetto Forces 229
  D. A Change of Policy 230
  E. David Blaustein 231
  F. New Conceptions 233
  G. Opposition 234
  H. Program of the Educational Alliance 236
  I. Experiences in Other Cities 237
  J. A New Departure 238
  K. Neighborhood Self-Activity 241
  L. Technical Education 241
  Questions 243

CONTENTS

xxvii

CHAPTER XVI

PAGE

JEWISH SETTLEMENTS AND NEIGHBORHOOD WORK............ 244
 A. The Settlement as a Social Service Agency: Origin of Social Settlements. Definition. Residents in Settlements. Charity in Settlements. The Specific Problem. Difficulties in Jewish Settlements................................. 245
 B. Jewish Activities in Settlement Work: Jews of Many Lands. Children's Clubs. Jewish Games. Activities for Adolescents. Community Forces...................... 252
 C. Religion in Settlements............................. 264
 D. Neglected Neighborhoods........................... 266
 E. Jewish Neighborhoods.............................. 268
 F. The Teaching of English............................ 271
 G. Employment....................................... 273
 H. True Americanization.............................. 276
 I. Expansion of Activities............................. 278
 J. Children's Work................................... 280
 K. Specialization..................................... 282
 L. Politics in the Settlement.......................... 284
 M. Co-operation...................................... 288
 N. Difficulties of a Jewish Settlement................... 289
 O. Juvenile Delinquency.............................. 289
 P. Crime Among the Jews............................. 294
 Questions.. 294

CHAPTER XVII

ORGANIZATION AND ADMINISTRATION....................... 295
 A. Leadership.. 295
 B. The Selection of Leaders........................... 296
 C. Persistency in Office Holding....................... 298
 D. Qualifications of Leadership........................ 299
 E. The Board of Directors............................ 300
 F. Meetings.. 301
 G. The Paid Worker.................................. 302
 H. Qualifications of a Social Worker................... 304
 I. New Positions..................................... 306
 J. Difficulties of a Social Worker...................... 308

	PAGE
K. Attitude Towards the Board of Managers	310
L. The Attitude of the Social Worker to the Community	315
Questions	317

CHAPTER XVIII

VOLUNTEER SERVICE.. 318
    A. Friendly Visitors as Adjuncts of Relief Societies......... 318
    B. Modern Conceptions of Lady Visitors.................. 320
    C. The Problems of Friendly Visiting: The Health of the Poor. Infant Welfare. Protection of the Health of the Children of the Poor. Tuberculosis, the Scourge of the Poor. Indiscriminate Charity. Proper Housing. Sufficient Feeding, an Index to Normal Life. Apportionment of Work Day. Proper Clothing. The Career of the Children of the Poor. The Struggle for Existence. Recreation and Amusement.. 322
    D. Settlement Volunteer Workers........................ 331
    E. The Big Brothers and Big Sisters Movement............ 333
    F. Education of Jewish Social Workers.................... 335
    Questions.. 336

CHAPTER XIX

ADMINISTRATION.. 337
    A. Budget Making....................................... 337
    B. Analysis of Budgets.................................. 338
    C. Applications for Relief............................... 342
    D. Administration Facilities............................. 343
    E. Interviewing the Applicant: Granting Relief. Refusal to Grant Relief. Investigation........................... 344
    F. Record Keeping: The Record Book. Individual Records. Filing Records....................................... 350
    Questions.. 362

CHAPTER XX

THE FEDERATION AND THE SYNAGOGUE..................... 363
    A. Philanthropic Effort in the Synagogue.................. 363
    B. Philanthropic Effort Taken out of the Synagogue........ 364

CONTENTS

	PAGE
C. The Effort to Unite the Synagogue with Charity Endeavor	365
D. The Federation and the Synagogue	366
E. The Scope of Social Service in the Synagogue	368
F. Plan of Action	372
Questions	374
BIBLIOGRAPHY	375
INDEX	383

JEWISH PHILANTHROPY

JEWISH PHILANTHROPY

I

THE EXTENT AND SCOPE OF JEWISH PHILANTHROPY

A. THE PROBLEM OF MODERN PHILANTHROPY

Ours is the era of social service. Society is beginning to realize its responsibility for the care of those who have been cast out of the human mill. The question, now, is only as to methods,—means that are to be adopted toward the solution of this perplexing problem. The growth of social consciousness, once aroused, has been phenomenal. Private initiative has been extended, first to municipal agencies, then to state and national enterprizes, all directed toward the amelioration of the condition of the poor and the eradication of causes predisposing to poverty. *The waste of society is being reduced to a minimum.*

B. REASONS FOR PHILANTHROPIC AGENCIES SPECIFICALLY JEWISH

In the midst of these progressive tendencies on the part of society as a whole, it seems but natural that there should arise a question as to the real need for organizations specifically Jewish. It is frequently suggested that the same purposes served by Jewish organizations may be achieved through existing agencies catering to the general population. In this, as in other perplexing situations, history is helpful. Some light may be shed by the origin of the different Jewish philanthropic organizations in the United States.

1. *Sectarianism*

In years past, when Jewish communities were small and homogeneous and consisted of individuals from the Old World, steeped in an atmosphere of which Jewish charity was an integral part, it was but reasonable that these communities should embody the same spirit and organize societies to help their own. There were, naturally, few Jewish poor. But these could get no help save from their brethren, who, in their religion, considered this their duty. The first Jewish organizations in the United States of a philanthropic nature were relief societies. These were connected closely, sometimes organically, with the synagogue, and were sectarian in character. At that time, charitable endeavor, in general, followed denominational lines. Jewish charities were no exception. Moreover, the Jews provided for their own poor that the latter should not be compelled to seek assistance from sources sectarian and strange to their own beliefs. The fear of proselytism was well founded, and served as an additional impetus for philanthropic effort specifically Jewish. As early as 1832, the first Jewish orphanage was established in New York City, and the reason given for its organization was that the Jewish community felt it its duty to care for Jewish orphans, who hitherto had

had to be placed in non-Jewish, sectarian orphanages at that time the only institutions for child-caring. Later, the same underlying principles were given as the motive for the establishment of Jewish hospitals. These reasons for Jewish institutions have lost none of their potency through age, and still exist.

It has also been the position that the Jews need special institutions because they need Jewish influence, and Jewish atmosphere: The Jew must not be allowed to become de-Judaized but rather re-Judaized, for herein lies the hope and the promise of maintaining the positive characteristics of their individuality,—the guarantee of their good citizenship.[1]

Then again, the ardent adherent of orthodoxy demands not only institutions under Jewish auspices, but also institutions that observe strictly all the dietary and other laws which are not observed, as a rule, by institutions supported in large by the reformed wing. This is the great motivator of new and frequently duplicating Jewish institutions, hospitals, orphan asylums, homes for the aged, etc., that are springing up all over the country, initiated and supported by the newer settlers from Russia, Roumania, and Austria-Hungary.

2. *Promise of the Jews—Never to Become a Burden on the General Community*

As a general proposition, however, Jewish philanthropy presented a limited sphere of activity up to the

[1] Dr. David Blaustein, "Proceedings Fifth National Conference of Jewish Charities," Richmond, Va., 1908, page 126.

time of the large Jewish immigration from Russia in the latter part of the eighties. Then the demand for Jewish philanthropic activity suddenly developed enormously. It was unreasonable to expect the then existing philanthropic agencies, though quite advanced and free from sectarianism, to care for this new and tremendous additional burden. The Jews did not forget the promise given two and one-half centuries previously to Governor Stuyvesant ever to care for their poor in such a manner that they should never become a burden upon the community.[1] American Jews have fulfilled their pledge.

But that argument is of value no more. The Jews have become part and parcel of this country; they share its responsibilities with the rest of the citizenship and are entitled to the same privileges. The pride of the Jews that they will never become a burden on the community is to-day an empty phrase. Notwithstanding all the generous effort of private philanthropy, some of the burden of chronic dependency falls upon the state and the municipality. As a result of their participation in general welfare movements, the Jews of this country recognize to-day their right to avail themselves in common with the remainder of the American population of the general forces and agencies for the amelioration of the conditions of the poor. They are entitled, as taxpayers and American citizens, to the privileges of municipal and state institutions. As contributors and fellowmen, they need not decline to par-

[1] Judge Julian Mack, "Proceedings Fourth National Conference of Jewish Charities," Philadelphia, 1906, page 25.

ticipate as beneficiaries of the different private endeavors of a non-sectarian character,—be they relief agencies, educational movements, or social activities. They need not be separatists so far as their rights and privileges are concerned.

3. *Immigration*

The argument that Jewish philanthropy deals in the main with recently arrived immigrants is weakening. There can be little doubt that Jewish charity, dealing in the main with foreigners, aliens in speech and nationality, calls for special agencies to deal with this peculiarity. The country at large, however, is rapidly awakening to the importance of this problem. It is a matter of but a short time when ample facilities will be provided by non-sectarian agencies for handling this situation in its ramifications, thus obviating the necessity of providing private institutions to meet the specific demands of the immigrant Jew, as far as speech and other obvious peculiarities are concerned.[1]

In this respect Jewish philanthropy paved the way for reform, and served as a model in the method of immigrant care, education and Americanization, a problem which is not alone Jewish in character.

4. *The Specific Problem*

Thus, through the experience of a short time, different causes and reasons have been assigned in ex-

[1] Professor J. H. Hollander, President's Address, "Proceedings National Conference of Jewish Charities," St. Louis, 1910.

planation of the existence of Jewish philanthropy. The apologetic attitude is rather typical. The tie that connects the Jews is not due to a formula of practical reasoning. It lies deep in the emotional nature of humanity which is responsible for the intense feeling for kith and kin.

There is no need for analyzing the external motives of Jewish philanthropy, nor is there any reason for apologizing for the brotherly attitude toward the needy. Jewish philanthropy, as such, is growing and extending in every direction. The old agencies enlarge and intensify their activities, and are constantly supplemented by new organizations and institutions called into existence throughout the country. This phenomenal growth of Jewish philanthropy indicates the demand along these lines, and points to valid reasons why Jewish activities should be directed through specifically Jewish agencies. The problem of Jewish dependency is unique. Jewish poverty does not carry with it the burden of heredity, and is not characterized by a downward tendency, repellent of reclaiming influences. Though poor and economically disabled, the Jews never before constituted the lowest strata of society, nor were they the inhabitants of the slum districts of their native cities. Their difficulties were due to external conditions, which did not, however, succeed in crushing the spirit of mental and moral integrity dominant throughout the ages. Nay, possibly the very disadvantages of the Jews in fighting for the rights of existence were responsible for the strengthening of their inner powers that express themselves in the indomitable aspiration for higher ideals of achievement. If this assumption be correct, it follows that philanthropic effort among the Jews is capable of better results than are to be looked for in the general field of charitable endeavor. Neglect in this respect cannot fail to create a new strata among the Jews, unreclaimable, and presenting a permanent waste to society. The responsibility for such a situation would rest directly on American Jewry. In other words, we are dealing with the prevention of the slum, rather than with the reclamation of a slum inherited from former generations. The problem is both manifold and difficult. Spasmodic effort and the mere treatment of symptoms by establishing relief agencies, institutions, and so forth, cannot be considered a wise method. Jews are entitled to have their own organizations to meet situations which would otherwise escape proper consideration—provided that such institutions cover a field untouched by general organizations. The right is also conceded to the Jews to separate agencies if these agencies cover the field more efficiently.

C. The Extent of Jewish Philanthropy

The extent and scope of Jewish philanthropy is rapidly growing, and is assuming quite important dimensions. An investigation made in 1909, of this particular phase of the subject, shows that there were then 1,191 separate and distinct Jewish organizations,— not including mutual benefit societies, cemeteries, burial societies, trade unions, Zionists, Territorialists, and other organizations doing work of an international character. The character of the 1,191 organizations was as follows:

National organizations	7
Relief societies, including federated charities, relief societies, proper sewing societies, etc.	809
Institutions, including hospitals, dispensaries, orphan asylums, convalescent homes, sanitaria, nurseries, etc.	148
Educational institutions, including institutes, settlements, trade schools, etc.	227
Grand total	1,191

Reports of annual disbursements were received from only four hundred and eighty-nine organizations, These show total expenditures in round numbers, of approximately four million, seven hundred and seventy-nine thousand dollars ($4,779,000). The membership of four hundred and sixty-two organizations, was three hundred and thirty-two thousand dollars ($332,000).[1] Without going into further detail, it is patent that the amount of money spent by the Jews in the United States for philanthropic purposes and the number of persons interested in the field of endeavor, as indicated by the total membership of the different organizations, are sufficient to demand serious consideration. The figures cited refer to about one-half the organizations, and since this investigation, there has been both an intensive and an extensive expansion of Jewish organizations. The American Jewish Year Book registers for the period 1909–1915, eight hundred and nine addi-

[1] "Extent of Jewish Philanthropy in the United States." Monograph, Boris D. Bogen, 1909.

tional philanthropic agencies, making a grand total of about two thousand.

A conservative estimate, therefore, of the total amount spent by Jewish philanthropic agencies in the United States would be ten million dollars ($10,000,000). Estimating the Jewish population in the United States at about two million, and presuming that two per cent are dependent, we get forty thousand Jewish dependents in this country, whose maintenance would cost, at two hundred dollars per capita per annum, about eight million dollars. In the experience of philanthropic effort it requires at least one paid worker for the distribution of each thousand dollars, or eight thousand workers to administer to the dependent Jews. Of each four employés, one should be necessarily a professional, hence the number of persons requiring professional proficiency in dealing with the problem of Jewish dependency can be conservatively estimated as two thousand.

CHAPTER ONE. THE EXTENT AND SCOPE OF JEWISH PHILANTHROPY

QUESTIONS

1. What is the problem of modern Philanthropy?
2. What are the reasons given for philanthropic agencies specifically Jewish?
3. What is the specific problem of Jewish philanthropy?
4. Under what conditions are philanthropic efforts specifically Jewish legitimate?
5. What is the estimated number of Jewish philanthropic organizations in the United States?
6. What is estimated to be their total budget?

II
DEPENDENCY AMONG JEWS

A. Basic Principles and Specific Causes

The tendency of modern philanthropy is toward the elimination of the causes predisposing to dependency, rather than toward palliative measures affecting the symptoms of distress alone. There can be little doubt that the broad basic principles underlying the phenomena of poverty and misery in general are applicable to dependency among Jews. Economic maladjustment, ignorance, political disability and exploitation of labor produce inevitable results, irrespective of race, creed, or color. At the same time, there are, in the case of dependency among the Jews, special causes,—in addition to the basic reasons,—specific reasons deserving serious consideration, which may, perchance, suggest different treatment and unique measures.

B. Temporary Dependency Due to Immigration

The awakening of philanthropy on a large scale, among Jews in the United States as has been shown, dates from the mass immigration,—almost an exodus,—from Russia in the eighties. In those days the underlying cause of dependency,—the reason for philanthropic effort among the Jews,—was immigration. The immigrant was the problem, and the measures applied were mainly such that might Americanize the newcomer and help him to withstand the hardships of the period of adjustment and adaptation. The large majority of the immigrant Jews coming to this country were not dependent upon charity in their native land. The existent poverty among the Jews in Russia could be easily explained by the political and economic restrictions under which they lived. Even in the case of the dependent, the Jews did not represent the lowest strata in Russia. (Poor as the Jews are there, there is little pauperism among them. More important, throughout these centuries they have succeeded in maintaining their family ties, the sanctity of their homes.) It seemed reasonable to presume that in this country of equal and untold opportunities, equal political, economic, and social rights, the Jewish immigrants, as soon as they had adjusted themselves to their new environment, would gain their independence and would present no problem as far as charitable effort is concerned. Jewish philanthropy, during this period, limited itself to giving "first aid to the immigrant."

Conditions, however, have changed. The reports of various charitable organizations show that the number of people applying for relief who have been in this country less than three months is negligible.[1] It seems that it takes from two to five years before the strength of the immigrant peters out, when he and his family become dependent upon charity. Thus, the problem of

[1] "Report of the United Hebrew Charities," New York, 1912; "Report of the United Hebrew Charities," Chicago, 1914.

aiding the immigrant is fast losing its commanding position. The majority of immigrants now come to join relatives or friends, and under ordinary conditions do not apply for assistance to organized charity. The difficulty comes later, when the cause of dependency is deeper rooted, and when temporary and inadequate relief does not offer a solution. Thus, in this particular instance, we deal with a dependency of a comparatively recent origin,—a dependency caused by conditions under which the immigrant Jew lives for the first few years in his adopted country.

C. Chronic Dependency of Recent Origin

1. *Resistance Power*

While in many instances the inherent physical disabilities of the Jews may be responsible for their breakdown, there is, on the other hand, considerable resistance which is not met with in the non-Jewish population. Thus, there is practically speaking no intemperance, no shiftlessness; on the contrary, there exists an unconquerable ambition, an untiring energy, and an entire absence of that indifference to one's condition which Karl Marx has so aptly styled "Verdamte Bedürfnislosigkeit." This is true with respect to the recently arrived, but unfortunately not altogether correct as concerns those who have been in this country for a certain length of time, nor is it true with respect to the second generation. One need not be a close observer of society to notice that the main strength of the Jewish immigrant lies in his home. And so long as home ties are retained, so long as the family is the unit and the center of care and consideration, just so long will the centrifugal forces of modern society, which destroy the individual and produce the terrible effects of poverty, meet with a resistance that in most cases results in immunity from degeneration. This explains why in the majority of cases the immigrant Jew outlives his experience of readjustment, and escapes the permanent effects of his first struggle for existence. He soon moves from the so-called neglected neighborhood, and joins the normal groups found in American society.

2. *Formation of Permanent Slum Conditions*

Extensive as is this immunity from deteriorating and devitalizing influences, all too many succumb and fall by the wayside. The very character and extent of this negative phenomenon of Jewish life is new and therefore doubly discouraging. We deal with the effects of a formative process, we witness the disintegration of the social group, a disintegration that has just begun. The problem is quite different from that of the general situation where individuals are burdened with hereditary traits which weaken the initiative for higher and better life and where the conditions productive of misery originated generations before.

If the Jewish Ghetto is to remain permanent; and if from a temporary abode of immigrants, with its pathos picturesque and sympathetic features is to change into a permanent breeding place for the terrible human cancer, the slum, with all its concomitant, frightful attributes,—delinquency, degeneracy, and irresponsibility,—then the blame is upon the present generation. For in that instance we permit the condition to foment without grappling with the problem in a sufficiently forceful and energetic spirit.

3. *The Necessity for Jewish Agencies*

Should this prove to be the case, it is proper to assume that besides lessening or eradicating the negative conditions in neglected neighborhoods, we must utilize, develop and strengthen those features of Jewish life which have enabled the Jew to withstand persecution and hardships within the narrow confines of the European Ghetto; and who is more qualified to undertake this work than the Jew himself? Only a Jew, who is stirred by a feeling of powerful self-consciousness can hope to cope with a problem so novel and unique. Appreciating fully the advisability and desirability of social intercourse between Jews and the general population, the question is much discussed whether, in this stage of readjustment, care should not be taken that the Jew should not fall to the level of the other inhabitants of neglected neighborhoods and thus fail of ultimate rehabilitation. Hence it is evident that the treatment of the Jewish problem of dependency presents a specific character and necessitates separate and specific measures.

"I sometimes think," said President J. H. Hollander at the Sixth National Conference of Jewish Charities in St. Louis, Mo., "that 'das jüdische Herz' is not a thing of the heart but of the head, less of a warmer pity for need than the outcome of a clearer conception of how that need had arisen. This, then, is the essential need for a distinct ministration of social relief to Jews by Jews, and the prime warrant for an independent study of the problem in all its phases by those who are immediately concerned therewith. It is only a more complete carrying out of that rational tendency that has brought us to where we are now, full determination of the causes of distress and application of the more appropriate remedies by the most efficient agents. Since it is only the Jew, who by virtue of a subtle 'Gefühl,' historic identity, race consciousness, or religious brotherhood, can become cognizant of the special circumstances which have contributed to Jewish dependency, it is therefore primarily the Jew who should assume the problem of Jewish relief and in anticipation of his responsibility, should deliberate as to his procedure." [1]

CHAPTER TWO. DEPENDENCY AMONG JEWS
QUESTIONS

1. What is the relation of Jewish dependency to the general problem of poverty with respect to basic principles?
2. To what extent is Jewish dependency caused by immigration?
3. Wherein does the resistance power of the Jews lie?
4. What are the characteristic differences between the Ghetto and the slum?
5. Wherein lies the danger of neglecting the problem of Jewish dependency?

[1] J. H. Hollander, Presidential Address, Sixth National Conference of Jewish Charities, St. Louis, Mo., 1910.

III

CHARITY AMONG THE JEWS

In our complicated social order, system, organization, and efficiency are imperative in every line of human endeavor. Philanthropic effort is no exception to this rule. A glance at the history of Jewish charity shows that, owing to the Mosaic law and its application to the social conditions prevailing in the different lands and times, the Jewish people succeeded at an early period in attaining a remarkably high degree of organization. Indeed, they are generally recognized as the forerunners of modern methods of philanthropy, especially in regard to outdoor relief, while the poor laws in the various states and communities of Christendom and Islam have been taken over directly from Jewish legislation and practice.

A. Charity Based on Justice

Charity and benevolence are, of course, general traits of humanity, responsive to the call of sympathy with the suffering and helpless. Instances of these are found among all the nations of antiquity. Egyptian tombstones extol such virtues. To alleviate the pains and miseries of human life was the great monition offered by Buddha to his million of followers, to whom belongs the credit of having been the first to erect hospitals for the sick. So have Athens and Rome given to the world illustrious examples of glorious donations of great wealth for distribution among the indigent and starving masses. But it was the Jewish law that made Charity an obligation, and the consequence was that Charity and Justice became synonymous, the term *Zedakah* came to indicate both, since Charity was based upon the principles of Justice. It enjoined the duty incumbent upon men of means to provide adequately for those in want. Whatever the origin of the practice of leaving the corners of the field, the gleanings of the harvest, and the forgotten sheaf, to the poor, the stranger, the fatherless, and the widow may have been in a more primitive life, the Mosaic legislation withholds the right of proprietorship on these from the owner of the field and assigns it to the poor, at least in a moral sense. So also in regard to the growth of the seventh year and the tithes of the produce of each third year. (Lev. xix, 9–10; xxiii, 22; Deut. xxiv, 19–21; Ex. xxiii, 11; Lev. xxv, 23; Deut. xiv, 22–29.) Besides these, there are many other provisions made for the needy. (Ex. xxii, 25–27; Deut. xv, 7–11; xvi, 11–14.) Instead of leaving it to personal and temporary impulses to come to the aid of the poor and homeless, the Jewish law made it the general rule to offer them support and shelter and assessed the rich for the benefit of the poor. So does the prophet declare it to be God's demand "to deal thy bread to the hungry and to bring the poor that are afflicted to thy house; when thou seest the naked that thou cover him, and

that thou hide not thyself from thine own flesh."
(Isai. lviii, 7.) Typifying the ideal man, Job is represented saying, "I was eyes to the blind and feet to the lame, I was a father to the poor, and the case of litigation I knew not, I searched out for them." (Job xxix, 15–16; cf. xxxi, 16–22.)

Upon the basis of the holy Scriptures, then, the Jewish sages laid down as the leading principles of charity on the part of the individual the *duty* of the more fortunate to take care of the less fortunate, and on the part of the representatives of the community the responsibility for the material and moral welfare of those dependent upon the help of others. (Sifre to Deut. xv, 7–11; xxi, 7.)

B. Systematic Relief

Organized charity was one of the principal institutions of the synagogue, at an early age. Besides religious instruction and regular forms of worship, practical benevolence constituted, according to Simon the Just, one of the Men of the Great Synagogue in the Third pre-Christian century, one of the pillars of human society. There are seven branches of charity specialized in the older Jewish sources; 1, to feed the hungry and give drink to the thirsty; 2, to clothe the naked; 3, to visit the sick; 4, to bury the dead and comfort the mourners; 5, to ransom the captives; 6, to educate the fatherless and shelter the homeless; 7, to provide poor maidens with dowries. The pious ones in each city, the class called *Hasidim* (Essenes), divided themselves into special groups for the performance of these different practices which they claimed to have come down from Abraham and Melchizedek, and which they ascribed even to God as the pattern of such acts of kindness to man. It is to these very practices that the passage in Matt. xxv, 35–39, alludes, when the Son of Man, that is, the Messiah, as the Judge of the souls, is represented as saying to the righteous on the great judgment day, "I was a hungered and ye gave me meat: I was thirsty, and ye gave me drink: I was a stranger and ye took me in: Naked and ye clothed me: I was sick and ye visited me: I was in prison, and ye came unto (ransomed) me." And when the righteous ask, "When saw we thee a hungered, and fed thee? or thirsty and gave thee drink?" and so forth, the King answers, "Verily I say unto you, Inasmuch as ye have done it unto one of the least of these my brethren, ye have done it unto me" and so forth. The whole passage seems to have been taken over from an ancient *Hasidic* or Essenic source, and has its exact parallel in the Midrash to Psalm cxviii, 19, where King David has taken the place of the Messiah. "What you do unto the poor you do unto Me" is also said by God in the Midrash (Agad Shir. ha Shir. ed. Schechter, p. 27). The Essenes had, furthermore, in every town, probably connected with the Synagogue, a treasury in the so-called "Chamber of the Reticent" to enable the poor of worthy families to obtain the means of support in secret. (Tos. Shekalim ii, 16.) Far, then, from being the originator of organized charity, as is generally claimed, the Church took the whole system of relief from the Synagogue, and particularly from the class of the pious *Hasidim* or Essenes, who made of the charity work a life practice. It is of special interest in this connection to notice that, when St. Jerome had induced Fabiola, the wealthy Roman matron, to erect the first hospital for sick persons in Rome and another for strangers in Ostia, he greatly lauded her for "having transplanted a branch of the terebinth of Abraham to the Ausonian shore," thereby admitting that she simply followed the Jewish example of having the institution of a hospice for strangers, the origin of which was ascribed to the patriarch who used the terebinth at Beersheba, or the large oak tree at Hebron (see Targ. and Midrash to Gen. xxi; Sota 10^{ab}) for the reception of passers-by.

The collection and distribution of the charity fund was given in charge of the most prominent and most trustworthy men of the community, so that it was made a rule in very ancient times that he whose fathers belonged to the administrators of charity was qualified to marry into priestly families without further enquiry as to his pure descent. (Mishnah Kid. iv, 5.) We accordingly learn from Josephus (Ant. xx, 2, 5), that when, during a great famine, Queen Helena of Adiabene bought shiploads of wheat and figs and her son Izates sent large sums of money to aid the starving, these were handed "to the foremost men of Jerusalem for distribution, among the people."

The following system of relief prevailed in Palestine during the Mishnaic times. Each community had a charity box (called Arca by the Roman church), containing the funds for the support of the indigent townsmen, who received every Friday for the fourteen meals of the week, as well as for clothing, while the transient poor received only as much as was needed for the day, and on Sabbath eve for three meals. Besides this, there was what we may call a soup kitchen, a charity bowl, which contained victuals needed for immediate relief. The charity fund was in charge of three trustees, who decided on the merits of the applicants, the former social station and the parentage being especially considered. Beggars who went from door to door received nothing, or at best a pittance. Two men of the highest respectability were sent forth to collect the funds, and were empowered to tax the individuals in the community and to seize their property until the demanded sum was forthcoming. These collections were made weekly, by the two officers who were not allowed to separate while collecting or holding the money, in order to avoid all suspicion.

C. Principles of Relief

While almsgiving had become a passion with many, especially among the class of the pious, of Essenes, who made it their practice "to sell all and give it to the poor" (Pes. 57 a; Arak: IV, 2, 4; B. B. 133 b; cf. Matthew xix, 21, and Acts iv, 34), the rabbis at the synod of Usha in the second century established a rule that "no one should give away more than one-fifth of his fortune." (Ket. 50, Tos. Arak: iv, 23.) Each person should be considered from the point of view of his former social position if he is in reduced circumstances. (Sifre to Deut. xv, 8; Ket. 67b.) All secrecy should be maintained in order not to offend the recipient of charity. (Ket l. c.) "To help the poor by lending him money or otherwise facilitating his mode of support is more meritorious than to give him alms," says the Talmud. (Shab. 63^a; cf. Lev. R. xxiv.) The leading maxim is that the poor should never be put to shame by receiving charity. (Hag. 5^a.) No city is worth living in we are told, which has not a charity box, that is, a systematic relief instituted for the poor. (Sanh. 17^b.) Indeed, we have the testimony of the emperor Julian, (Epist. xxx, 49), that there was no beggar found among the Jews of his time. It is expressly stated in the Midrash, that the non-Jewish poor of a city may, for the sake of maintaining peace and good will among the inhabitants, also receive support from the Jewish charity fund. (Tos. Gittin V, 4; Gittin 61^a.) Inasmuch as charity partook of the nature of sacrifice, for which nothing that is abominable in the eyes of God may be used, it was made the rule not to accept gifts for the charity fund from men who were supposed to live on ill gotten gains. (Tos. B. K. XI, 9.)

Summing up the Talmudic rules, Maimonides, in his code, enumerates eight different grades of donors. (Mattenoth 'Aniyyim X, 7–13.)

1. He who aids the poor to support himself by advancing him funds or by helping him to some lucrative occupation.

2. He who gives charity without knowing who is the recipient, and without the recipient knowing who is the donor.

3. He who gives in secret, casting his money into the houses of the poor, who remain ignorant as to the identity of their benefactor.

4. He who gives without knowing the recipient, whereas the recipient knows the giver.

5. He who gives before he is asked.

6. He who gives after he is asked.

7. He who gives inadequately, but with good grace.

8. He who gives with bad grace.

D. Jewish Charity in the Middle Ages

The various branches of charity mentioned in the Talmudic sources continued in practice during the middle ages under modified conditions. Especial attention was given to the raising of orphans, which is also in the Midrash extolled as the highest form of charity (Tanh. Ki Tira, 116), but it was considered rather as a privilege of the wealthy than mere charity to become foster parents for destitute orphan children. Similarly was the provision for dowries for poor girls, especially orphan girls, for a long time a matter of individual generosity.

As the number of poor travelers increased, owing to the many expulsions of the Jews, in the various lands, different methods of relief came into use. Besides the food distribution which concerned chiefly the resident poor, there were first the rich men in each town who,

following the example of Abraham and of Hana bar
Hanilai, in Babylonia (Ber 58b; cf. Testament of Job
iii, 11), extended the hospitality of their homes to the
homeless poor, called already in Mishnaic times char-
acteristically "Guests." Then arose as a general rule
in each town a Travelers' Inn, called by the Christian
people of Spain and France the Jews' Inn for the
lodging and feeding the poor and the sick by way of
revival of the ancient hospice. Finally, the increasing
needs called the different charitable societies into existence, in the course of time, which were to attend to
the various branches of relief in response to the great
demands of the community. For general relief, the
funds were raised in each congregation by the assess-
ment of its members, in accordance with their means, by
officials appointed as charity directors. The collections
were made either weekly or monthly, or three times a
year. The assessors were empowered to tax each member according to their capacity to give, and in case of a
refusal, to seize the amount fixed for him. Besides these
regular assessments, voluntary contributions were made
on occasions of joy or on anniversaries of death, and
the like. Such donations were given in the form of
vows, made publicly in the synagogue, a practice found
as early as the Mishnaic times (Tos. Ter. i, 10; Shabb
xvii, 22), and at festal banquets.

The average Jew was expected to give one-tenth of
his income to charity (Ket. 50^a; Yer. Peah I, 75^b; Maim.
l. c. vii, 5), and the rabbis of the middle ages endeavored to make this a legal tax rather than a mere

voluntary contribution. For some time the giving of the tithe became a common practice among the pious Jews of Germany and elsewhere.

As early as the eleventh century, we meet with a Jewish hospital under the name of *Hekdesh* (a home consecrated to God for the benefit of the needy) in Cologne, and they are found in every large Jewish community used both as an Inn for the poor as well as for the sick and the aged. Jewish orphan asylums were not known before the seventeenth century, the one established in the Sephardic Congregation in Amsterdam in 1648 being the first recorded in Jewish sources. The one in Bavaria was established in 1703.

One of the most prominent forms of charity was the ransoming of captives, declared in the Talmud to be of the most meritorious. (B. B. 86.) Talmudic sources tell us of a class of the pious *Hasidim*, who devoted their whole lives to the performance of this most pressing obligation in Roman times. During the middle ages, the wars on land and the pirate ships on sea turned the prisoners into slaves, and to purchase the freedom of Jewish slaves required large funds which only the concerted efforts of the community could supply. Especially along the Mediterranean shores were the Jewish congregations, which, whether of Spain and Portugal or of Italy and the Greek Islands were taxed to the utmost, and had to unite for intercommunal action. Later on we find the Jewish communities of Turkey and of Germany banded together for the liberation of the Jewish prisoners. Yet this very fact often led the pirates and occasionally the rulers of Christendom to resort to all sorts of extortions for the sake of obtaining large sums of money from the Jews.

E. Charitable Societies

As stated above, there existed already in ancient times associations of the pious who devoted their time to the performance of special acts of charity. One of these was to visit the sick, another to attend to the dying and bury the dead. From the thirteenth century on we find societies organized all over Europe for the support of the poor, for the education of the children of the poor, for endowing poor maidens, for the raising of orphans, for visiting and aiding the sick, for sheltering the aged, for free burials, and for the ransom of prisoners. But it was only with the beginning of the nineteenth century that the beginning was made in Paris, London, and then in various cities of the United States of amalgamating the different charitable societies and institutions and organizing the whole work of relief along modern lines and methods.

Chapter Three. Charity Among the Jews

Questions

1. What place does Jewish endeavor occupy in the development of philanthropic organization?
2. What was the ancient Jewish conception of charity?
3. What was the system of relief in Mishnaic times?
4. How did Maimonides classify donors to charity?
5. Describe Jewish charity in the middle ages.

IV

NATIONAL ORGANIZATIONS

A. THE BARON DE HIRSCH FUND [1]

1. *Baron Maurice De Hirsch*

The name of Baron De Hirsch is well known as that of the greatest benefactor among the Jews. He was born in Munich on December 9, 1831, and he died near Brek-Ujar, Hungary, on April 21, 1896. He started his phenomenal career as a bank clerk, where he later married the daughter of the president. He became interested in the building of railroads through the Balkan States, to Constantinople. During the prosecution of this work, he became intimately acquainted with the deplorable conditions of the Jews in the Orient. In the beginning he placed large sums of money at the disposal of the Alliance Israélité, to whose endeavors he was kindly disposed, and with whose work he was satisfied. In 1885, Baron De Hirsch drew up an elaborate scheme for improving the conditions of the Russian Jews. At this time he was opposed to emigration as a solution, and so he offered the Russian Government fifty million francs to be used for educational purposes. The offer was rejected. He next turned to

[1] Eugene S. Benjamin, "The Baron De Hirsch Fund," "Proceedings National Conference of Jewish Charities," Philadelphia, 1906.

emigration as a possible solution and toward it he directed all of his strength.

2. *The Jewish Colonization Association*

After considerable effort, Baron De Hirsch succeeded in forming an international organization called the Jewish Colonization Association, popularly known as the I C A. The nominal capital of two hundred thousand pounds was contributed entirely by the originator of the scheme. The objects of the Association, as formulated by the founder, were:

"To assist and to promote the emigration of Jews from any part of Europe and Asia, and principally from countries in which they may be for the time being subjected to any special taxes or political or other disabilities, to any part of the world and to form and establish colonies in various parts of North and South America and other countries, for agricultural, commercial, and other purposes."

In the beginning the possibilities of forming colonies in Argentine formed the major part of the extensive program of the Jewish Colonization Association. With the sudden and extraordinary immigration of the Russian Jews to the United States, however, the Baron's attention was directed to the needs of this country.

3. *Formation of the Baron De Hirsch Fund*

In 1891, he was instrumental in forming the Baron De Hirsch Fund with an initial capital of two million five hundred thousand dollars, which was later considerably

NATIONAL ORGANIZATIONS

augmented. The original trustees were Meyer S. Isaacs, Jesse Seligman, Jacob H. Schiff, Oscar S. Straus, Harry Rice, James H. Hoffman, Julius Goldman, Meyer Sulzberger, and William H. Hackenburg. The board was co-optative. The purposes of the fund, as expressed in the deed of trust, are as follows:—

1. Loans to emigrants from Russia and Roumania, agriculturists, and settlers within the United States, upon real or chattel securities.

2. Provision for the transportation of immigrants selected (after their arrival in any port in America) with reference to their age, character, and capacity, to places where it is expected that conditions of the labor market or the residence of friends will make them self-supporting.

3. Provision for training immigrants in a handicraft and contributing for their support while learning such a handicraft, for furnishing the necessary tools and implements and other assistance to enable them to earn a livelihood.

4. Provision for improved mechanical training for adults and youths—immigrants and their children—whereby persons of industry and capacity may acquire some remunerative employment, either by payment of apprenticeship or tuition fee, or the instruction of adults or minors in trade schools or otherwise with contributions for temporary support.

5. Provision for instruction in the English language, and in the duties and obligations of life and citizenship in the United States, and for technical and trade education, and the establishment and subvention of special schools and workshops and other suitable agencies for promoting and maintaining such instruction.

6. Provision for instruction in agricultural work, and improved methods of farming, and for aiding settlers with tools and implements and the practical supervision of such instruc-

tion, conducted upon suitable tracts of land and the necessary buildings.

7. Co-operation with established agencies in various sections of the United States, whose duty it shall be in whole or part to furnish . . . relief, and education of needy and deserving applicants coming within the classes designated herein.

8. Contributions toward the maintenance of individuals and families, while temporarily awaiting work, or when settled in the new homes in which they may be established.

9. Such other and further modes of relief and such other and further contributions to education and in other departments of knowledge as the said trustees or their successors shall from time to time decide.

A portion of the capital was spent immediately under the provision of the trust, the balance of the principal has been kept intact by the trustees. In 1906 it amounted to three million, eight hundred thousand dollars and only the income thereof is used. The Fund is also augmented from time to time by special appropriations from the Jewish Colonization Association of Paris. The precise amount of the income of the Baron De Hirsch Fund of America cannot be secured, as there is no official account of disbursements, but it can be estimated at approximately two hundred and fifty thousand dollars per year.

4. *The Agricultural and Industrial Aid Society*

The agricultural and industrial removal work became so extensive that in 1900 it was necessary to found a separate society to take charge of these activities. Accordingly there was organized the "Agri-

cultural and Industrial Aid Society," which is maintained partly by funds donated from the Baron De Hirsch Fund and partly by contributions from the Jewish Colonization Association of Paris; also the Industrial Removal Office which is entirely supported by the I C A. These activities of the Fund at present fall under the following heads:
1. Baron De Hirsch Agricultural School, Woodbine, N. J.
2. Baron De Hirsch Trade School, N. Y.
3. Woodbine Land Improvement Company.
4. English instruction to Immigrants.
5. Relief work.

B. THE NATIONAL CONFERENCE OF JEWISH CHARITIES

The National Conference of Jewish Charities was organized in 1899. The objects of this association are to discuss the problems of charities and to promote reforms in their administration; to provide uniformity of action and co-operation in all matters pertaining to the relief and betterment of the Jewish poor of the United States, without, however, interfering in any manner with the local work of any constituent society.

The Conference succeeded in introducing the "Transportation Rules," an arrangement which makes each community responsible for the care of its own poor, and cope effectively with the problem of transient applicants for relief.

The Conference devoted considerable time to the study of the problem of the care of dependent children, and is responsible for great many improvements in the Jewish child-caring agencies as well as for the spread of the child-placing policy and, together with the introduction of the widow pension practice, the forerunner of the present state pension allowances. The Conference has given considerable thought to the question of tuberculosis and only recently caused a scientific study of the situation in Denver. The Conference was instrumental in organizing the National Desertion Bureau.

The Conference has promoted the spirit of social service in the different communities and has prompted the organization of federations, etc.

The Conference now conducts a Field Bureau, which is serving as an information agency, making it possible for organizations to utilize the services of the secretary and other experts in organizing and revising their activities.

1. *Membership*

There are one hundred and forty-five constituent organizations of the Conference, representing eighty cities and thirty-five states.

Any regularly organized Jewish society of the United States having charitable and philanthropic purposes may become a member of the association on application made to the secretary and on payment of the membership dues.

The annual membership dues in a city where federation exists shall be for such federation one-tenth of one per cent of the annual amount expended by it for its corporate purposes during the preceding year; not less, however, than five dollars ($5) nor more than fifty dollars ($50) and dues of five dollars ($5) for any constituent member of such federation that shall desire membership in this Conference.

In cities where no federation exists the annual membership dues for each society shall be five dollars ($5) where its expenditures as above are less than five thousand dollars ($5,000) and ten dollars ($10) for all others.

Individuals may become subscribing members upon the payment of one dollar ($1) dues annually, for which they shall be entitled to all the publications of the Conference, but they shall have no vote.

Each constituent society shall be entitled to one delegate, but may appoint as many as it sees fit to attend the biennial meeting. All such delegates shall be entitled to participate in said meeting, but each society shall have but one vote.

"Jewish Charities," the bulletin of the Conference, is issued monthly.

C. THE INDEPENDENT ORDER OF B'NAI B'RITH

Organized as early as 1843, the Independent Order of B'nai B'rith was originally a mutual aid society, but for some years the organization has abandoned, practically speaking, all the features of exclusive aid to its members, and at present devotes its funds to charitable and educational work on a scale more or less national. The following institutions in the United States were founded by the Order:

Hebrew Orphan Asylum, Atlanta, Ga.
Free Employment Bureau, Chicago and Pittsburg.
Jewish Widows and Orphans Home, New Orleans, La.
Home for the Aged and Infirm, Yonkers, N. Y.
Jewish Orphan Asylum, Cleveland, O.
Relief Committee, Hot Springs, Ark.
National Hospital, Hot Springs, Ark.
Home for Jewish Orphans, Los Angeles, Cal.
Immigrant and Sabbath schools in a number of cities.

In 1915, a special department of Jewish Social Service was inaugurated, with a paid worker at its head. The Order has four hundred and forty-two lodges (some in Europe, Asia, and Africa) with a membership of forty thousand and eighty-three individuals.

D. NATIONAL INSTITUTIONS FOR THE CARE OF CONSUMPTIVES

There are three national institutions for the care of consumptives. The National Jewish Hospital and the Jewish Consumptives Relief Society are both situated in Denver, Colorado. The former was founded in 1889 and the latter in 1904. The phase that these two institutions represent in Jewish philanthropy in the United States is interesting to note. They represent the rivalry in the sphere of charity between the older American Jewry (the Reform element) and the newer and orthodox element, which arrived in our country during the last thirty years. Another national organization was started in Los Angeles in 1914, and is known as the Jewish Consumptive Relief Association of Los Angeles.

E. NATIONAL FARM SCHOOL

The National Farm School was founded in 1896, primarily through the herculean efforts of Dr. Joseph Krauskopf, to promote agricultural training and education among Jewish youths, and to prepare experts and leaders for the Jews engaged in this particular occupation. The school is situated at Doylestown, Pa., and is largely supported by Jews all over the United States.

F. THE COUNCIL OF JEWISH WOMEN

The Council of Jewish Women was organized in 1893, and consists of seventy-three senior sections situated all over the United States. Besides social and religious activities, the Council is actively engaged in philanthropic and educational activities.

G. THE HEBREW SHELTERING AND IMMIGRANT AID SOCIETY OF AMERICA

The Hebrew Sheltering and Immigrant Aid Society of America cares for, and offers protection to the immigrant. Formerly a Hebrew sheltering house, this new organization assumed, in 1909, the entire care of the newly arrived immigrants.

H. THE EDUCATIONAL LEAGUE

The Educational League, organized in 1896, has for its purpose the providing of means for the higher education of orphans.

I. THE NATIONAL JEWISH IMMIGRATION COUNCIL

The National Jewish Immigration Council was organized in 1911 for the purpose of general supervision of all work for Jewish Immigrants at the seaports of the United States.

J. THE NATIONAL UNION OF JEWISH SHELTERING SOCIETIES

The National Union of Jewish Sheltering Societies was organized in 1911 for the purpose of helping worthy wayfarers, to put a stop to habitual wanderers, and to prevent wife deserters from using the *Hachnosis Orchim* as a means of escape from family responsibility.

K. THE AMERICAN JEWISH COMMITTEE

On November 11, 1906, the American Jewish Committee was organized for the purpose of preventing the infraction of the civil and religious rights of the Jews in any part of the world, to render all lawful assistance, and to take appropriate remedial action in the case of threatened or actual invasion of such rights, or of unfavorable discrimination with respect thereto, to secure for Jews equality of economic, social, and educational opportunity, to alleviate the consequences of persecution and to afford relief from calamities affecting Jews, wherever they may occur, and to compass these ends to administer relief funds which shall come into its possession or which may be received by it in trust or otherwise for any of the aforesaid objects or for purposes comprehended therein.

L. THE JOINT DISTRIBUTION COMMITTEE

The Joint Distribution Committee was organized for the distribution of funds for the Jewish War sufferers in Europe, and represents three national committees collecting funds for this purpose, namely, the American Jewish Committee, the Central Relief Committee, and the People's Relief Committee. Each of these committees retains its autonomy as far as the collection of funds is concerned, and uses its own methods, while the distribution is attended to by a joint committee consisting of representatives of the constituent committees.

CHAPTER FOUR. NATIONAL ORGANIZATIONS. QUESTIONS

1. Outline the career of Baron De Hirsch.

2. What are the purposes of the Jewish Colonization Association?

3. Describe the formation and the aims of the Baron De Hirsch Fund.

4. State the reason for forming the Jewish Agricultural and Industrial Aid Society.

5. Give the origin and purposes of the National Conference of Jewish Charities, and describe its membership.

6. Describe the Order B'nai B'rith.

7. What are the national institutions for the care of Jewish consumptives?

8. Describe the National Farm School.

9. Explain the organization and activity of the Council of Jewish Women.

10. What is the purpose of the Hebrew Sheltering and Immigrant Aid Society of America?

11. Characterize the activities of the Educational League.

12. What are the National Jewish Immigration Council and the National Union of Jewish Sheltering Societies?

13. Describe the organization and purpose of the American Jewish Committee.

V

METHODS OF FUND RAISING FOR JEWISH PHILANTHROPIC AGENCIES

A. DIRECT BEGGING

From time immemorial it was the business of the indigent themselves to seek out those persons who would contribute towards their maintenance. The profession of the "schnorrer" was the highest evolutionary type of this direct method of raising funds by the recipients themselves. Each *schnorrer* had a certain route of contributors, whom he visited at definitely recurring intervals. When in need no longer of making the rounds himself, he would not infrequently sell this privilege, and so transmit his income to his successor.[1] This method of direct soliciting of funds by the poor themselves carried with it the advantage of personal contact on the part of the giver with the actual conditions of the recipient. The supreme objections to this method, however, are, first, that the poor are humiliated by the necessity of begging, second, that they do not receive adequate relief from any one source and are compelled to gather the needed funds spasmodically in irregular amounts, third, that they have no definite assurance that their needs will be met by the generosity of the giver. Still, in former times, when social relations

[1] See Israel Zangwill's "The King of Schnorrers."

were simple, and social cleavage was not so clearly marked, this method could satisfactorily serve its purpose. In the present complexity of modern society it carries with it serious difficulties. In Jewish philanthropy, however, this method is still in vogue, especially in regard to the large number of traveling "scholars," rabbis, and so forth who collect donations from a generous community and change their location as soon as the ground has been covered.

B. THE PUSHKA METHOD [1]

The *pushka* or charity box in the synagogue was another primitive form of raising charity funds. This box was, as a rule, supplemented by collectors, who canvassed the homes and the business districts for contributions to definite works. Simon Kaftan, in Russia, one of these private collectors, was one of the large number of picturesque charity workers. Entering a house while on his continuous mission of mercy, he would place his tin collecting box behind himself, and say, "Put in as much as you can or take out as much as you need." Deborah Esther, of Vilna, devoted her life to building up one particular institution, the free loan society of that city. Going around hurriedly from morning until night with her box in her hand, sitting in front of the passers-by in the market place in rain, in storm, and in cold, she collected, kopeck by kopeck, not less than three hundred roubles a week. This noble

[1] "Jewish Charitable Activities in Russia": Dr. David Blaustein and Prof. H. L. Sabsovich, Proceedings Fifth National Conference of Jewish Charities, Richmond, 1908.

work she prosecuted until the end of her days. She died at the age of ninety, and the entire population, in gratitude for her devoted service, followed her remains to the grave. The collections of charity funds by means of a charity box and synagogue donations during the holy days, while inoffensive in itself as a method, unfortunately gives no assurance that each member of the congregation does his duty in proportion to his means, nor does it presuppose either a definite income or a certain manner of distribution with guarantee of efficient, ultimate disposition. The charity box method is extensively used in the United States, not only in the synagogues, but also in private homes by the so-called *Halukah* organizations, whose purpose is the collection of funds for the support of the poor in Jerusalem and their maintenance in the Holy Land. In this instance, besides the negative value of the charity box method, the cost of collection and the lack of centralized control of expenditure make the system most unwholesome and undesirable. The same can be postulated with regard to the different private collections made by self-appointed individuals who usually approach persons for a donation either for a poor family or for a sick person.

C. Charity Taxes

Between 1826 and 1851 the Russian government variously established special taxes, a part of the income from which was to defray the cost of Jewish charitable institutions. This impost is either a tax on *Kosher* meat or a duty on the candles used every Sabbath eve in the home of the pious Jew. It is interesting to note that with the customary impartiality of the Russian government towards its Jewish subjects, the major portion of the revenue accruing from these imposts is used for rather alien purposes, such as the building of roads or even for the erection of Greek orthodox churches. Voluntary taxation has frequently been adopted in the United States; for instance, the B'nai B'rith organization sets aside a certain portion of its membership dues for the maintenance of the various charities of the Order.

D. Endowments

Frequently the bulk of the initial expense of an institution is contributed by a single individual, often as a memorial to a departed member of the family. Only in individual cases are these institutions sufficiently endowed to obviate dependence on outside support for their maintenance or expansion. The Baron De Hirsch Fund is an example of this, an endowment upon a gigantic scale. In a number of institutions, donations are also received in small sums, in memory of the departed. Tablets are placed to perpetuate the names of the donors, and again, *Kaddish* (prayer) is recited for the dead by the inmates of the beneficiary institution receiving a certain compensation in the form of a charity subvention. This form of income is quite an item in the orphanages and homes for the aged and infirm, etc. Permanent endowment funds in charitable endeavor undoubtedly carry with them many advantages. They obviate the necessity for continuous raising of funds, and provide a definite income and reduce to a minimum the expense of collection of revenues. On the other hand, however, the danger in endowment funds is that, frequently, the conditions calling for the endowments disappear, whereupon unnecessary institutions are perpetuated. This continuation by endowment of institutions rendered obsolete naturally weakens the interest of the community in social welfare and makes the management of such funds more or less bureaucratic and exclusive. It is imperative, therefore, that bequests of this character should be extremely elastic, and that the use of the funds should be determined by the needs of the times. In the same light should be considered those donations made for charitable purposes and extended to perpetuate the memory of the departed.

With the growing demand upon charitable activities, there is a strong sentiment to designate charity bequests for immediate actual needs rather than to transfer them into permanent sources of income. This is the principle advocated by the great philanthropist of Chicago, Julius Rosenwald. Another principle is expressed in the statement of the Federation of Charities in Philadelphia, which refuses to accept the donations of institutions unless they are endowed sufficiently to guarantee the expenses of operation.

E. Charity Socials

Frequently, charity funds have been raised through social enterprises. For instance, to liquidate a mort-

METHODS OF FUND RAISING 43

gage upon the Educational Alliance and the Hebrew Technical Institute in New York City, over a quarter of a million dollars was raised on a fair in 1900. In some cities, the charity ball is an annual affair, and is a source of considerable income. Besides, minstrel shows, tea parties, dramatic evenings, guessing parties, raffles and what not else, are used to raise funds for philanthropic purposes. In quite recent years, these questionable methods are becoming rapidly displaced by regular periodic subscriptions, which guarantee to the institutions a definite income without additional expense or obligation. The temptation to raise funds for charity through entertainments has been very great, and was abused to such an extent as to justify the indignation of the public. Frequently a large part of the funds raised were consumed in the enterprise which produced them, and the net income was disproportionate to the effort expended. This became a burden upon communities and annoying and obnoxious to the generous donors.

F. THE FEDERATION IDEA

1. *Federation Experiences*

While the methods enumerated above are still practiced and a certain merit cannot be denied them, there can be no doubt that they are being more and more replaced by the so-called subscription method, in which the contributors subscribe a certain sum periodically for the given philanthropy. While in its older form this method presupposed a collector, usually paid for his labor, it has been gradually adjusted to a way by which the subscribers send in their contributions by mail, thus avoiding unnecessary expense. In attempting to simplify the method of collection and to save the contributors unnecessary annoyance, the Jews were the first in the field of social work to introduce the "Federation" idea.

The Federation is an attempt to unify the different philanthropic efforts of a community. In some cities it is simply a central collective agency, in others, the relief department is an integral part of the Federation, and again, in some, it is a central administrative agency for all organizations.

In New York, the United Hebrew Charities as its name implies, was the result of a combination of several institutions which pooled their resources in the year 1874, and have continued their combined activities since that day. We find that in 1895, in Boston, some form of a Federation was established, but the first true Federation was established in Cincinnati in 1896. Here nine institutions of the city combined while two stayed out of the Federation and still remain unaffiliated. At present, there are forty-five cities that have followed suit. In every case, Federation has produced an increase, both in subscriptions and in numbers of contributors.

Special mention should be made of affairs in Baltimore, where a Federation of what may be termed the "up-town" institutions of the older established Jewish inhabitants of that city was effected in 1907. The later arrivals, seeing the advantages of union, but declining for various reasons to combine with their fellow-Jews, made a Federation of their own, under the title of the United Hebrew Charities of Baltimore. These two Federations appear to co-operate in all matters in which they can. Something similar has occurred in Chicago, where the Federated Orthodox Jewish Charities was organized in 1913.

Meanwhile, the tide of Federation had reached New York and an attempt was made to apply its methods to the largest Jewish community in the world. In the year 1908, the heads of some forty-five institutions of New York City met in a series of conferences to determine whether it would be feasible to bring them all into a Federation. One of the persons who took a great interest in the movement in favor of Federation in Manhattan was Mr. Louis A. Heinsheimer, who devoted much time and energy in promoting this scheme. Shortly after, unfortunately, he died, but left a magnificent legacy for the purpose of such a Federation of Jewish Charities in New York City when once established, conditional upon five institutions named going in. His brother Alfred, the residuary legatee, offered the one million dollars ($1,000,000), provided four of the five agreed. Even this magnificent inducement did not overcome the opposition to the Federation in New York, and as Mr. Heinsheimer had set a time limit to his bequest, the plan fell through. One section of greater New York was not affected by this unfortunate deadlock, and the leaders of the Brooklyn Jewish Charities combined in 1910 the chief charitable organizations of that borough. Lately, the sentiment in favor of a Federation in New York City has been again awakened, and the study of this subject has been renewed.[1]

On June 6, 1916, a committee on Federation adopted a plan for the Federation of Jewish Charities in New York City to take effect when agreed to by societies receiving two-thirds of the total amount collected in membership dues and subscriptions of designated societies. The scope of the Federation is limited to organizations ministering to the needs of the Jews of the Boroughs of Manhattan and Bronx though not necessarily within those territories. Charitable and relief agencies, organizations for the care of the sick, the dependent and delinquent, societies for general educational and social activities are included within the plan. However, because of the special problems they present, religious, educational, and national institutions, even though ministering to the specified localities, are, for the time being, excluded from the plan.

The Federation is to act chiefly as a clearing house for the collecting of funds for its constituent societies though these will be permitted to retain their own memberships. Representation and voting power on the governing body will be apportioned on the basis of gross income. Provision is made for the grouping of

[1] "What Federation in the Interior Cities can Teach New York." Morris D. Waldman, in the "American Hebrew," March 5, 1916.

societies, with incomes too small to deserve representation, for the election of joint representatives. A number of persons not connected with the executive boards of any constituent societies are to be elected trustees by the members. The board of trustees, the governing body, is to control the securing of funds, but to have no say in the management of any society.

An emergency fund of three hundred thousand dollars for local emergencies only is provided. Constituent societies are guaranteed an income equal to that which they received in 1915.

2. *Advantages of Federation*

The first advantage found for the Federation throughout, has been the distinct increase in the amount collected. Persons are often of the erroneous impression that they are contributing largely to charity when sending their gifts in driblets, and are frequently surprised at the comparative smallness when the different items are added up. They are, therefore, prepared to make considerably greater sacrifices, especially when not likely to be worried more than once a year.

This kind of increase naturally did not continue after the Federation had entered. It is almost a universal experience that the second, third, and fourth years after Federation do not show a marked increase, certainly no more than the normal increase in population and affluence would have warranted if no Federation had taken place. It is also a general experience, that after three or four years, another jump takes place in the receipts, after which another pause occurs.[1]

The second benefit accruing from Federation is the elimination of indiscriminate, unauthorized, solicitation. The third advantage is that Federation tends to prevent the increase of unnecessary institutions; and the fourth claim advanced is that Federation eliminates duplication and overlapping of the activities of the constituent societies.

But apart from the material benefits which result from Federation, the whole plane of Jewish philanthropy is raised by this more dignified method for collecting and distributing the means by which charity lives. Then again, the community in which the institution exists learns to regard it as an organized member of the community, rather than pet institutions of a limited number of families. When occasions arise on which a greater appeal has to be made for charity purposes, it would, perhaps, come with more force from a central bureau representing all the philanthropic activities of the community rather than if it emanated from the directors of a single institution.

On the other hand, it is claimed that Federation fails in the promotion of new enterprises, that it does away with private initiative of the different constituent societies, and in many instances does not achieve a definite and just apportionment of the funds.

[1] "Federation" by Dr. Joseph Jacobs. "American Jewish Year Book," 1914.

METHODS OF FUND RAISING

G. THE SUBSCRIPTION METHOD

Concomitant with the spread of the Federation principle, private subscriptions have almost displaced the foregoing methods and have become the only legitimate way of raising funds, though some of the different methods enumerated above are still practiced and a certain merit cannot be denied them. With the introduction of the Federation idea, however, the possibility of raising funds without these extraordinary and sometimes illegal enterprises became self-evident. The contributing public cheerfully met the proposition that henceforth subscribers to the Federations should be relieved of the necessity of contributing in any other way and should not be obliged to purchase tickets, and to attend the various affairs given, presumably, for philanthropic purposes. Thus, Federation has eliminated a considerable amount of waste.

H. EFFICIENCY TESTS FOR RAISING FUNDS

The problem of raising funds for philanthropic purposes, as expressed in the modern term of efficiency, is to secure the greatest amount of money with the least possible expense and effort,—to provide a permanent regular income for the maintenance of existing activities, and to conserve the interest, as well as the resources, of the community, in the field of philanthropy. The Federation plan fully meets these tests.

I. Methods of Getting Subscriptions

1. *The Card Catalogue*

The experience of several Federations suggests certain methods for raising funds through annual subscriptions. First, a thorough canvass of the community should be made, and a card catalogue compiled of all potential subscribers of the organization. This catalogue should include all of the members of the different congregations and clubs, donors and subscribers to the existing charities, and members of fraternal orders. In some cities, the names found in the telephone directory were secured, and having a telephone was taken as prima facie evidence of ability to donate to charity. Real estate owners, as well as property owners of business establishments were included in the catalogue.

2. *Circulars*

When the catalogue is compiled, a circular letter is sent, enclosing a subscription blank and requesting the addressee to become a subscriber.

3. *Personal Solicitation*

This is followed by a personal solicitation by the membership committee, which is formed for this purpose. In this campaign the city is divided into districts, or each one of the committee men takes for solicitation the names of those with whom he is acquainted or with whom he comes more or less in contact. Usually both methods are utilized.

4. *Arguments*

In the circular letter that is mailed, as well as in the personal appeal that is made by the committee, the general purpose of the charity organization is set forth, and the following arguments advanced:

First, that the subscriber will henceforth relieve himself of the annoyance of continual solicitations for charity funds.

Second, that the organization will get rid of the professional beggar, and that the deserving poor will receive adequate and scientific treatment; and last, that the subscriber has the opportunity to refer all applications for relief to the central organization, and be assured that the applicant will receive proper attention.

5. *Special Help*

In some cases, especially in the case of large donors, repeated efforts will have to be made before success is achieved, and a special committee, having close connections with the party in question, will have to take it upon itself to secure the special subscription. Chicago should be given credit for organizing a Young Men's Auxiliary Society, which is endeavoring to raise money among the younger element for the Federation. Other cities have emulated Chicago's lead.

6. *After Numbers*

The present tendency is not only to get as large an amount of contributions as possible, but a large number of subscribers as well. It is interesting in this connection to examine the tables of comparative contributions for charity in the different cities.[1]

Cities	Contributions	Jewish Population	Per Capita
Cincinnati	$117,372	28,000	$4.19
Chicago	482,809	125,000	3.86
Baltimore	122,714	42,500	2.89
Pittsburg	112,000	45,000	2.49
Philadelphia	250,000	110,000	2.27
Rochester	12,728	6,000	2.12
St. Louis	97,500	47,500	2.01
Cleveland	91,500	50,000	1.83
New York	1,250,000	750,000	1.66
Detroit	25,000	16,500	1.51
Boston	90,000	65,000	1.38
Indianapolis	11,000	9,000	1.22
Brooklyn	102,500	300,000	.34

7. Special Donations

It is but natural that certain activities or institutions should appeal to individual donors more than others. This legitimate choice is often responsible for large endowments, bequests, or donations to these particular activities or institutions. It is consequently the duty of those who are at the head of philanthropic agencies to popularize their workings, thus giving the public an opportunity to judge of the relative merits of the different activities. Frequently a new activity will require a

[1] " Jewish Charities," vol. 1, No. 8, page 3, 1911.

METHODS OF FUND RAISING 53

large initial outlay, and this had best be covered by special donations.

8. *The Spirit of Rivalry*

Chicago was especially successful in instilling a wholesome spirit of rivalry and has raised considerable amounts of money in this way, not only in these large donations, but through large numbers of subscribers, and amounts of small annual contributions as well. As a rule, however, these whirlwind campaigns are spasmodic, and can be successful only in an emergency. The method is especially effective in raising funds for building purposes, establishing new activities, and especially for those institutions that supply an educational activity that will serve the community at large, rather than a purely charitable enterprise intended primarily for the poor. The raising of funds through annual subscriptions is of prime importance, and if carried on effectively and consistently, obviates the necessity for these sporadic attempts.

J. STATE AND MUNICIPAL SUBVENTIONS

In no small number of instances, Jewish institutions administering to a certain definite clientele are entitled to and are utilizing state and municipal subventions. Again, many relief agencies refer cases of dependency to state and municipal institutions, thus lightening the burden upon private philanthropy. This is the case with a number of hospitals, orphanages, and also in the case of outdoor relief in many cities, and in the instance of state funds to parents.

K. Outside Contributions

In but a few instances do Jewish charitable institutions apply for support to a constituency other than their own. While this may be a matter of necessity in these few cases, there is no doubt that outside contributions invariably weaken the independent spirit of the community, and lead to an attitude of dependency with its demoralizing effects.

L. Collections by Mail

In some cities the arrangements are so successfully completed that the subscribers realize the importance of minimizing the expenses of collections and co-operate to such an extent that all the subscriptions are sent in by mail, leaving only a few who require additional reminders. In others, however, it becomes necessary to engage a paid collector, who receives a salary, or is paid in proportion to his collections.

M. Publicity

1. *Reports*

In the last analysis, the financial success that an organization achieves is directly proportional to the amount of wholesome publicity that it receives. For this reason, it has been customary for organizations to publish an annual report. This includes an account of the different activities, with special emphasis upon special policies and acquisitions of the year, the names of the officers of the organization, and a list of the subscribers with the amounts of their contributions. For a time it was thought advisable to omit the amount of the contribution, thus putting all the subscribers on the same basis. Intended originally to prevent embarrassment on the part of those who cannot contribute large sums, it is also a recognition of the fact that the small subscriber deserves the same consideration as does the large contributor, since the small contribution in many instances represents a larger proportion of a man's income than does the large donation. This ethical consideration rapidly gave way to a more practical consideration, namely, the desire to make public the amounts contributed by different individuals and thus make them do their full share, and to give special acknowledgment to those who contribute large amounts. Besides this, some cities publish the subscriptions of the previous year, and so give mention to those who have increased their contribution.

2. *Pocket Editions*

In the last few years, pocket editions have been substituted for the usual quarto size, and outside of the statistical and financial statements of the organization, only a few pages are devoted to the description of the activities. Other information is inserted, calculated to induce the subscriber to carry the report in his vest pocket and use it for propaganda.

3. The Daily Press

Some cities use the daily press and other publications in which they periodically insert accounts of their activities and even the names and amounts of their contributors and contributions. Other organizations issue their own bulletins for the use of their subscribers.

4. Moving Pictures

In this discussion of publicity, we cannot help mentioning the newest departure in fund raising, used by the Federation of Jewish Charities of Brooklyn, New York, where the motion picture was used as a medium in a fund-raising campaign. This, naturally, carries publicity to an extreme, and may, unless judiciously presented, do harm, injuring the very elements whom the Charities are to serve.

There can be little doubt that in the question of raising funds for philanthropic purposes, the Jewish charities have made great strides and have achieved results much better than similar endeavors of non-Jewish agencies. It is worth while mentioning that only in 1913, Cleveland organized what is known as the Cleveland Federation for Charity and Philanthropy—the principles of which are modeled after the Federation idea in vogue in Jewish organizations for the past decade. Similar movements are occurring in many cities at the present time.

N. EMERGENCY FUNDS

While under ordinary conditions the subscription method is universally recognized as the most efficient,

METHODS OF FUND RAISING

in emergencies there is considerable deviation from this principle. In handling relief situations caused by calamities like the San Francisco earthquake, the Chelsea fire, or the floods in the Ohio valley, the work is usually delegated to the Red Cross Society and there is little done under specifically Jewish auspices. However, the great demand and the unusual conditions of the Jews of the War Zone at the present time required additional efforts on the part of the American Jewry, and special committees were organized for the purpose of raising funds. In this particular instance the organizations dealing directly with Jewish charitable effort in this country did not initiate this particular movement. At first the I. O. B. B. issued a call for funds but the response was inadequate. Then the American Jewish Committee organized its own machinery and collected money under its own auspices all over the United States. Almost simultaneous with this the orthodox element of the Jews had organized another committee known as the Central Relief Committee, and this was followed by a still other organization, the People's Relief Committee, which has chosen its sphere of action among the large masses of Jewish workingmen. Within a very short time these three committees had combined as far as the distribution of relief was concerned, under a composite organization known as the Joint Distribution Committee. It is interesting to observe that in this particular instance every kind of method was and is being used in raising funds. While subscriptions represent the larger donors, we find all different plans in operation, intended to attract contributors who otherwise would not be ready to give their share toward the alleviation of the suffering of the Jews in the War Zone. Thus concerts, flower days, entertainments and bazaars, are quite in vogue for raising funds for this purpose. Within two years the Jews of America have collected more than $6,000,000 for the relief of the war sufferers.

CHAPTER FIVE. METHODS OF FUND RAISING FOR JEWISH PHILANTHROPIC AGENCIES

QUESTIONS

1. What are the objections to begging?
2. Discuss the charity box method.
3. What is the taxation method of raising funds?
4. Discuss the endowment method.
5. What are the objections to fund raising through spasmodic campaigns and charity socials?
6. Define the Federation idea.
7. Describe the advantages of Federation and its disadvantages.
8. What is the criterion of efficiency in raising funds?
9. State the methods of organizing a subscription system.
10. Discuss the different sources of funds of Jewish philanthropic activities.
11. Describe different methods of publicity.

VI

TRANSIENTS

The sine qua non of Jewish Charities is a relief agency. There are over seven hundred of these agencies, situated in the different cities of the United States. These societies are, presumably, to serve as agents for the various forms of relief to the poor and are expected to come into direct contact with the needy. While in small communities, where social intercourse between the rich and the poor is not so restricted as in the larger cities, the knowledge of the exact economic condition of a family applying for assistance or requiring help without an application is a matter of personal contact, in larger communities, with their complicated system of social relationships, this knowledge of the poor of the community becomes a special problem and merits serious consideration. While each and every case must receive individual attention and more or less individual treatment, still, in the practice of a charity relief office, applicants fall into certain classifications and are treated accordingly.

A. The Stranger in the Past

The most striking distinction in the treatment of cases arises in the method of handling transient cases as contrasted with the treatment of residents. In former times, the stranger was the most welcome applicant for assistance. No stranger was allowed to depart without proper allowances. Every Jewish home was open to him. There he found food and lodging. There he was the guest of the family, and if he was to proceed to other localities, he was assisted in continuing his journey. The stranger would be met on the way, and he would not be asked any questions as to his name or condition until his first needs were satisfied. (Gen. R. xxiv, 3.) The rabbis quote as models of hospitality, Abraham and Job, the doors of whose houses were open at each of the four corners, so that strangers coming from any direction might find ready access. (Gen. R. xlviii, 7 et seq.)

In the middle ages, the itinerant students were distributed among the households of the towns, and a system of *pleten*, that is, *Billeten*, bills for which the poor traveler received meals and lodging at a household was introduced.

B. The Modern Conception

Under present conditions, such a patriarchal arrangement would be difficult to imagine. Charity, once private, direct, indiscriminate, is delegated to special agencies, and the entire attitude is changed. The stranger is no longer considered a legitimate charge to the community. We begin to realize that each community must care for its own indigents, and that the passing on of applicants for relief is not a fair proposition. It means, as a rule, additional hardships upon the dependents, and prevents constructive work. In addition, this indiscriminate relief based upon the principle of "hospitality to the stranger" promotes "wanderlust" and creates a special class of paupers, the traveling beggar, who, in the extreme, becomes a confirmed tramp,—a man without a home and without a desire to acquire one. This passing on creates a psychological condition in which a person can do nothing continuously, has no thought for the future, has no ambition, energy, or plan in life.

C. THE PASSING-ON POLICY

The ever growing numbers of these kinds of applicants in the experience of organized Jewish charities became alarming; it was therefore thought expedient to propose and to inaugurate measures which would eliminate the passing on of dependents from place to place. It had become an almost universal practice to supply transportation to the needy to some other city. In quite a number of instances, communities have attempted to relieve themselves of the burden of a permanent dependency by shipping the dependent to some other city. Then, too, the number of itinerant applicants to charity became so great that it caused just alarm on the part of many communities, especially the communities in the Middle West. This situation was one of the causes leading to the formation of the National Conference of Jewish Charities, and received a good deal of consideration at the first conference which was held in Chicago. The constituent societies of the Conference adopted resolutions condemning the practice of forwarding dependents from city to city, and also agreed upon certain regulations which should control the providing of transportation.

D. THE TRANSPORTATION RULES

This agreement is expressed in the so-called Transportation Rules of the Conference, which have since become the guiding principle in the work of the relief agencies of the country. These Rules were as follows:

1. A transient shall mean any person (including his family) who shall have become a charge upon the city where he may be, within nine months of the time of his arrival in that city, unless he shall have become dependent through unavoidable accident.
2. A telegraphic code shall be used for the prompt and economical exchange of information regarding the transportation between the constituent associations, and each association agrees and binds itself to reply to all inquiries submitted to it as soon as the necessary investigation can be made.
3. No applicant for transportation shall be forwarded from one city to another, nor shall half rate tickets, paid for by the applicant, be furnished, without the advice and consent of the city of destination, but should the applicant be a transient within the meaning as above defined, he may be returned to the city where he last resided not as a transient, or to any other city where transportation shall have been furnished him, in neither case at the expense of the city to which he shall have been returned, provided that statement as to residence shall have been verified.
4. The initial city shall in all cases furnish transportation through to the city of destination. In the event of any violation of this rule, the receiving city shall, at its option, after investiga-

TRANSIENTS 63

tion, transport the applicant to his destination or to the city from which he came, at the cost of the initial city.

5. Any woman wishing to seek or desiring to join her husband shall not be assisted with transportation under any circumstances without the consent of the city where it is claimed that the husband resides.

6. Any violations or disputes or misunderstandings between constituent associations under these rules shall be referred to the executive committee, who shall investigate the same, and whose decision shall be final and binding.

The telegraphic code referred to in the rules has sunk into disuse, due to the reduced rates for telegraphic communications. The rules, however, proved to be of great value in their practical application. They were, on the whole, strictly observed by all the societies, and violations became more and more rare. The transportation agreement was dedicated to the proposition of eliminating the practice of forwarding transients in the full meaning of the word.

E. EXTENSION OF THE TRANSPORTATION RULES

Further experience, however, proved that this rule could be applied also where a dependent individual or family was sent from one city to another with the bona fide intention of solving the problem of dependency in the case, wherefore in a number of cases, differences between the constituent associations arose; these differences were finally brought to the executive committee of the Conference, which appointed a standing transportation committee, to decide the merits of the controversies. The decisions of this committee which form interesting material depicting complicated and recondite problems in charity work, serve as amendments to the original rules.

F. SPECIAL DECISIONS

Number One. S. versus E.

Decision: Justice to the communities in the health resorts requires that no families be furnished with transportation unless the investigation is first had and permission obtained.

Number Two. L. versus P. and
Number Three. L. versus N.

Decision: When an applicant, being a transient, applies for assistance in any city, such city may return him at its own expense to the city where he really belongs. Answers to inquiries must be definite, and if evasive, a counter-inquiry should be sent.

Number Four. C. versus T.

Decision: A city is responsible for sending a family to another city with the intention of forwarding the family to Denver, though the case may be transient and originally coming from a city which does not belong to the National Conference of Jewish Charities.

Number Five. L. versus C. and
E. versus F.

Decision: A case sent by the Industrial Removal Office does not become a resident of the city before the expiration of nine months; no matter what the mutual agreement of the Industrial Removal Office and the city may be. An illness that develops from causes not existing at the time of resi-

TRANSIENTS 65

dence in the former home is to be deemed an unavoidable accident within the meaning of Rule 1. A suburban locality, whether technically a part of the city or separate municipalities in the same county or state, or even in another state, is a locality for practical purposes, as far as the Jews are concerned, forms a metropolitan community, and should be considered as such within the meaning of the transportation rules.

Number Six. L. versus C.

Decision: Excuse of a community that its finances would not permit sending of the dependent to the place of destination, and therefore the transportation was granted to a nearer point is to be considered as a clear violation of the rules.

Number Seven. D. versus G.

Decision: A city is responsible for sending a woman and her children to join her husband although she had a letter from her husband that he was willing and able to support the family.

Number Eight. L. versus M.

Decision: The officials of a society may properly feel that the best interests of the applicant require that transportation be furnished, irrespective of the consent or approval of the city of destination, and if such an applicant thereafter becomes a charge upon the latter organization, the former should cheerfully reimburse. For the purposes of promoting harmony it may at times be well to overlook trifling or minor infractions of the rules, and it may be doubted whether it is good policy for an organization to claim compensation in each and every case.

Number Nine. C. versus R.

Decision: No organization should be held liable or responsible because a citizen of its community chooses to seek a new field of activity unaided and becomes an applicant for relief in some strange city. But when such citizen is assisted to leave, the organization so aiding him, without the consent of some responsible organization in the city of his destination, must be held to assume the chance of his becoming an applicant for charity elsewhere, and if this does happen, to be responsible for the expense. These expenses must be limited to the amount that it would cost to transport the applicant to his home city.

Number Ten. C. versus B.

Decision: Members of the Conference should be solicitous to convey to one another the fullest information on cases under consideration. The mere consent to transportation does not imply an agreement to accept a person as a citizen and charge upon the community.

It operates solely as a waiver to the right to be indemnified against expense. It does not refuse the city granting permission from returning the applicant at its own expense in the event that he should become dependent during the period in which he would otherwise be considered a transient.

Number Eleven. B. versus M.

Decision: There seems to be no power vested in the Committee or in the Conference to enforce the payment of what seems to be the legal and moral obligation of a city. The Transportation Rules are a gentleman's agreement, and are binding only in honor.

Number Twelve. B. versus M.

Decision: If a man lives in a city even more than nine months but his family is residing in another city, he is still not to be considered a resident, and when his family arrives, it remains transient for the period of nine months.

It is quite evident from the examples just quoted above that judicial interpretation of transportation rules has considerably extended the original scope and intention. Primarily adopted to eliminate the vicious passing on of dependents from city to city, the rules are now applied to cases where the dependent is not merely a transient (in the original connotation of the term) but also where the dependent is sent to another locality with the expectation that the subjective cause for dependency may be eradicated, and that the case may become self-sustaining. There can be little doubt that the rules have effectively curtailed, if not entirely eliminated, the passing on of transients, but the question is now, however, as to how far the responsibility of a city extends in regard to its dependents, and how long is it responsible for the care of its charges, even when those charges are removed to other cities. For example, when a family is sent to a community known as a health resort, and after the family becomes self-supporting, how long must it remain in the city in the self-sustaining position to acquire residence, and how long will it take to release the sending city of its responsibility for the care of the family? Further, where the time required by municipalities and states for establishing a residence is not co-terminous with the nine months' period as provided by the transportation agreement, what shall be the responsibilities of the cities concerned?

The Industrial Removal Office cases offer still further difficulties. The above enumerated difficulties were not foreseen in 1902, when the present rules were drawn up and adopted. The subsequent rulings are rather indefinite and vague. It is now felt, in some quarters, that a new code should be adopted to meet the demands for regulating and defining precisely the responsibility of a city with regard to its dependents that are not residents in the strict sense of the word. At the Memphis conference, in May, 1914, the Conference passed upon certain aspects of the situation, and a Committee was appointed to revise the transportation rules, adapting them to the present conditions. At the conference in Indianapolis in 1916 the following were finally adopted as amendments.

G. NEW TRANSPORTATION RULES ADOPTED AT THE NATIONAL CONFERENCE OF JEWISH CHARITIES, INDIANAPOLIS, 1916

1. (a) A transient shall mean any person (including his family) who shall apply for aid or become a charge upon the charities of the city where he may be within *one year of* the time of his arrival in that city, unless he shall have become dependent through unavoidable accident, in which shall be included illness developing from causes not existing at time of residence in former home.

(b) Within the meaning of the Transportation Rules all suburban localities which for practical purposes are parts of the metropolitan community and which have no Jewish organized charities of their own are to be considered part of that city.

2. A telegraphic code shall be used for the prompt and economical exchange of information regarding transportation between the constituent associations and each association agrees and binds itself to reply to all inquiries submitted to it as soon

TRANSIENTS 69

as the necessary investigations can be made. Any city failing to respond with reasonable promptness to inquiries from other cities may be held liable for expenses incurred through delay.

3. (a) No applicant for transportation shall be forwarded from one city to another: nor shall half-rate tickets paid for by applicants be furnished: nor shall transportation in whole or in part be requested on behalf of applicant from railroads or other organizations: nor shall *cash relief be granted* to enable applicant to purchase transportation at charity rate or full fare, without the advice and consent of the city of destination.

(b) Any transient within the meaning as above defined may be returned to the city of his last legal residence, the cost of transportation to be borne by returning city, excepting in the event that transportation to that city shall have been furnished by the city of origin, in which case he shall be returned at the expense of the city of origin.

(c) Persons who have become dependent or have applied for aid within one year of the time of their arrival may be returned to the city of origin at any time thereafter at the expense of the returning city, whose consent to receive family is not a waiver of the right to return.

(d) Whenever transportation is furnished, even if paid for by the applicant, notice shall be sent to the city of destination.

4. The initial city shall in all cases furnish transportation through to the city of destination. In the event of any violation of this rule, the receiving city shall at its own option, after investigation, transport the applicant to his destination or to the city from which he came at the cost of the initial city.

5. Any woman wishing to seek or desiring to join her husband shall not be assisted with transportation without the consent of the city where it is claimed her husband resides.

6. Any violations, disputes or misunderstandings between constituent associations under these rules shall be referred to the Transportation Committee of the National Conference of Jewish Charities, who shall investigate the same, and whose

decision shall be final and binding. It shall also be possible for organizations to submit to this Committee the facts in doubtful cases for advice before action is taken.

Rules Adopted 1914

1. A deserter cannot acquire residence away from his family, even though the family be cognizant of his whereabouts.

(A deserter within the meaning of the Transportation Rules shall be any person who leaves his home city and in his absence wilfully fails to provide for his wife and children.)

2. Persons sent by the Industrial Removal Office to any city shall acquire residence in the meaning of the Transportation Rules from the moment of their arrival at destination.

The committee further suggests the following:

1. That the Transportation Rules finally adopted by the 1916 Conference, together with a digest of all decisions rendered, be published and placed in the hands of all members of the Conference.

2. That a digest of all transportation decisions of each year be published once every year by the Conference.

3. That, through the office of the Field Secretary or in some other way, the Conference enlist the membership of the Organized Jewish Charities in non-member communities in order that it may be possible to secure widespread observance of the letter and the spirit of the Transportation Rules.

4. That, if possible through the Field Secretary, national registration of transient persons and families be effected, this to include special work with Jewish Shelter Houses throughout the country.

H. Violations of the Transportation Rules by Outside Agencies

Although the indiscriminate passing on from city to city has practically ceased on the part of organized effort, there remains, however, a great deal yet to be corrected in this regard. The existing organizations as shelter homes, *Hachnosis Orchim*,—and there are about thirty-two of them,—frequently refuse to recognize the wisdom of the proposed regulations, and make private subscriptions for the transportation of transient dependents, despite the strict policy of organized agencies. Frequently the synagogue, still clinging to the old maxim of indiscriminate assistance to the stranger, procures funds and helps the transient to get to another city by the old vicious route. Again, small communities, not constituent societies of the National Conference, are indifferent to the rules controlling the distribution of transportation. Although the transportation rules have had a decidedly salutary effect upon the transients who apply for relief, the problem is not entirely solved. While it can be safely stated that there are no transients on account of the Rules, there are, however, a great number of transients in spite of the Rules. Their treatment merits serious consideration.

I. Hachnosis Orchim

In the treatment of transients, the institutions of "Hachnosis Orchim" play an important part. A great number of large cities have special shelter homes for the temporary cases of transients, organized and maintained, in most cases, by the Orthodox constituency. The largest of these institutions is that of New York, where it is operated in connection with the Hebrew Sheltering and Immigrant Aid Society of America, and is primarily intended for the care of the recently arrived immigrant. This institution has modern accommodations and sanitary appointments. In the interior cities, the Hachnosis Orchim are open to all strangers, men, women, and children. They represent a very primitive arrangement, and are, as a rule, lacking in all necessary sanitary accommodations. The management of these institutions is vested in a board, and the stranger, by applying to either the individual members of the Board or to a specially assigned member, receives a ticket entitling him to one or more days' shelter and board. The manager of the Hachnosis Orchim is usually the janitor, his wife serving as cook and matron. In some cities the relief societies of the Federation utilize the facilities of the shelter home for their applicants, and in this case pay a certain amount to the shelter homes for maintenance. The buildings of the Hachnosis Orchim are either rented, or, even if owned by the organization, are not especially adapted for the purpose they serve. Very few of them are supplied with bathing facilities; there are no provisions made for the fumigation of clothing; in many instances the beds are shared by two or even three lodgers, and in general the entire régime is far from being modern. Very few of these institutions keep any records of their constituency, and only in a few instances do they co-operate with the organized effort of the city. An attempt has been made to organize and concentrate the work of the various shelter homes. Initiated by the Hebrew Sheltering and Immigrant Aid Society of America, the first convention took place in New York City in July, 1911, but results have yet to materialize.

J. Professionals

Transients fall into one of four categories. The first class is composed of the professional. From time immemorial, the Jews were blessed with a specific class, who made it a business to go on the road and to live upon the generosity and sympathy of their coreligionists. Sometimes they gave in return the products of their knowledge in the shape of discourses and lectures (*Droshes*). At other times, they offered merely their companionship. The traveling rabbi, preacher, and chazan, should not be classed with the genuine tramp, although they do make a practice of going from place to place, depending upon charity. They, in their turn, can be subdivided. First comes the rabbi or chazan, who has acquired his profession abroad, and who has emigrated in the hope of securing a position where he can utilize his learning and talents. He is often disappointed at his first destination, usually New York City or Chicago, and then commences his weary march to smaller communities in search of a pulpit. Often he is tempted upon the road by an advertisement in one of the Jewish newspapers; again, his traveling may be incited by the advice of a friend who claims to know of an opening. He is never a skilled mechanic, nor has he ever done any manual labor at which he might earn a livelihood.

Some of these traveling rabbis or chazanim possess

vast knowledge in their special field and an excellent delivery. Others may have superb musical ability. They speak or sing in a synagogue where a collection is made and are invited to return. Some have regular routes, which they periodically cover. Frequently, they strike a vacancy and make a settlement. They are not a dependent class as such, but consider themselves entitled to reduced transportation rates and free meals and lodgings wherever they may be. Others of these traveling rabbis or chazanim have permanent locations, but travel periodically to augment their meager earnings. The constant shifting of rabbis, chazanim, and even *shochetim* contributes in no small extent to the number of persons of this profession who follow the road.

In this, as in every other profession, there are impostors,—rabbis who are ignorant, teachers who know nothing about teaching, and chazanim who cannot sing. This is rather an annoying situation, but as long as there is no other way to discriminate except by personal contact, the orthodox constituency will have to stand the risk of being duped. It is becoming a practice, however, to refuse the privilege of the pulpit to strangers until they have proven their merits. A better organization of our synagogues, an absolute refusal to permit the traveler the use of the pulpit, unless by previous engagement through a central agency, are possible ways to reduce the number who are dependent upon charity. Then the situation will be easily controlled, and the traveling chazan will be considered just as legitimate a proposition as the visiting theatrical troupe, or the début of the renowned Sirota.

Meanwhile, it is deplorable to observe that this class of dependents is, in the majority of cases, treated in the same manner as other transients. Private homes do not offer them shelter, and they are seldom invited to a meal. In cities where there are shelter homes they are referred as strangers to these institutions, there to mingle with the indigent sick, suffering with tuberculosis, or some other highly communicable disease. Besides, the moral contact is not in all cases productive of good. It is pathetic to see to what risks these unfortunates are put, due to indiscriminate methods of what may be called organized effort in philanthropy.

K. Temporary Dependent Transients

The second class, temporary dependent transients, including a number of recently arrived immigrants, who because lacking in knowledge of the language or in other ways handicapped are induced by friends, upon whom they happen to have fallen as a burden, to try their fortune in some other city. They are usually supplied with transportation, and the rest is left to the philanthropic agencies in the separate localities. Often, this type of transient is attempting to reach a town where he expects to meet an acquaintance, or relative, or "landsman" who he hopes will care for him until he has secured work. It is reasonable that this new arrival is easily satisfied, his standards are low, and he is usually contented with very little,—a few meals, some clothing, a night's lodging, and a few cents to enable him to continue his journey is all he expects from a community. A frightened figure, he presents a very pitiable aspect of maladjustment. Organized effort has very little to do with these, their special field is the synagogue and a few orthodox families. They are most emphatically not of the tramp type. Most of them have families abroad, and are only too anxious to settle down, and to send their earnings, no matter how meager, to their families. They change from place to place, no one wants them, and they are not in position to settle down. These transients are easily reclaimed. All that is necessary is a job, which will enable them to exist here and to send some money abroad to parents or wife. They should, by all means, be discouraged from traveling, for once the habit becomes ingrained, it is hard to surmount. This is especially typified by some of the Industrial Removal Office cases. Sent to an interior city, they frequently leave it, endeavoring to find better opportunities in other localities. Frequently, in recent arrivals, we find cases of "nostalgia." Nothing but a change will satisfy. This is, however, a purely fancied condition, and should be discouraged. Frequently, however, the transient is reduced to his present condition by a false promise or an expectation of work that did not materialize. Some are brought out by employment agencies, and put to work on railroads or mines, frequently while a strike is going on, from which they usually escape and begin their weary march. An example is a Russian student, who beat his way to Cincinnati from the mines, on a freight train. Eating nothing for two days but coffee grains which he found in the box car, he was almost famished. One year later he was part owner in the hot tomale trust—in Cincinnati an industry in the hands of the Russian immigrants.

L. SICK AND DEFECTIVE

The traveling defective, cripple, or person suffering with a contagious disease, presents a pitiful sight. This traveling is frequently encouraged by communities which, in the effort to get rid of these dependents, supply them with transportation to the next available city. Often they bring letters, recommending pity.

The traveling consumptive is a pitiable sight. Between 1896 and 1911, fifty-five transients afflicted with tuberculosis applied to the United Jewish Charities of Cincinnati. Many of these were neglected cases of other communities. There were also the restless sick, who had no patience to take up the long and tedious course of treatment, and again, those who were making their way, either to Colorado and California, or to other places renowned for the climatic treatment of tuberculosis, or those who were on their homeward journey from these localities after a fruitless search for health. Some had been compelled to give up the cure because of lack of funds. All were miserable and helpless, most of them in advanced stages of the disease, the large majority assuming all the characteristics of the repulsive tramp. Four of these unfortunates found their graves in Cincinnati; many of them having received temporary assistance, failed to return; some were sent to their destinations where they belonged; one was sent to Russia; six were sent to the National Hospital for Consumptives; nine were placed in the Branch Hospital in Cincinnati. Of all the above fifty-five cases, there is only one who is known to be self-supporting now in Cincinnati. The rest have either died or their fates are unknown. Some probably are still drifting around, others may be cured. The drifters are lost souls, strangers and still suffering brethren—the unlovable and the human—they are the results of neglectful communities and they constitute a challenge to organized philanthropy.

In all these cases of transients, we are dealing with causes over which, in the majority of instances, the individual has no control, and for which he is not to be held responsible. Although every case presents some peculiar angle, making the treatment of great significance, there are, nevertheless, great possibilities of rehabilitation, of real help, of saving life and preventing unnecessary waste to society. The more personal attention the individual receives, the better are his chances of ultimate reclamation. It is sadly true, that even among these enumerated classes of transients, there are quite frequently impostors. However, the benefit of the doubt should always be given the dependent. The burden of proof is always with the charitable agency. It is far better for any philanthropic agency to be duped repeatedly than that one deserving individual should be mistreated. Moreover, it is self-evident that in the treatment of these cases, the specific Jewish organization may prove of great value. It is in a position to handle the individual cases better, it probably possesses greater facilities for investigation, securing of employment, co-operation with agencies in other cities, and so forth. The Jewish organization can better understand the recently arrived immigrant. It is in a unique position to reconcile families, and is usually able to detect fraud more quickly. Quite a perplexing problem is presented by the refugee from justice. Frequently an applicant will apply for assistance and claim that he is either an escaped prisoner or one who ran away from his city of residence to avoid criminal prosecution. The duty of the social worker is rather doubtful. It lies between the enforcement of Justice and the demand to assist the authorities, and implies on the other hand, a breach of confidence toward the applicant.

M. The Tramp

The fourth class is composed of the true tramp. Extensive argument is not necessary to show that this category should not be encouraged by charitable endeavor. No help should be given except an opportunity to work. If no steady employment is available, this class should be offered any manual labor to enable it to earn maintenance—just enough for the bare necessities. The standard must always be far below that offered to the bona fide dependent. The labor yard where tramps can earn enough for food and lodging is all to which they are entitled. If this treatment is strictly adhered to, in the majority of cases they forget their wanderlust, and settle down if legitimate employment is offered. At any rate, they do not then form an undesirable and illegitimate burden upon the community. The tramp is the most important part of the transient problem. The genuine tramp is aptly characterized by Mrs. Solenberger as a "class of parasites."[1] This class contains the confirmed wanderer, criminals, impostors, begging letter writers, confidence men, etc., besides a great number of all kinds of chronic beggars, local vagrants, and kindred types. While our classification indicates sufficient characteristics to distinguish the individuals of each class, it must be remembered that this classification is, in the ultimate analysis, very arbitrary. Quite frequently we meet with a composite type, belonging to two or three classes simultaneously. Often it is impossible to trace the gradual transition from one class to the one below.

This class of parasite is the most annoying problem modern charity faces. The reclamation of the true tramp is one of the most thankless and hardest of tasks. Attempts to combat this evil are really worldwide. There is no doubt that here we are dealing with psycho-pathological phenomena. The restless spirit, the desire to live without labor and without responsibility, the lack of attachment to any social group is abnormal and vicious. It is anti-social and dangerous.

[1] Mrs. Alice Solenberger, "One Thousand Homeless Men."

Authorities are in accord that only the most stringent methods and definite policy of handling this class will reduce the evil to a minimum.

In this class, as well as in the aforementioned three other classes, there are some specific characteristics that distinguish the Jewish tramp from his non-Jewish confrères. The Jewish tramp, as a rule, takes it for granted that his co-religionists owe him a living; he does not cherish the idea of depending upon non-Jewish charity, though he is very unscrupulous in accepting assistance. If there is a synagogue he does not fail to appear there, in a larger city he usually remains over Saturday, so as to be sure to get all he can from the pious Jew who comes to the House of Worship; he knows well that he is welcome to the shelter home, if there is any in existence, and he utilizes the privilege to the fullest extent. At last he takes to organized charity, and in the majority of cases scrapes together sufficient money for railroad transportation, at least to the next point, where he can repeat his operations. A Jewish tramp does not like the excitement of jumping trains, and while occasionally the use of freight trains is accepted, as a rule, he prefers the slow but sure way of going from one town to another and paying for transportation. He has considerable pride. He objects to being arrested as a vagrant, and in fact, does not want to be treated like a non-Jew. Intemperance plays a very insignificant part in the life of the Jewish tramp, but gambling seems to be an ever present characteristic.

Chapter Six. Transients

Questions

1. What was the attitude of the Jews in the past towards the stranger?
2. What is the present attitude, and what caused the change?
3. What is the "passing-on policy" and what are the objections to it?
4. What are the transportation rules of the National Conference of Jewish Charities?
5. Discuss the most important decisions.
6. What is the present status of the transportation rules?
7. Describe the institutions of Hachnosis Orchim.
8. Discuss the four categories of transients.

VII

THE IMMIGRATION PROBLEM

In accepting the rough classification of applicants for relief on the basis of length of residence in the city, into transients and residents, we must also consider as a separate category, the recently arrived immigrant, who in length of residence is not a resident, and in characterization is not a transient. In this connection it is interesting to note that even the law of the land is rather indefinite on the privileges of residence of the stranger within our gates. Even after his admission he is not to become a public charge, and if he temporarily halts or stumbles in his progress toward acclimatization, adjustment, and naturalization, he is liable to the dreaded deportation. A humanitarian interpretation of the law is given in practice, however, and generally speaking, only in cases where the dependency is of a chronic nature, or had originated before immigration, is deportation resorted to. On the other hand, from the standpoint of the relief agency, the recently arrived immigrant can in no wise be treated like a transient. As a result, we must add a second class called "Recent Arrivals" to our rather arbitrary division. They present a special field of specific Jewish philanthropy, which for want of a better name we may term "first aid to the immigrant."

This particular sphere of philanthropic effort has been especially well developed among the Jews of the United States, where, in the beginning, the entire raison d'être of Jewish charity was the helping of newly arrived immigrants. It is only lately that the country at large has begun to realize that the proper care of the immigrant is of great moment to the commonwealth in general. We see the different attempts to handle the situation on a national scale. For a long time, however, this care of the stranger after he had been admitted to this country was left to mere chance and to the sympathy of those with whom he came in contact. In this regard the Jews have not been backward in ameliorating the hardships of their co-religionists who came after them.

A. Early Jewish Immigration to the United States

The first impetus for Jewish immigration to the New World came with the Spanish Inquisition. Immigrating, first to South and Central America, the Jews later extended their objective points to Mexico and the West Indies. In the seventeenth and eighteenth centuries they settled in parts which now belong to the United States. When, in 1654, twenty-four Jews, fugitives from the Portuguese persecution in Brazil, arrived in New Amsterdam, Peter Stuyvesant, the governor, applied to the directors of the Dutch West India Company for authority to exclude them. Since large Jewish capital was invested in the company, and because Jews had assisted in the conquest of Brazil, the directors promptly denied his request. The company permitted the Jews to trade and to settle in the New Netherlands, but a year later enjoined the Jews from building a synagogue, and somewhat later, from holding public office.

The community at Newport owes its origin to the unfriendly attitude of Stuyvesant. Some of the Jews sought the kindlier atmosphere of Rhode Island, where Roger Williams had exerted his influence for absolute freedom of conscience. In colonial times, the colony at Newport attracted the renowned rabbis the world over, and before the revolution, numbered one thousand, one hundred, and seventy-five Jews.

The Jews seem to have suffered the greatest curtailments of their civil and political rights in Maryland.

In Georgia, the Jews appeared immediately following the first settlers. Despite the opposition of his trustees in London, Oglethorpe saw no reason to refuse to Jews admission to his colony, and a number of them were included in grants of public lands in Savannah.

At the beginning of the nineteenth century, the Charleston Jews formed the most important Jewish community in the United States.[1]

B. BEGINNINGS OF JEWISH CHARITY IN THE UNITED STATES

There is no doubt that even at this early period the Jews did not neglect their brethren and endeavored to

[1] "Jewish Encyclopædia," Vol. xii, "United States."

help their co-religionists. Although most of the Jews of that time were widely scattered, we find that as early as 1746, in New York City, there was a school attached to the existing synagogue, where provision was made for the free instruction of the children of the poor. In those days, the community directed the administration of its charities exclusively through its synagogue and other congregational channels. The beginning of the organization of independent Jewish charities dates back to as early as 1812, when the number of Jews in New York City was not more than five hundred.

In the first quarter of the nineteenth century, a large number of German Jewish immigrants arrived. In 1818, the existing congregation, Shearith Israel, in New York City, was rebuilt, to accommodate the increasing number of worshipers, many of them newly arrived immigrants. In 1822, the Hebrew Benevolent Society was organized with the residue of a fund raised by popular subscription two years before for the maintenance of a poor Jewish veteran of the Revolutionary War. In 1825, Sampson Simpson, the first Jewish member of the bar, was one of the leaders in Jewish charitable work.

Although there was little or no communal life, the interest of the Jews in their own brethren, even outside the limits of the United States, was not foreign to them. As early as 1825, Mordecai M. Noah, a native of Philadelphia, and prominent in politics, journalism, and civic affairs, originated a plan of establishing a Jewish colony on Grand Island, in the State of New York. He received, however, little encouragement or co-operation from his co-religionists, who, in fact, opposed and ridiculed both the plan and its author.

C. Early Immigration

Just as the explorer, before him, had to fight for his rights, so the immigrant in early days had difficulty before he was admitted to an existing settlement. There were certain requirements and qualifications that he had to meet before he could join a community. The Jews had additional difficulties to overcome. During the early period, from colonial times to 1835, immigration was taken as a matter of course. The only legislation enacted, and in fact, the only law proposed, was the law of 1819 for the regulation of the steerage passengers at sea. This law, besides, provided for the collection of statistics relative to immigration to the United States.

The second period—from 1835 to 1860—is chiefly characterized by the growth of the Native American or Know Nothing movement, which was based largely, if not exclusively, upon an opposition to the immigration of Roman Catholics. Many strenuous attempts were made to pass restrictive and repressive measures, but no laws were enacted to that end.

D. Immigration of 1848

As a consequence of the sudden and large increase in immigration from Europe between 1848 and 1850, the old prejudice against the foreigner was revived. This sentiment grew so strong that in 1855, an effort was made to elect a president upon an anti-immigration platform. The movement of immigration was made up in no small part of Jewish immigrants from Germany, principally from Bavaria and the Rhine provinces. The condition of the immigrants in those days was deplorable. Legislation enacted in New York State clearly indicates the existing situation. In 1847, a resolution was adopted, memorializing Congress to limit the number of passengers which might be carried by steamships and also to prescribe the method of carrying, so as to ameliorate the bad conditions previously existing. Among other things the resolution states "that almost weekly some vessel, swarming with human beings, arrives at our ports, and the details of their suffering, arising from the crowded state of such a vessel, a neglect of the master to see secured a sufficiency of water and provisions for the voyage, and the convenience for preparing food, the inattention of such master to the cleanliness of the steerage, and the comfort and health of the passengers, are shocking to our sense of humanity, and a disgrace to any country possessing the power to prevent the recurrence of such enormities." [1]

This was just the time when, as has been stated above, the larger proportion of the Jewish immigration came from Bavaria and the Rhine provinces. The immigrants at that time began to present a distinct problem. While the American Jews enjoyed social equality and partook with their Christian fellow citizens

[1] "Reports of the Immigration Commission," Vol. 39, page 767. Washington, 1911.

in the organization of clubs, dancing assemblies, and other social functions, we find that after 1848 there arrived a large number of Jews who disturbed the tranquillity of the old settlers. Almost all of the Jewish immigrants during this period arrived wholly without means, and for many, peddling was at first the only means of a livelihood. There was no doubt that the Jewish immigrant received considerable aid from his co-religionists. Private relief agencies were then organized, and they assisted the newcomer by establishing him in a home, and giving him a start in the new country.

E. Polish Immigration

Individual Russian and Polish Jews, more especially the latter, emigrated to the United States at the time of the American Revolution. The Russian ukase of 1827, drafting Jewish boys at the age of twelve for military service, and that of 1848, extending the conscription to Russian Poland were the initial incentives which led to a larger stream of immigration, which first flowed to England and thence to America. The epoch-making revolutionary period of 1848 and the Polish revolt in 1863, were potent factors in the increase of this immigration.

F. Russian Immigration

The Russo-Jewish exodus, en masse, however, did not begin until 1881. With the anti-Jewish riots of April 27, 1881, at Yelissavetgrad and the later riots at Kiev and other cities of South Russia, Jewish immigration from that country to the United States assumed very large proportions. The first group of this newer class of immigrants, consisting of about two hundred and fifty members of the Am Olam (eternal people) Society arrived in New York on July 29, 1881. This was followed later by a large stream of refugees.

The following table gives the number of Russian Jews who emigrated to the United States during the several years of this decade, according to the figures of the United States Immigration Commission and the United Hebrew Charities of New York:

Year	From Russia	Year	From Russia
1881	8,193	1886	17,309
1882	17,497	1887	28,944
1883	6,907	1888	31,256
1884	15,122	1889	31,889
1885	16,603	1890	33,147

The immigrants that came so suddenly and in such large numbers attracted the attention of the general populations of the United States. No wonder that their co-religionists were eager to do their bounden duty in helping the newcomers, in need of immediate assistance. While it must be recalled that the immediate causes of the large mass of immigration of the Russian Jews were the riots and political and religious persecution, underneath the movement was the economic disability under which the Jews labored in Russia. They came here without means. Unlike other immigrants, they came with families, and the families

THE IMMIGRATION PROBLEM 91

were large. The large majority came to New York, and intended to settle there.

G. IMMIGRATION FUNDS

Funds to aid the Russian Jews were raised everywhere. In Philadelphia, twenty-five thousand dollars were raised early in 1882. The Hebrew Immigrant Aid Society of the United States collected three hundred thousand dollars, and the New York Russian Relief Fund, seventy thousand. In 1883, sixty thousand dollars more were collected, and temporary quarters were erected on Wards Island and at Greenpoint, L. I. About three thousand immigrants were temporarily housed and maintained there until employment could be secured.

H. FEDERAL LEGISLATION

The beginning of the large Russian Jewish immigration coincided with the beginning of our Federal legislation for the control and regulation of immigration in general. The first general immigration law was approved August 3, 1882. This law provided for a head tax of fifty cents to be levied on all aliens to be landed at any port in the United States, the money thus collected to be used exclusively to defray the expenses of regulating immigration and for the care of immigrants after landing.

On February 26, 1885, the first act of Congress forbidding the importation of contract laborers was approved. This law was later amended in 1887, giving authority to the Secretary of the Treasury to return within the year any immigrant landed contrary to this act.

These restrictive laws did in no wise affect Jewish immigration. The new arrival did not belong to the excluded categories, but needed help and assistance. The American Jews nobly came to the front and collected money, not only sufficient to meet the emergency here, but also to send large sums of money to Russia for improving conditions there.

I. First Aid to the Immigrant

But what was the problem that confronted American Jewry? The question of settling the immigrant was most important. Accommodations were secured to house the new arrival. Clothing was distributed, food and clothing were supplied. The dependency of the immigrant was temporary, the assistance given was intended to carry him through until he found employment. There was no doubt but that as soon as he was established he would need no help. All organized effort was directed to the new arrival. Jewish philanthropy at this period limited itself to "first aid to the immigrant." Through the experience of those few years, the Jews learned the necessity and wisdom of thorough organization of relief agencies. As a result the Jews have succeeded in instituting system and efficiency in the administration of relief.

J. The Exodus from Russia and Roumania

The new and more repressive measures inaugurated by the Russian Government in the early nineties resulted in still another increase in Jewish immigration, as can be seen from the following table:

Year	Total [1]	Year	Total [1]
1891	42,145	1896	45,137
1892	76,417	1897	22,750
1893	35,626	1898	27,321
1894	36,725	1899	24,275
1895	33,232	1900	37,011

This stream of Russian Jewish immigrants was augmented by large numbers of immigrants from Roumania, due to the continual persecution of the Jews in that country, and to no inconsiderable extent from Austria.[2] The question of extending relief to

---

[1] Jewish immigration at the port of New York.

[2] The following tables prepared by the Hebrew Sheltering and Immigrant Aid Society of America give the Jewish immigration at the port of New York for the calendar year 1914, classified by sex, country of birth, and destination within the United States:

Sex		Country of Birth (cont.)	
Male	26,880	Roumania	1,394
Female	24,543	Turkey (European)	420
		Greece	217
Grand Total	51,423	Serbia	37
		Bulgaria	10
Country of Birth		Italy	7
From S. and E. Europe—		Syria	7
Russia	38,064		
Austria	9,272	Total	49,428

94 JEWISH PHILANTHROPY

large numbers of immigrants became a perpetual problem. The United Hebrew Charities of New York

Country of Birth (cont.)
From other countries—

England	648
Turkey (Asiatic)	469
Germany	298
France	81
South America	61
Holland	47
Belgium	44
Egypt	36
Denmark	30
Switzerland	27
South Africa	20
Ireland	22
Scotland	15
Sweden	14
Norway	9
Australia	7
Central America	6
West Indies	6
Mexico	5
Wales	5
Persia	2
San Domingo	1
Canada	22
United States	120
Total	1,995

Destination
States—

Alabama	51
Arkansas	1
California	161
Colorado	46

Destination (cont.)
States—

Connecticut	1,017
Delaware	12
District of Columbia	51
Florida	19
Georgia	62
Illinois	1,825
Indiana	130
Iowa	73
Kansas	6
Kentucky	22
Louisiana	21
Maine	36
Maryland	246
Massachusetts	1,327
Michigan	499
Minnesota	194
Mississippi	7
Missouri	360
Montana	14
Nebraska	114
Nevada	7
New Hampshire	23
New Jersey	2,166
New Mexico	6
New York	38,753
North Carolina	6
North Dakota	30
Ohio	760
Oklahoma	8
Oregon	42
Pennsylvania	2,025
Rhode Island	171
South Carolina	15

City felt the burden of immigration, probably more than did any other organization, and in its annual reports the officers of that organization called attention to the deplorable conditions under which the immigrant lived and the urgent necessity for extensive funds to handle the situation. The following table gives Jewish immigration from 1901 down through the outbreak of the war. It will be seen that the war caused a falling off in immigrant arrivals of over 90 per cent. Another interesting phenomenon is found in a study of the proportion of Russian Jews among the total. Beginning with 1915, there is a marked decline, more and more immigrants coming from "English-speaking" countries to use a phrase adopted by the Immigration Commission of 1907.

Destination (cont.) States—		Destination (cont.) States—	
South Dakota	4	West Virginia	13
Tennessee	56	Wisconsin	242
Texas	37	Wyoming	2
Utah	2	In transit	645
Vermont	11		
Virginia	35	Grand Total	51,423
Washington	70		

For more detailed analysis, information, and statistics of immigration to the United States see Samuel Joseph's "Jewish Immigration to the United States from 1881 to 1910" and Isaac A. Hourwich's "Immigration and Labor."

Year [1]	Total	From Russia	Per cent
1901	37,152	21,214	57
1902	54,954	29,280	53
1903	60,815	34,196	56
1904	89,442	66,536	75
1905	100,388	77,564	78
1906	147,269	118,620	81
1907	109,603	80,503	74
1908	62,326	45,465	73
1909	54,223	38,460	71
1910	71,256	49,007	69
1911	63,032	44,513	71
1912	61,903	42,554	69
1913	95,286	65,636	69
1914	77,719	56,646	73
1915	6,247	3,629	58

K. Additional Legislation

Meanwhile, in 1891, additional legislation was proposed, and in due time, passed. Polygamists, and persons suffering from loathsome or contagious diseases were added to the classes excluded by the act of 1882. Provision was made that "assisted persons unless affirmatively shown that they do not belong to any of the excluded classes" should be deported. All decisions of the inspection officials refusing an alien the privilege of landing were final, unless appeal were made to the Secretary of the Treasury This law was of great consequence to Jewish immigrants, a large number of whom suffered from trachoma (granulation of the conjunctiva of the eyelids, attended by in-

[1] Jewish calendar year September 30th to October 1st, inclusive.

flammation) which was classed by the United States Public Health and Marine Hospital Service as a dangerous contagious disease within the meaning of the immigration act of 1891. This caused the deportation of a considerable number of immigrant Jews. Others were debarred from landing because in some way or other they had been assisted in emigrating. Still others were deported as likely to become public charges. The fact that the decisions of the immigration inspectors were more or less final permitted a rather severe interpretation of the law, and the possibility of wrong judgment, and the further fact that not unfrequently certain immigration inspectors became arbitrary and dictatorial, in their attitude toward the immigrants, provided the incentive for organized effort for the protection of immigrants. This resulted in the establishment of an agency whose duty it would be to secure for the immigrant fair treatment at the hands of the inspectors, and to take appeals to the Secretary of the Treasury, as provided by law in the cases of threatened deportation.

The immigration law of 1893 provided that the judgment of one inspector was not sufficient to exclude an immigrant. It now became his duty to detain for special inquiry each immigrant who, in his opinion, was not qualified to land. Special inquiries were to be conducted by not less than four inspectors. In 1894, the head tax was increased from fifty cents to one dollar. It is necessary to refer here to the American Protective Association, an atavistic form of the old

Know Nothing movement, which again became prominent about this period. The Junior Order of the United American Mechanics and the Patriotic Sons of America were claimed to be sympathizers and co-operators. In 1890, the Association claimed a membership of close to two million, five hundred thousand persons. At that time it seemed probable that the Association would grow in influence and power, but in reality it never progressed beyond the stage of agitation.

In 1903, the Department of Commerce and Labor was established, and a Commissioner General of Immigration was placed under the jurisdiction of that Department. By the law of 1906, providing for a uniform rule for the naturalization of aliens, the designation of the Bureau of Immigration was changed to the Bureau of Immigration and Naturalization.

L. The Immigration Law of 1907

In 1907, a bill was approved which is practically the present immigration law, and contains the following special provisions: The head tax is now four dollars, and is to be paid by every alien entering the United States. The classes of aliens excluded from the United States are as follows: (1) idiots; (2) insane persons; persons who have been insane within five years previous to arrival, and persons who have had two or more attacks of insanity at any time previous; (3) imbeciles; (4) feeble-minded persons; (5) epileptics; (6) paupers; (7) persons likely to become a public charge; (8) professional beggars; (9) persons afflicted with tuberculosis or with a loathsome or dangerous contagious disease; (10) persons not included within any of the foregoing excluded classes who are found to be mentally or physically defective, such defect being likely to affect the ability of such aliens to earn a living; (11) persons who have been convicted of, or admit having committed a felony or other crime involving moral turpitude; (12) polygamists, or persons who believe in polygamy; (13) anarchists, or persons who believe in or are advocates of the overthrow by force or violence of the government of the United States, or of all governments; (14) prostitutes; (15) persons who procure or attempt to bring in prostitutes or women or girls for the purpose of prostitution; (16) contract laborers; (17) persons who have been deported within one year from the date of application for admission to the United States, as being under contract or promise to perform labor in this country; (18) any person whose ticket or passage was paid for with the money of another, or is assisted by others to come, unless it is affirmatively shown that such person does not belong to one of the foregoing excluded classes; (19) all children under fifteen years of age unaccompanied by parent or guardian, at the discretion of the Secretary of Commerce and Labor; (20) any alien accompanying another alien, helpless from sickness may be deported with such alien.

The following are excepted from the provision of the act with regard to contract laborers: professional actors, artists, lecturers, singers, ministers of any religious denomination, professors for colleges or universities; persons belonging to any recognized learned profession; or persons employed strictly as personal or domestic servants; and skilled labor if its kind is not to be found in this country. A diseased wife or minor children of a resident alien may be admitted if without danger to the public. The importation or holding of any alien woman or girl for purposes of prostitution is forbidden under penalty of five thousand dollars or imprisonment of not more than five years for each offense. Any alien woman or girl found an inmate of a house of prostitution or practicing prostitution within two years of landing within the United States shall be deported.

Unless the inspector clearly thinks that the immigrant is entitled to admission, he must hold him for special inquiry, which is conducted by a Board of Special Inquiry, appointed by the Commissioners of Immigration at each port of arrival. Each Board consists of three men. The alien or any dissenting member of the Board may appeal to the Secretary of Commerce and Labor through the Commissioner of Immigration and the Commissioner General. No appeal may be taken from their decision, made upon the basis of certification of a medical officer in the case of aliens afflicted with tuberculosis, or a loathsome or dangerous contagious disease.

If any alien shall have entered the United States and become a public charge from causes existing prior to landing, he may be deported within three years after the date of entry.

Any alien liable to be excluded as likely to become a public charge or because of physical disability other than tuberculosis or a dangerous or loathsome contagious disease may be admitted, if otherwise admissible in the discretion of the Secretary of Commerce and Labor, upon the giving of a suitable bond that such alien will not become a public charge. This act also established a division of Information in the Bureau of Immigration, whose duty it is to promote a beneficial distribution of aliens among the states and territories desiring immigrants.

In 1910, an important amendment to this law of 1907 was enacted. The following were added to the classes excluded from landing: persons who are supported by, or receive in full or in part, the proceeds of prostitution. The agitation of the subject known as white slavery resulted in the enactment of the Mann Act, an act prohibiting the transportation between states of persons for the purposes of prostitution. Subsequently the Department of Commerce and Labor was divided into two departments. The Commissioner General of Immigration is now an officer of the Department of Labor.

M. THE ECONOMIC STATUS OF THE JEWISH IMMIGRANT

Practically speaking, all the above laws, as enacted, limit immigration to persons who are not likely to become charity recipients, and at least at their arrival possess some means to preclude the possibility of their becoming a burden on the community of their destination. In this connection it is interesting to note that the average amount per capita shown by Jewish immigrants for the fiscal years 1904 to 1910 was thirty-two dollars and nine cents. Again, the majority of the Jewish immigrants in later years came to join relatives and were assisted by the latter. Statistical tables show that for the years 1908 to 1910, both inclusive, 142,369 immigrants reported that their passage was prepaid by some relative, 1,053 by others than self or relatives, and 101,777 by self. In other words, 58.5 per cent were paid for by someone who was ready to help the immigrant if necessary, and so make it unnecessary for them to apply to organized charity. This change in the very setting of the new immigrant explains the small number of recently arrived immigrants who apply to relief agencies as shown by the reports of the latter. Thus, the United Hebrew Charities of New York, in 1914, reports only 967 of 7,208 applications, as being less than five years in America, while Chicago, of 2,324 applications, reports only 97 as being less than one year in this country; Baltimore reports only 227 out of 5,229 applications.

N. Protection of the Immigrant at the Port of Entry

Although the relief phase of the first aid to the immigrant is of far less importance than in years previous, the immigrant requires a considerable amount of assistance which only organized effort can provide. The Government attempts to guard the interests of the new arrival, and makes considerable provision for their supervision. Municipalities in many instances offer instruction in English, and other facilities for the rapid Americanization of the newcomer. In the large majority of cases, however, the present day immigrant, coming to relatives, applies to organized charity for assistance only in exceptional cases, and so the field of the so-called "first aid to the immigrants" is changing in its application. There are a few features in this particular field of philanthropic effort which are still the functions of an organized agency, and cannot be performed by individuals not equipped with the knowledge or machinery which is imperative in this sphere. Thus, the question of the admission of aliens at times presents considerable difficulty. With the more complicated immigration legislation pertaining to the exclusion of aliens, an immigrant is liable to be rejected for no other reason than for some misunderstanding or for inability to answer the formal requirements of the law. Often he makes statements that are detrimental to his own interests; he may have difficulty in locating his friend because of a wrong, illegible, or lost address; he may misunderstand the question propounded, and at times may meet with an unforeseen situation which properly explained would not debar him from admission. Hence, the necessity of providing some definite system of protection of the immigrant at the port of entry. The Hebrew Sheltering and Immigrant Aid Society of America and the Council of Jewish Women are especially active in this connection.

The anti-white slavery agitation emphasizes the importance of protective work among immigrant girls. The National Council of Jewish Women has taken charge of this important activity. The organization maintains connections with various European societies which watch over girls who are traveling either to or from Europe, especially the sick, excluded upon arrival, or the insane deported after a stay in America. They thus have some friendly agency to guard their interests from the time they leave to the time they reach their destination. At the various points of entry the Council maintains women agents, who are ready and anxious to give advice and aid in solving, as far as possible, the many difficulties that present themselves to anyone coming from foreign shores. The agents of the Council also protect the immigrant girls against exploitation of any nature. They follow up the girls in their homes, and maintain wherever necessary or expedient a proper supervision over them. The organization has sections all over the country, so that the work is pushed far into the interior, especially in the larger cities.

The United Hebrew Charities of New York in former years maintained a special agent at Ellis Island for this purpose. For the past eight years, however, this work has been assumed by the Hebrew Sheltering and Immigrant Aid Society of America which has a very pretentious program besides. From the annual reports of the Hebrew Sheltering and Immigrant Aid Society of America we can secure a definite idea of the scope of its program. The expenditure of the organization in 1913 was $72,093.78. This society maintains two representatives at Ellis Island. In order to prevent, as far as possible, deportation of those who should be released, their duty is to scrutinize the lists of immigrants who are refused admission on primary inspection. Thus they aid in the administration of justice, and serve as volunteer attorneys for the immigrants, seeking to protect them from misinterpretation of the law, the abuse of the discretionary powers vested in the Boards of Special Inquiry, and in the medical officers as well. They guide the immigrant also through the maze of rules and regulations that enmesh and bewilder him from the moment that he arrives in this country, at a time when he does not know where and how to locate the friend or relative whose presence he so sorely needs.

The number of Jewish immigrants arriving in New York during 1913 was 103,869. The Society dealt with 3,726 cases, or 3.6 per cent of the total. One thousand nine hundred and forty-four, or 51.5 per cent of the detained or excluded, were admitted on rehearings before the Boards of Special Inquiry, often reversing their own decisions on the presentation of supplementary evidence. The Society appealed 736 cases, of which 461 were admitted. Altogether, only 1.2 per cent of the total immigration were deported. All the Jewish immigrants giving New York as their destination are taken in charge by the Society until they are safely placed with their relatives or friends, or otherwise disposed of. In cases where the friends or relatives cannot be located the Society provides food and shelter, inserts advertisements in the Jewish dailies, and spares no efforts to locate them. Twenty-five thousand three hundred and nine immigrants, 24.4 per cent of the total number of Jewish immigrants in 1913, received this guiding assistance from the Society. In addition, the Society conducts an employment agency, and a temporary shelter house with accommodations for about one hundred, maintains educational work upon lines of Americanization, and attempts to use the follow-up system with as many immigrants as possible. A special branch has been recently organized on the Pacific Coast. There are also immigrant aid societies in Baltimore, Philadelphia, and Boston, which work in co-operation with the Society in New York.

With all these agencies, specifically engaged in first aid to the immigrant, there is very little need for other organizations carrying on general welfare work to devote considerable attention to this particular phase of the problem. Occasionally, however, in individual cases, a philanthropic agency may be called upon to assist a newly arrived immigrant. In the main, this assistance means merely to refer the case to the special agency, to enter into correspondence with the same, and to give co-operation which the latter may require in securing whatever information is needed. Again, in some instances, the relief society may have some immigrants who need actual monetary assistance, either through unavoidable accident, sickness, and so forth, simply because the natural guardian, the relative or friend whom the immigrant joined is unable, or in some isolated cases even unwilling further to assist. These cases, as we have mentioned before, are comparatively rare, and after the first aid, be it establishment in a home, or temporary relief, they present no difficulties—except the somewhat large initial outlay. There need be no fear that adequate relief given to the recently arrived immigrant will lead to dependency.

O. THE ANTI-RESTRICTION MOVEMENT

Although the actual work along lines of first aid to the immigrant seems to present few difficulties and is rather well in hand, there has been lately thrust upon American Jewry the urgent necessity of maintaining an agitation for defense against restrictive tendencies and discriminatory effects of laws advocated and often initiated by enemies of a liberal immigration policy.

1. *The Immigration Commission of 1907*

By an Immigration Act of Congress of February 20, 1907, a special commission was created, consisting of nine members; three senators, to be appointed by the vice-president, three representatives, to be appointed by the speaker of the House, and three laymen, to be appointed by the President. The Commission was to make full inquiry into the subject of immigration, to report to Congress the conclusions reached by it and make such recommendations as in its judgment shall seem proper. The Commission was subsequently appointed and organized in April, 1907. The complete report of the Commission comprises forty-two bulky volumes, and contains, on the whole, some valuable contributions. The work of the Commission was watched with intense interest by both the restrictionists and those who favor a liberal immigration policy.

On the appointment of the Immigration Commission in 1907,[1] the American Jewish Committee sent a communication to Chairman Dillingham, asking that the Committee be given an opportunity to express its views on immigration, more particularly, if not solely, as it refers to the Jews. On December 4, 1909, the Committee, together with delegates from the Independent Order of B'nai B'rith was accorded a hearing and in 1910 the Committee presented written recommendations concerning the revision of the existing immigration laws and regulations. The Committee maintained that the existing laws are, in the main, satisfactory, that the immigrants are entitled to due process of law, and opposed proposed amendments, which, first, increased the head tax, second, repealed or modified the bonding provision, third, established a literacy test, fourth,

---

[1] The personnel of the Commission was as follows:
Hon. Wm. P. Dillingham, of Vt., chairman; Hon. Henry Cabot Lodge, of Mass.; Hon. Anselm J. McLaurin, of Miss. (Substituted in 1908 by Hon. Asbury C. Latimer, of S. C. on whose death in 1910, Hon. Le Roy Percy of Miss. was appointed.) Hon. Ben. F. Howell, of N. J.; Hon. Wm. S. Bennett, of N. Y.; Hon. John L. Burnett, of Ala.; Mr. Charles P. Neill, of Washington, D. C.; Professor Jeremiah W. Jenks, of N. Y.; Professor Wm. R. Wheeler, of Cal.

THE IMMIGRATION PROBLEM 109

prescribed physical examination for immigrants such as is prescribed for admission to the United States army, fifth, established monetary requirements, sixth, required moral certificates for admission, particularly from Russian refugees, seventh, abolished the bonding provision, eighth, established as an excluded class, persons found to be economically undesirable, ninth, required all aliens to secure registration under heavy penalties, tenth, increased from three to four years the period within which deportation may be ordered on the ground of being a public charge, and lastly, established a race and color test for admission of aliens, contrary to the fundamental principles of our government and in violation of treaty rights.

2. *The Jewish Issue Before the Commission*

The specifically Jewish issue was encountered by the Commission when, in adopting the classification of immigrants by races, the Commission found difficulty in placing the Jews by this scheme in a separate category. At a hearing before the Commission, December 4, 1909, the Hon. Simon Wolf of Washington, D. C., representing the executive committee of the Board of Delegates on Civil Rights of the Union of American Hebrew Congregations, appeared to oppose the use by the Commission of the word Hebrew in a racial connection. Hon. Julian W. Mack of Chicago, made a similar argument. Mr. Wolf explained, moreover, that the Jews are by no means unanimous in denying their racial status, but that a certain portion of the Jewish people, notably the

Zionists, claimed that the Jews are a distinct race. The Commission also received several communications from Hebrew organizations, urging the continued use of the word Jew or Hebrew to designate a race or people, one of these petitions being in the form of a resolution, adopted by the Federated Jewish Organizations of New York. The Commission decided that it was justified in using the term Hebrew as designating a race or people.

3. *The Burnett-Dillingham Bill*

In 1910, the Committee made every legitimate effort to prevent the passage of the bill introduced by Senator Dillingham, which contained among other features, a provision for a reading and writing test. In April, two years later, the House Committee on Immigration finally reported a bill by Representative Burnett of Alabama. This bill would generally exclude aliens over sixteen years of age unable to read. It contained a clause, however, excepting from this provision those who can prove that they are seeking admission solely for the purpose of escaping religious persecution.

The Immigration Bill, a combination of the Dillingham and Burnett Bills, passed February 19, 1913, but was vetoed by President Taft. The Senate passed the bill over the President's veto, but in the House the veto was sustained. Subsequently, in February, 1917, practically the same Bill was passed in both Houses of Congress over the veto of President Wilson, and is now law. While the American Jewish Committee has an extremely wide scope, as its constitution provides, most of its activities prove that at present, at least, it is pre-eminently concerned with combating hostile immigration legislation. This work is undoubtedly of great positive value to those who, without this guardian of their rights, would not be allowed to land and become good American citizens.

P. THE GALVESTON MOVEMENT

In June, 1910, a considerable number of Jewish immigrants came through the port of Galveston, and were ordered deported on the alleged ground, either that they had come in violation of the contract labor laws, or were liable to become public charges. These immigrants came through the Jewish Territorialist Organization, which was then trying to divert the stream of immigration from New York to Galveston, where the Jewish Immigrants Information Bureau was attempting to distribute these immigrants so arriving according to the best interests of the immigrants and the attendant interests of the country. However, this logical attempt to divert immigration at its fountain head was construed to bring it within the meaning of stimulating immigration from Russia to America.

CHAPTER SEVEN. THE IMMIGRATION PROBLEM

QUESTIONS

1. Why do the "recent arrivals" form a separate class?
2. State the history of immigration laws.
3. State the restrictive laws from 1882 to 1907.
4. Enumerate the provisions of the present law.

5. Describe the work of the Immigration Commission of 1907.
6. What are the provisions of the Burnett-Dillingham Bill?
7. What is the anti-restriction movement, and what are the functions of the American Jewish Committee in connection with it?
8. Describe the early Jewish immigration to the United States.
9. Describe the attitude of the American Jews toward the immigrants from Germany, Poland, etc.
10. Give the history of the Russian Jewish immigration of the eighties.
11. Describe the raising of immigration funds.
12. Discuss the economic status of the Jewish immigrant.
13. State what protection the Jews offer to the Jewish immigrants at the port of entry.
14. Describe the work of the Hebrew Sheltering and Immigrant Aid Society of America.
15. What is the Anti-White Slavery Crusade?

VIII

DISTRIBUTION

While the Jews advocate a very liberal immigration policy, and a liberal interpretation of the existing laws, and are great believers in the potential good that foreigners bring to America, they are, at the same time, quite aware that great danger lurks in the unreasonable congestion in the limited territory. As a result, the Jews are firm believers in the policy and efficacy of adequate distribution of immigrants. Thus, at the earliest inception of the Russian mass immigration, the Baron De Hirsch Fund was ready to supply transportation to those immigrants who have expectations of employment outside of the larger cities, or who have relatives or friends willing to receive and care for them at their destination. This distribution was done in individual cases alone, and no organized effort was made to make this movement counteract the tendencies of the immigrant to remain in the ports of entry, particularly in New York City.

A. THE INDUSTRIAL REMOVAL OFFICE

In 1900, the so-called removal work was delegated to a special agency known as the Industrial Removal Office. It was self-evident that if this work of distribution was to succeed and reach the immense scope that, in this field, was the criterion of efficiency, it was necessary not only to supply funds for transportation, but also to secure the co-operation of the different communities to which the immigrants were to be sent. Organizations had to be effected in the different localities to help the removals in the first instances, for it became patent that immigrants without friends or relatives must be removed from the congested centers, so that the immigration which that individual induced would come to him in an interior locality, instead of to the already overcrowded centers.

B. Co-operation

In 1901 Leo N. Levi, late president of the Independent Order of B'nai B'rith, issued a circular calling upon the lodges of the Order for close co-operation in the work of the Industrial Removal Office. At the Detroit Conference of the National Conference of Jewish Charities in 1902, the work of the Industrial Removal Office was the main topic for discussion. It was at that meeting that Cyrus Sulzberger made his memorable appeal to the delegates from the different cities. There was not a dry eye when he described the conditions in the New York Ghetto. From that time on, the work of the Removal Office proceeded in earnest and upon a large scale.[1]

In the beginning, a central office was opened in New York City, and a number of traveling representatives

[1] "The Removal Work," Simon Wolf. "Proceedings of the Third Conference of Jewish Charities," New York, 1904.

presented to various communities all over the country the object and functions of the Removal Office, and its methods of procedure.

This educational program was essential to bring home to the Jewish community at large that the stream of immigration had to be diverted away from New York, that the problem of Jewish immigration to the United States was not a local one merely because, by sheerest accident, the vast majority of ocean steamers disembarked their human cargoes at the harbor of New York, and since the question of immigration was of national interest, that it was therefore incumbent on the Jews of the entire community to help in the assimilation of these friendless refugees and to help make them self-supporting.

C. Local Agencies

Later, the Industrial Removal Office provided a paid agent in a number of communities, who devoted part or whole time to the individuals or families who were sent from New York, and who became known in the parlance of Relief Offices as "I. R. O. cases." The Industrial Removal Office usually provided an allowance of twenty-five dollars in the case of a family, and ten dollars in the case of an individual.

D. Classification

It is claimed, and justly so, that besides the direct benefit that the Industrial Removal Office produces upon those who are sent out, it also "creates nuclei of

immigrants which will in time attract to themselves a natural stream of Jewish settlers, just as the pioneer Jewish settlers of the eighties of the last century who settled in the interior attracted the hundreds and thousands who followed them." Thus, the Industrial Removal Office divides its applicants into three broad categories called:
1. Direct or Original Removals.
2. Request Removals.
3. Reunion Removals.

The individuals in the first division are those who have no definite locality to which they wish to be sent, and who, as a result, leave the selection of the destination to the judgment and discretion of the officials of the Office.

The second category, "request" cases, are sent to their destination only after the community to which the applicant desires to be sent has been notified and has been afforded the opportunity of signifying its pleasure or displeasure in the matter.

The above privilege is also accorded the community with respect to removals of the third class, where the head of the family has left his family either in New York or abroad. The community must ascertain whether the man has established himself sufficiently well to enable him to receive and support his family in the new settlement.[1]

[1] "The Removal Work, Including The Galveston Movement," by David Bressler. Sixth National Conference of Jewish Charities, St. Louis, 1910.

E. Methods

The handling of the I. R. O. cases presents quite a number of peculiar features that tend, at times, to lead to difficulties. There can be no argument as to the duty of the interior Jewish communities to relieve the situation in New York City. In fact, as soon as the situation was presented in its true light, a large number of cities were willing to do their share and anxious to co-operate in this movement.

The question arose, however, as to what criteria should be used in the selection of those who were to be sent and the points of destination. It was decided that the application for removal should be received by the office in New York; various facts pertaining to the desirability of the applicant were to be secured by the office and verified; these facts were then to be submitted to the prospective destinations where the co-operators were to judge whether, in their opinion, the particular case in question might properly be sent. These requisitions for permission to send a case include, besides the name, age, social state, nationality, and so on, the trade, earnings, duration of unemployment, etc. Should the community decide to accept the applicant, it so notifies the office in New York. The applicant is furnished his transportation, funds for incidental expenses on the road, and a letter of introduction to a local agent, who has been informed, usually by telegraph, of the time of arrival, to provide temporary shelter and food and to make efforts to secure work as speedily as possible. In the great majority of cases this arrangement has worked out admirably.

As the success of the movement depended as much upon the prospective applicant as it did upon any other influence, it became necessary to carry on a systematic propaganda among the immigrant classes in the city of New York. To accomplish this, various methods were employed. 1. "The Experiment at Ellis Island": the services of a well-known Yiddish orator and Rabbi were secured to meet the immigrants at Ellis Island, there to talk with them, explaining the situation in New York, the difficulty of finding work and the evils resulting from the overcrowded conditions in the Metropolis. In addition, pamphlets in Yiddish setting forth salient facts, were distributed among the immigrants. Another man was engaged to supplement the above work, by visiting the immigrants in their homes, to explain the purpose of the Removal Work. Still another man was engaged to address the various lodges and societies on the East Side with a view to presenting the movement in its true light and to give people the opportunity of learning something about the interior of the United States. All this propaganda was not engaged in for the purpose of coaxing people out of New York City against their will, but merely to bring people's notice to the existence of the office. It succeeded in arousing the interest of the population to such an extent, that within a very short time after the office was inaugurated, all further propaganda was discontinued because of the large number of applicants that came to the office

DISTRIBUTION

determined to avail themselves, if possible, of the opportunity to start life anew in more favorable surroundings in the interior.

However, other forms of propaganda were resorted to from time to time by means of literature and expositions, showing the settlement of Jews in the United States; the general and the Jewish population in various localities; photographs of living conditions in the interior as contrasted with conditions in the overcrowded Jewish sections of New York; cost of living in the interior; the industrial activities of various cities and towns in the country; public lectures illustrated by slides, articles in the Jewish press, etc.

Within a few years after the movement was first inaugurated, the work of the office, and the number of applicants thereto, assumed such large proportions, that it became possible to discontinue practically every form of propaganda, as the momentum itself, of the work, and the reports of the successful settlement of the great majority of persons sent by the office in the interior, brought to the office daily, a far larger number of desirable applicants than for whom it could properly make provision. Occasionally, however, the Yiddish press was resorted to for advertisements calling for special types of highly skilled artisans—such as were not usually included among the general type of applicants.

F. Reception of Newcomers

The question as to the first reception of the removal case is quite important. In some cities a special boarding house is patronized where all of the I. R. O. cases are placed upon their arrival. In other cities, different places are patronized so as not to form a center, which may cause dissatisfaction and hinder the progress of all through the failure of one. It was found necessary to provide educational and social features and facilities for the newcomers, for in the absence of these, many of the removal cases became homesick. They missed the social life and atmosphere, and not unfrequently left for another city or returned to New York before making a thorough effort to orient themselves in the city of destination.

While in some cities the entire work is vested in the hands of a paid agent of the I. R. O. who works under the supervision of a small committee composed of representative members of the community, in other localities it is a function of the Independent Order of B'nai B'rith with a large committee at the head. Again, in other cities, especially in the smaller communities, the Jewish Congregation takes charge, with the Rabbis in charge of the actual work.

G. Relation to Relief Agencies

The work of the I. R. O. cases requires great tact and much patience. This is probably the reason that it was found advantageous to employ a special agent to look after these cases. In isolated instances, the Industrial

DISTRIBUTION 121

Removal Office case becomes dependent and falls a burden on the local community. As a result of several of these instances, controversy arose as to the residence of the dependent. It was finally decided at the Memphis Conference of Jewish Charities in 1914 that the Industrial Removal Office case becomes a resident in the city of destination immediately upon arrival and need not wait the customary nine months' probationary period.

Because of the peculiar origin of the Industrial Removal Office cases that become dependent, the danger of making the applicant more or less dependent is extremely great. This tendency is often responsible for a cooling off of the desire on the part of communities for further co-operation with the Industrial Removal Office. On the whole, however, the progress made by this movement is controlled almost exclusively by economic conditions. Thus, cyclical fluctuations of labor demand are reflected in the number of removals.

H. Results of the Industrial Removal Office Work

An intensive survey of the work of the Industrial Removal Office was presented in its twelfth annual report, and gives a definite idea of the character and scope of the work achieved. From 1901 to 1912, inclusive, 59,729 people were sent from New York City. The number of cities and towns reached was 1,474, situated in every state of the Union. Quite a number were sent to Canada, one to Argentine, and nine to Brazil. Besides this, the two branches in Boston and Philadelphia during an existence of nine years distributed 5,817 persons, making a grand total of 64,546.

I. THE GALVESTON MOVEMENT

The work of removal discussed thus far refers to the immigration to the Atlantic seaboard, more especially, if not solely, to New York City. A radical and rational departure from this particular problem and as a corollary principle of the Removal Office is presented by what has since become known as the Galveston Movement.[1]

Inaugurated and supported by Jacob H. Schiff, this movement was initiated and dedicated in 1907 to the deflecting of some part of the large immigration which had been flowing almost exclusively to the ports of the North Atlantic States, and directing the deflected portion toward the gulf, with a view of distributing these immigrants over the American "hinterland" west of the Mississippi. Galveston was chosen as the most available port of entrance, and a Jewish Information Bureau was established there for this purpose. With the co-operation of the Jewish Territorialist Organization (I. T. O.) propaganda was conducted in Russia and Roumania to acquaint the prospective emigrants with the advantages of settling in the less densely populated section of the United States west of the

[1] "The Galveston Movement," Jacob H. Schiff, in "Jewish Charities," Vol. IV, No. 11, June, 1914, Baltimore.

Mississippi River and for this purpose to enter the United States through the port of Galveston, rather than through the congested North Atlantic ports of entry. Upon their arrival, the immigrants were met by a representative of the Bureau of Information, who directed them efficiently over the territory between the Mississippi and the Pacific and the Gulf of Mexico and the Dominion. The amount expended for the distribution of immigrants, maintenance until employment had been secured, and other incidentals of the movement, is given for seven years, up to 1914 as $300,000. During this period there have been distributed from nine to ten thousand immigrants who have come to Galveston. The existence of but one steamship line from Bremen to Galveston, and a long ocean voyage, lasting twenty-three days, caused considerable dissatisfaction among the immigrants. Unfortunately the United States Government did not always show itself as sympathetic with the movement as the committee believed it was justified in expecting.

CHAPTER EIGHT. DISTRIBUTION

QUESTIONS

1. What is the problem of distribution?
2. What are the functions of the Industrial Removal Office?
3. What were the co-operative agencies?
4. Describe the local organization.
5. State the three classes of Removal Office cases.
6. State the method of handling Industrial Removal Office cases.
7. Discuss the difficulties.

8. Describe the reception of newcomers and their relations to relief agencies.

9. State the result and progress of the Industrial Removal Office work.

10. What was the Galveston Movement, and why was it abandoned?

IX

THE BACK TO THE SOIL MOVEMENT

Among the different attempts to cope with the problem of congestion and in general to divert the Jewish population from the large cities, the plan to induce the newcomer to follow farming as a pursuit deserves special mention. It is an interesting phenomenon in Jewish philanthropy that an attempt is made to utilize the new immigrant in experiments tending toward the redemption of the name of Israel.

A. EARLY ATTEMPTS

The ambition of the American Jews to develop Jewish farmers is not of recent origin. As early as 1820, an attempt was made to establish a settlement at Grand Island, N. Y., and then again in 1837. These settlements known as Shalom, in a few years were given up as failures. In 1853, a society was organized known as the American Hebrew Agricultural Association, for the purpose of establishing an agricultural school. Individual attempts to settle "on land" were made at different times and at different localities, colonies of various descriptions were planned and some of them settled, but all of these enterprizes made little impression, and with but a few exceptions their lives were short.

The real beginning of Jewish agricultural movements in the United States dates from the large influx of Russian immigrants. In 1881 a colony was started in Sicily Island, La. The Alliance Israelité Universelle assisted in this project. The following spring one of the Mississippi floods devastated the entire colony. Some of the remaining pioneers attempted to settle on Government land in South Dakota, and named their new place Cremiet. Here the results were also unfortunate; the colony was abandoned after three years of hard struggle. In 1882, two colonies were started, by the Immigrant Aid Society of New York, one in Colorado and the other in New Jersey, and still another by philanthropists of New York and Philadelphia. Quite an interesting attempt was made by a group of Russian immigrants—socialists,—settling in a colony named New Odessa, in Oregon. They called themselves the Sons of the Free. This also proved a failure. The St. Paul Community tried to help a group of people who occupied Government lands in North Dakota, while Cincinnati Jews were interested in a colony in Kansas. In the latter state, three other colonies were established by the Montefiore Agricultural Aid Society of New York. All these, as many other pioneer efforts in this direction, had similar careers and resulted in the same sad ending.

The only colonies of this early period that were destined to continue their existence were those of New Jersey. Despite considerable hardships and many disappointments, these colonies succeeded in coping

THE BACK TO THE SOIL MOVEMENT 127

with the difficulties. While natural advantages were few, the proximity of these colonies to New York and Philadelphia kept them in touch with sources where they could affect, and actually received, timely financial support. Many a crisis was thus arrested.

B. THE AGRICULTURAL AND INDUSTRIAL AID SOCIETY

The movement for Jewish agriculture received great impetus in the organization of the Baron De Hirsch Fund and the establishment of the Jewish Agricultural and Industrial Aid Society. The fundamental activity of the Jewish Agricultural and Industrial Aid Society is the rendering of financial assistance to those desiring to become farmers, and to enable those who are already on the farm to maintain their foothold. The financial assistance consists of granting loans for the purchase of the farm, equipment or other urgent needs. The rate of interest is 5 per cent and the principal is payable in small installments. Most of the loans are on second mortgages. In some instances loans are granted on third and even fourth mortgages, supplemented sometimes by chattel mortgages or other collateral. Up to 1916, the society made 3,714 loans to 3,151 individual farmers, amounting to $2,100,263.89. It is interesting to notice that over one-half of the loans are already repaid.

Since 1908, the society has published an agricultural paper in Yiddish, the "Jewish Farmer" edited by Joseph Pincus. It conducts a farm labor bureau for the purpose of giving the Jewish young men an opportunity of learning something at least of practical farming, and incidentally, to find out to his own satisfaction whether he is fit for it by inclination or otherwise. It organized nineteen credit unions, the first and so far the only co-operative agricultural banks in America. The Society was instrumental in the organization of the Federation of Jewish Farmers of America, with sixty-three constituent farmers' associations, and a total membership of over 1,500. It also assisted the organization of a co-operative fire insurance company, and other co-operative enterprizes among Jewish farmers.[1]

C. THE EXTENT OF JEWISH FARMING

The extent of Jewish farming at the present time is difficult to ascertain definitely. However, the statistical data of the Jewish Agricultural and Industrial Aid Society is quite illuminating. The organization came in touch with 3,118 Jewish farming families, comprising an estimated population of 18,590 souls. There are 3,438 farms with an estimated total acreage of 437,265 acres, and land value of $22,196,335; value of equipment of $4,166,329. This, according to the opinion of the United States Immigration Commission, represents only seventy-five per cent of the Jewish farmers in the country. A fair estimate of the extent of Jewish farming in the United States would, therefore, be about 5,000 families, comprising a population of about 25,000 souls, occupying an acreage of about

[1] "American Jewish Year Book," 1915-16.

THE BACK TO THE SOIL MOVEMENT 129

600,000 acres and having a value in real and personal property of about $33,000,000.[1] While Jewish farmers are to be found in every part of the United States, the most important settlements are those in New York, New Jersey, Connecticut and Massachusetts in the East; Ohio and Michigan in the Middle West, and North Dakota in the Northwest. In 1891 the Baron De Hirsch Fund assumed the care of the South New Jersey Colonies, whereupon they were transferred to the Agricultural and Industrial Aid Society. Besides making loans of money to farmers, an attempt has been made to encourage industry, so as to provide employment for the non-agricultural element, as well as for the farmers and their children in poor seasons. The paternal supervision of the colonies, however, has been gradually curtailed; industrial subventions have been systematically reduced; and the economic independence of the older colonies has been practically established.

D. Recent Efforts

For the last few years, new attempts have been made to promote agricultural colonies. An organization of Jewish immigrants, largely residents of Philadelphia, formed the Jewish Agricultural and Colonial Association, and purchased, in 1911, directly from the State of Utah, a tract of land of about six thousand acres of plateau lands. The plan calls for the settlement of

[1] "Agricultural Activities of Jews in America," Leonard G. Robinson, "American Jewish Year Book," 1912-13.

one hundred and fifty families. The entire tract was to be cultivated on a co-operative basis until the settlement is completed, when it will be parcelled out into forty-acre tracts for each family. The Utah Colonization Fund was incorporated by a number of prominent Jews of Salt Lake City to finance the individual members who may settle on the land.

In 1912, a five-thousand acre tract of land was bought in Texas by the Jewish Farmers Association of St. Louis, who are establishing an Ida Strauss Colony there, named in memory of Ida Strauss, who, with her husband, Isidor Strauss, perished in the Titanic disaster. All these efforts represent only a weak endeavor and have been given up as unsuccessful ventures.

E. WOODBINE

The most striking attempt along the establishment of a Jewish Agricultural Colony on a larger scale has been made in Woodbine, New Jersey, founded in 1891 by the Baron De Hirsch Fund. A tract of five thousand three hundred acres of land was purchased at seven dollars an acre and placed in charge of an agriculturist, Professor H. L. Sabsovich,[1] to whose untiring energy and self-

[1] Professor Sabsovich was born in Russia in 1860, where he received a general education. Later he took a three years' course at the Agricultural School of the Federal Polytechnicum in Zurich, Switzerland. He was agricultural chemist at the University of Odessa, emigrated to the United States in 1888 and occupied the post of agricultural chemist of the Colorado State Agricultural College. When in Russia, Professor Sabsovich took active part in Jewish communal affairs, was organizer of the Committee of Safety in Odessa during the anti-Jewish riots of 1881, and later was one of the founders of the *Am Olam*,

THE BACK TO THE SOIL MOVEMENT

sacrifice is due in no small measure the success of the Woodbine colony.

It is difficult to describe the obstacles that were met with in Woodbine by the pioneer settlers. The land was covered with a dense growth of scrub oak and pine; the settlers were housed in a temporary shack; they were not used to manual labor, nor prepared for the great task that confronted them. Their families were left in New York until the land could be cleared, and housing facilities provided. The pioneers were paid for the work they performed, but, even then, many left, unable to do the hard labor. However, the settlement succeeded; considerable land was cleared, houses built, and about fifty families moved to Woodbine. Agriculturally, Woodbine made little progress. The soil and the climatic conditions were poorly adapted to general farming, and required unusual efforts to make it successful. From the very beginning, a certain area was designated for a town site and here is where Woodbine developed rather as an industrial settlement.

F. The Industrial Settlement

Now a new idea was propounded. If it could be possible to establish industries in the rural districts, the workers would leave the city and go where their earning was assured. Thus by certain grants a clothing factory

one of the intellectual groups that emigrated to the United States in the eighties.

When appointed as leader of the new enterprize, Professor Sabsovich gave himself to the cause, and relentlessly applied himself to make Woodbine a success.

was induced to start operation in Woodbine. Later other industries were instituted,—a machine shop, a hat factory, a knitting factory, and so on. These factories were housed in brick buildings built by the Baron De Hirsch Fund, operating what is now known as the Woodbine Land and Improvement Company.

G. SELF-GOVERNMENT

In 1903, Woodbine, by act of the Legislature, was made a separate borough. It is unique in being the only municipality in the country in which all the offices are filled by Jews. Now the town presents quite a prosperous appearance, the streets are wide, lighted with electricity, well made. The houses are quite artistic, a number of them built of concrete. Lawns and trees add to the general impression. There are a number of public buildings, including a townhall, schools, synagogue, etc. The population is about two thousand. Most of the inhabitants are employed in the different factories. There are quite a number of retail stores, a hotel, two moving picture shows, dance halls, a garage, and other comforts of city life. The schools in Woodbine are especially good. There is a high school and three primary school buildings. There are a large number of social organizations, showing a great deal of social spirit, a volunteer fire brigade, a brass band, a civic club, and so on.

The Baron De Hirsch Fund has performed functions usually undertaken by a real estate development company, in laying out streets, building factories, a power house, waterworks, and so on, but it has sedulously refrained from eleemosynary gifts, its altruistic purpose being expressed in the elimination of promoters' profits and in bearing all risks and administrative expenses.

H. THE BARON DE HIRSCH AGRICULTURAL SCHOOL

In connection with Woodbine, consideration should be given to the Baron De Hirsch Agricultural School, established there in 1894. The School was primarily intended for the children of the colonists, but later its scope was enlarged, and a regular course in agriculture was introduced catering to the boys of the city, who in this way could prepare themselves for agriculture. Between the years 1894 and 1912, eight hundred and ninety-one students attended this school, of whom four hundred and nine completed the course and were graduated. The school has also had quite a stormy career. The curriculum has had to be changed quite frequently. This idea of preparing plain farmers was not an easy matter, the boys were too ambitious and strove for higher callings. Many of them made good, and distinguished themselves in the service of the United States Department of Agriculture, became teachers, veterinary surgeons, or continued their educations at college. It was then suggested that general scientific instruction be eliminated and the course shortened. It is rather curious to mention that on many occasions the pupils have rebelled, organized strikes, and caused considerable confusion. However, matters seemed to have been adjusted, and the school is operating smoothly. The last annual report states that from thirty-seven to forty per cent of the graduates remain in agricultural pursuits.[1]

I. THE NATIONAL FARM SCHOOL

In 1896, Rabbi Joseph Krauskopf founded another agricultural school at Doylestown, Pennsylvania, known as the National Farm School. This school is picturesquely located in one of the best farming sections of eastern Pennsylvania, and occupies about four hundred acres. It aims especially to afford agricultural training to young men who are not prepared to enter State Agricultural Colleges. The institution is supported by private subscriptions from all parts of the country and by annual appropriations from the State of Pennsylvania. Since 1901, the school has graduated about one hundred and seventy-four students, many of whom have since distinguished themselves as experts in various branches of agriculture as teachers and farm managers. The success of this school is chiefly due to the devotion and enthusiasm of Dr. Joseph Krauskopf. At the National Conference of Jewish Charities in Philadelphia, in 1906, Dr. Krauskopf read a paper on "Agricultural Education,—its Possibilities in Preventive Charity" in which he eloquently presented the shattering influences of city life and pleaded that the different organizations composing the Conference set aside annually a sum sufficient for part payment of a

[1] Report of the Superintendent of the Baron De Hirsch Agricultural School, 1915.

number of tracts of arable, properly located, lands, and for the expense involved in the starting of a new settlement. "It will be a philanthropy that, though involving a considerable expense at first, will be cheapest in the long run. It will make laborers instead of paupers, bread producers instead of bread beggars." This plea was not followed by any definite action.

J. General Suggestions

Dr. Morris Loeb commenting upon progress of the various Jewish agricultural activities in America expressed very deep thoughts as to the lesson that the experiences of the past suggest, and among other things says: "Those who try to foster agricultural tendencies among the Jews must seek means that do not differ in principle from those to be adopted in connection with any agricultural movement. Wherever this common sense rule is neglected, wherever colonists are planted in localities not suitably chosen, wherever the colonists themselves are not selected with regard to their intellectual, physical, and moral fitness, wherever they are not sufficiently equipped with agricultural implements, as well as agricultural knowledge, wherever they lack the means to await the harvesting of the first successful crop, the colonies are bound to fail; and it is the neglect of one or other of these essentials that has caused so many bitter disappointments in the past among the innumerable agricultural settlements, Jewish and others—which have been placed in so many different parts of the world during the past fifty years. The worst mistake of all is that of placing paupers in an agricultural colony with the idea that they must succeed there, when they have failed in industrial or financial pursuits. The true pauper lacks the essentials for the successful farmer in the same degree; namely, will power and the capacity for sustained effort. An agricultural colony, composed largely of industrial failures, will be an agricultural failure as well. On the other hand, it must be remembered that paternal administration of a colony will certainly repel the ablest and most progressive settlers, and it is for this reason that the Alliance Israelité Universelle, the Jewish Colonization Association, as well as the American organizations dealing with the same problems, are endeavoring, as far as possible, to reduce the paternal system in the form of administrators dwelling within the colonies, and to substitute therefor local self-government, with the aid of traveling agricultural and administrative advisers. The results seem to have been most encouraging, and such colonies have not only succeeded in retaining their original membership, but have attracted additional energetic settlers. An artificially-planted colony, however, is, at best, a makeshift as compared with voluntary acquisition of land by the settler himself, and it is here that the greatest development must be expected in the future, inasmuch as this follows the natural course of events and is free from any artificial stimulus, whose removal might lead to a collapse of the enterprise." [1]

[1] "Afterword," by Professor Morris Loeb, "Jewish Year Book," 1912-13.

THE BACK TO THE SOIL MOVEMENT

Quite an interesting experiment was made by the Agricultural and Industrial Aid Society in establishing a test farm at Kings Park, L. I.[1] A tract of five hundred acres of good land was purchased there and equipped with modern buildings and farming implements. Houses were erected for twelve families. The heads of the families were provided with work as farm laborers, thus learning American methods of agriculture. They were also allowed a small plot of ground for raising the garden truck needed for the use of their families. After a few years, this experiment proved unsuccessful, and the plan had to be given up.

CHAPTER NINE. BACK TO THE SOIL MOVEMENT

QUESTIONS

1. Describe the first attempts in establishing Jewish Agricultural Colonies.
2. State the different activities of the Agricultural and Industrial Aid Society.
3. What is the extent of Jewish agriculture in the U. S.?
4. What are the recent attempts towards Jewish colonization in the United States?
5. Describe the building up of the Woodbine colony.
6. What role did industry play in Woodbine?
7. In what way did the Baron De Hirsch Fund avoid pauperization of the colonists?
8. Describe the Baron De Hirsch Agricultural School.
9. Describe the National Farm School.
10. What are the important suggestions of Professor Morris Loeb in regard to the promotion of Jewish agriculture?

---

[1] "The Baron De Hirsch Fund," by Eugene Benjamin, National Conference of Jewish Charities. St. Louis, 1906.

X

RESIDENT-DEPENDENTS

The largest part of Jewish organized philanthropic effort of to-day deals with a more or less chronic dependency, a dependency of people who have acquired their residence, and whose condition is due to circumstances beyond their control.

A. THE SICK

The most important of these elements is sickness. While a family, under normal conditions may be able to retain itself on a self-supporting basis, in case of sickness, it is compelled to apply for outside assistance. Free medical help is the most popular form of relief in this instance. Because of the urgent need and the appealing nature of the work, agencies giving free medical aid readily find generous support, and with the anxiety on the part of the medical profession to utilize the large material of the indigent patient, there is seldom difficulty in getting free medical service. Thus we find free dispensaries, clinics, and hospitals, supported and maintained by Jewish contributors, attended by Jewish physicians, and patronized by Jewish patients.

With the development of municipal and state facilities, it would seem that the necessity for specifically

Jewish agencies would become of lesser and lesser importance. However, when the Jewish dispensary is able to reach its patients more effectively, where, because of its limited scope it is capable of offering better and more thorough attention, where, because of the close connection with the very life of the patient, the follow up work can be more successfully carried out, the existence, nay even the establishment of new agencies, is quite justifiable. There is a possibility that, because of loose system and a multiplicity of agencies, the patients, instead of deriving benefits from one center, will, in search of a remedy, utilize a number of agencies, and thus get negative results. Therefore, a strict and persistent system of records and a legitimate stringency in the acceptance of new patients is absolutely necessary. It is a moot question whether the free dispensary should receive a fee from patients. The one who is able to pay should apply to a private physician. A dispensary, however, serving indigent patients, should put no additional hardships upon its constituency. In many instances, the dispensary is an adjunct of a relief agency.

Free medical attendance is, after all, material relief given in the form of service. Its administration, therefore, should be careful and intelligent, and the services offered should be efficient. The close connection of the dispensary with a relief agency, if properly conducted, answers the purpose. The responsibility here is placed with the attending physician, and the medical services are supplemented by social services, which play an important part in the course of treatment. At all events, the poor must be provided with the best possible medical aid, for to the poor, health is the only asset upon which they can rely to preserve their equilibrium and to save themselves from becoming permanently dependent upon outside assistance. Efficient, skilled diagnosis, made in time, saves many a life and leads to speedy recovery, preventing innumerable complications. Hence, no effort should be spared in affording the poor the best medical aid obtainable. The utilization of the dispensary facilities for work of prevention, vaccination, dental work, frequent examination of children, milk stations, etc., makes this particular agency of inestimable value and serves as a great educational factor in the community.

While it is natural that in many instances medical aid offered free attracts a great number of patients with minor ailments, it easily gets the reputation of detecting serious sicknesses. Besides the dispensary and clinic, the poor are frequently in need of the physician's aid in their home. The sick are not anxious to go to the hospital with minor ailments; the patient may be bedridden, but if it is only for a short time he would rather remain at home. Then again, there are the so-called "non-hospital cases" that are not welcomed at the hospitals, and again, there may be some other circumstances that make hospital treatment impossible. The practicing physician among the poor usually has his quota of free visits, the different philanthropic agencies usually having some arrangement to meet this particular demand. The visiting nurse saves time for the doctor. Frequently, the doctor is called though there is no urgency at all, and again, in some cases, the patient can call at the dispensary instead of the doctor having to pay a home visit. Thus, in many cases, the nurse is sent first, and decides whether a doctor's help is needed. Miss Lillian Wald thinks that in many instances the home treatment produces better results than the hospital, and refuses to enforce a strict rule as to the disposition of the sick.[1]

Maternity cases especially are frequently attended at home, and special societies are in the field for providing this particular aid. This includes the doctor, nurse, and temporary relief whenever it is necessary.

A number of cities have one or more Jewish dispensaries. A typical example of a complete arrangement is the West Side dispensary in Chicago, which is a part of the Jewish charities of that city. For the year 1915 "more than 64,000 patients passed through the dispensary for consultation, and were distributed among 13 departments. The dental department now has two dentists; 6,500 patients attended this clinic. A member of the staff of the Michael Reese Hospital has taken charge of the children's department and infant welfare work. Mothers come to be taught the care and feeding of their infants. There is a trained social service director who follows the mothers to their homes to see that instructions are followed correctly. Attendance at these departments was about 7,500. Of

[1] Lillian Wald, "Home Medical Treatment for Needy Families."

more than 64,000 applicants at the dispensary, only a little more than 500 were sent to the Michael Reese Hospital, and about the same number to other hospitals, where contagious diseases are taken. These figures show the value of the dispensary as an outpatient department of the hospital. The dispensary has three salaried physicians, who call at the homes of patients unable to come to the dispensary. These patients are usually on the verge of becoming hospital cases, but the necessity of sending them to the hospital is often avoided. The social service department has three trained nurses."

In the treatment of the sick more and more attention is being paid to prevention. The general advance of infant welfare work has also been undertaken in the Jewish field. Pre-natal care is given to the expectant mothers. Special milk stations and welfare stations are conducted in the congested districts. An educational campaign among Jewish speaking mothers is carried on in Yiddish, and provision is made for the temporary care of babies in the country.

It has been observed in Europe by many statisticians, and in America by Dr. John Billings, that the birth rate is lower among the Jews than among the general population. Leroy Beaulieu tersely expresses it thus: "to make up for the small number of births, they (the Jews) lose almost everywhere a perceptibly smaller number of children by death." Dr. Maurice Fishberg ascribes this phenomenon to the devotion of the Jewess as a mother; to the fact that Jewish mothers largely nurse their children themselves to the exclusion of patented foods said by the sellers to be "just as good as mother's milk." [1]

Interesting results of Jewish infant welfare are found in the work of the after care circle, Jewish Maternity Hospital, presented by Elinor Steinholtz, at the National Association of Jewish Social workers in 1913.[2] Of 462 cases, only 6 died, a mortality rate of a little over 1 per cent. The returns of the Health Department of the City of New York for the same year showed 17 per cent. A study of Jewish infant mortality in Cincinnati for the year 1915 shows that of 344 babies born, only 16 died, or 4.3 per cent, whereas the Board of Health reports a general infant mortality of 7.8 per cent.

B. School Hygiene

Special attention has lately been given to the health of school children. In many cities the Council of Jewish Women initiated Penny Luncheons. Systematic medical examinations of school children are conducted in connection with a number of Jewish agencies, relief societies, settlements, and so forth. The United Hebrew Charities of New York found that there is a large number of children physically handicapped, needing medical attention, special nourishment, and so forth. This leads to the enlargement of the facilities for a country stay for the children in summer. In New

[1] Dr. Maurice Fishberg, "Leaves from a Doctor's Note Book." "Jewish Charities," January, 1904.
[2] "Jewish Charities," 1913, Vol. III, No. 11.

York, three Jewish agencies are engaged in this particular line of work and are especially helpful to children who are anæmic and pre-tubercular. Special nurses are in the field, endeavoring to get for the children the necessary medical attention, securing for them the necessary facilities and giving them attention as far as hygiene and sanitation are concerned. In many instances this work is supplementary to the efforts of municipal agencies.

C. DEFECTIVES

The problem of the care of the Jewish blind has been only recently taken up by the Jews of this country. Occasionally a relief agency would take care of some individual case, but no systematic effort was made to do work among the blind, outside of the existing agencies for the general population. In some states, the blind get a pension from the state. In New York it averages fifty dollars per person per year. In 1914, a Hebrew Association for the blind was organized in New York City. The object of this association is to improve the condition of the Jewish blind and prevent blindness, to endeavor to publish an accurate Yiddish and Hebrew literature for the Jewish blind, to provide guides for blind people when needed, to help the Jewish blind to become self-supporting. The Council of Jewish Women is also active in this campaign. The Society for the Welfare of Jewish Deaf was organized in New York in 1910. It is acknowledged that the United States has efficient schools for the deaf and that on the whole the deaf receive quite a satisfactory training. The trouble, however, begins after graduation, when the students are to gain their own livelihood and become self-supporting. The above mentioned society conducts an employment bureau, arranges socials and entertainments, provides religious services, and gives necessary material relief either in the form of loans or as grants. There are two congregations of the Jewish deaf, one in Manhattan, the other in Brooklyn. The number of Jewish deaf in the United States is not definitely known, however; the aggregate estimated by those who handle the problem is about five thousand.

There is undoubtedly a goodly number of Jewish children that fall into the classes of feeble-minded and retarded. This is a neglected problem. The states are just now awakening to a realization of the magnitude of the situation, and only a small portion of the children requiring custodial care are supplied by the existing institutions. In different places, private initiative is awakened and it is only a matter of but a short time when the Jews will respond to their duty on behalf of these unfortunates. Meanwhile, it is important to know the exact number of defective children, who are still without any training or receive regular schooling, so ill adapted to their needs. Here is a field almost untouched in Jewish philanthropic effort.

D. Hospitals

In quite a number of cities we find special Jewish hospitals, which, as a rule, are supported by Jewish funds, but which do not limit their clientele to Jewish patients exclusively. The first hospital of this kind was established in Cincinnati in 1845. The original reason for the establishment of these hospitals is to be found in the lack of general facilities for the treatment of the sick of the community. In places where the existing hospitals were under the auspices of strictly sectarian groups, the need for special hospitals was self-evident. In some instances, the Jewish physicians initiated the movement, frequently because of their inability to attach themselves to any of the existing agencies. Lately, we find also, an endeavor to establish new hospitals on the plea that the patients require kosher food, not to be found even in the hospitals bearing the name Jewish. This has been the case in Chicago, New York, and other cities. The growth of efficient municipal institutions should diminish the necessity for specifically Jewish hospitals. The Jewish hospital, as a rule, besides receiving charity cases, has also accommodations for the care of private cases, from which it receives an income paying the larger part of its expenses. The arrangements by which the well to do and the indigent are cared for by the same institution are often responsible for the sentiment that the poor are not treated with the same consideration as those that are in a position to pay for their services. In quite a number of hospitals, schools for nurses have been established, but it is only recently that Jewish girls have entered this profession. The relations of the relief agency to the hospital are quite varied. In some instances the hospitals make their own investigations as to the financial position of their applicants. In others, the investigations are made by the relief agencies, and no free patients are accepted unless under recommendation of the relief society, and again, in a few cities, as Louisville, the hospital is a part and parcel of the Federation. The management of Jewish hospitals in general is quite modern, and the achievements of Dr. Goldwater of New York in Mount Sinai have been taken as a model in hospital management. While, as a rule, there seems to be no difficulty in getting funds for the establishment of hospitals, in many instances the maintenance is quite a great burden on the community, as in Chicago, where the community was obliged to discontinue the orthodox Jewish hospital in 1915. Mention should be made of the new National Hospital for Rheumatism and Blood Diseases, established in Hot Springs, Arkansas, by the B'nai B'rith and known as the Leo N. Levi Memorial Hospital.

The most recent development in Jewish hospitals, as well as in hospitals in general, is the organization of social service departments. This has been especially necessary when a hospital lacked connections with a relief society. The initiative in this particular service has been taken by the Free Synagogue in New York, which has organized Jewish hospital social service departments in connection with Bellevue Hospital, and which has extended its scope to other hospitals in New York City. This is at present an important part of the social service work of other cities.

E. TUBERCULOSIS

One of the most frequent diseases among the poor, producing continuous dependency, is tuberculosis. In 1906, Dr. Theodore Sachs of Chicago, estimated that there were from four to five hundred thousand tubercular individuals in the United States, and that in Chicago alone there were not less than twenty thousand active cases of consumption.

To a certain extent, it is known that the Jews are not so frequently apt to get tuberculosis as their neighbors. The reasons are: the limited use of alcohol, home life, good food, regularity of habits, and so forth. Still, the White Plague is a problem with the Jews as well as with non-Jews, and while there is nothing specific in the disease to make it particularly Jewish, it requires serious consideration. With the general inadequacy of treatment of tuberculosis, the specific efforts of the Jews in this respect, even in their limited sphere, are quite important. The appalling condition of the growth of tuberculosis among the Jews was first brought to the attention of the public in 1899, when a large number of the victims of the White Plague found their way to Denver, Colorado, where the climate was supposed to have a curative effect. Then the National Hospital for Consumptives in Denver was established, which was the first institution to start the procession for the elimination of tuberculosis among the Jews of this country. In 1904, another national institution for the treatment of Jewish consumptives was established in Denver, the Jewish Consumptives Relief Society. This institution belongs to a new type, supported and initiated by the Orthodox group. In the beginning, it was intended primarily for the advanced cases, in opposition to the work of the National Hospital for Consumptives, which treated incipient cases only. The unhealthy spirit of rivalry and competition compelled both institutions to deviate from their original restricted activities, and at present, we find patients in all stages of tuberculosis housed in both institutions. Another sanitarium has been established recently in Los Angeles.

Yet with all these institutions, located in favorable climates, the facilities are exceedingly limited, and the growing contention that consumptives can be cured without change of climate has resulted in the establishment of sanitaria in different localities, as in New York, Chicago, Baltimore, Philadelphia, and other cities. Special mention should be made of the Workingmen's Circle Sanitarium, located at Liberty, New York.[1] This sanitarium is supported by the organization, which is essentially a mutual aid society. It is thus free from the stamp of charity, and presents an interesting experiment of what workingmen have achieved by intelligent co-operation. All in all, however, the capacity of all the Jewish institutions for the treatment of tuberculosis hardly exceeds one thousand, and can relieve only an exceedingly small proportion of the number who need sanitarium treatment. It is no wonder, therefore, that while all these institutions are very much over-

[1] Strunsky Survey, 1915.

crowded, the Jews also utilize, to a large extent, the state and municipal institutions, which are steadily increasing in their efficiency and in their accommodations.

Outside of the dietary laws, which by the way are observed only in very few Jewish institutions, the state and municipal institutions will eventually make it unnecessary to maintain specific Jewish sanitaria. This can be noted in the change that has already taken place, where the general facilities are making progress. Thus, in Ohio, with the establishment of a State Tubercular Sanitarium, a number of Jewish patients were sent from Cleveland and Cincinnati, cities that had formerly used the Denver Hospital for this purpose.

1. *Home Treatment*

Though sanitarium treatment is indispensable, though the results of treatment in incipient cases are gratifying, and though the importance of isolation of advanced cases, if nothing else, is of great value, still, we are beginning to realize that sanitarium treatment plays only a minor part in the cure of the tubercular patient. Tuberculosis, affecting the breadwinner spells misery and dependence of the entire family. Unless the latter is adequately provided for, the patient is exposed to worry and anxiety which interfere with the successful process of recovery. Quite frequently, the patient neglects the cure, prematurely leaves the sanitarium compelled to look for work, while he ought to be treated for the disease. The municipalities provide institutions for the treatment of consumption, but they are not taking care of the families of consumptives; this is the sphere that the private agency can enter without fear of duplication. In the case of the Jews, considerable has been done in this direction. Provision is made in almost every city for the care of the family while the breadwinner is undergoing the cure at the sanitarium. In quite a number of instances, the sanitarium treatment is unattainable, either because the patient is not willing to enter and go through a continuous stay, or because, for some reason or other, the removal of the patient from his family is difficult. In such instances home treatment is necessary. Some cities have endeavored to remove the families of tubercular patients to the suburbs, and by strict supervision and ample relief maintain the necessary isolation and standard. An interesting experiment in this direction was made in Cincinnati in 1910, where a few families were removed to a hill suburb in the neighborhood of the local tubercular sanitarium. This particular suburb had had previously, few Jewish inhabitants, but since then it has become quite populous, and at present harbors a large Jewish community, composed mainly of families that moved there on account of their health.

2. *After-Care of Consumptives*

An investigation into the subsequent histories of about one thousand cases discharged from tubercular sanitaria, made by the Council of Jewish Women, emphasizes another phase of the problem. Though the patient leaving the sanitarium may be benefited by the treatment, and discharged as either cured or improved (in this investigation only 20 per cent showed that they were progressing or unimproved when discharged) it is only a matter of a short time, after his return to the unfavorable conditions and after he has to meet the full burden of the struggle for existence, before he relapses and the entire effect of the sanitarium treatment is nullified.[1]

3. *The Cincinnati Method*

The United Jewish Charities of Cincinnati recognized the importance of the after-care of tubercular patients as early as 1902, and since then ample provision has been made, not only for the treatment of the patients, but also for their rehabilitation to such surroundings that their health might receive proper care. Thus, for some time, the United Jewish Charities sent all cases of incipient tuberculosis to the National Hospital for Tuberculosis at Denver, and provided adequate relief for their families while the patients were in the sanitarium. When the patients were ready to be discharged, the families were sent to Denver to join them, and were established in Denver. The United Jewish Charities supplied the funds necessary for the rehabilitation of the families and in the majority of instances placed the former patient in an occupation;

---

[1] "The Subsequent History of Patients discharged from Tubercular Sanitaria." Department of Health, New York. Monograph Series, No. 8, 1913.

e. g., peddling, storekeeping, etc., that the patient was capable of pursuing. Under no condition were the patients allowed to leave Colorado after they were discharged from the sanitarium. This was known among charity workers as the "Cincinnati Method." Though expensive, as far as the initial outlay was concerned, the results were quite gratifying. But the continuous responsibility that the United Jewish Charities of Cincinnati assumed proved to be an unreasonable arrangement, which prevented the continuance of this policy.

The return of patients from Denver to the place where the disease originated proved to be detrimental, as the majority of them, acclimated to higher altitudes, easily relapsed under the unfavorable conditions. This has been the experience of other cities, and at present the treatment of tubercular patients in the Colorado climate is used only in individual cases, while the majority are availing themselves of the growing facilities of local institutions. It has been demonstrated beyond the possibility of doubt that as far as sanitarium treatment is concerned, the local sanitaria are capable of producing similar results to those obtained from the treatment in the sanitaria situated in the specially favorable climatic locations. However, the main problem, as was demonstrated by the study of the Council of Jewish Women in New York and corroborated by similar studies in Baltimore and other cities, is in regard to the treatment of patients after their discharge from the sanitarium.

Patients whose after-care is neglected, invariably relapse and succumb to the disease. The possibilities of efficient after-care treatments are demonstrated by the experience of the United Jewish Charities of Cincinnati. In a strictly scientific study of seventy-one cases of tuberculosis that were treated in this city and followed up for a period of not less than five years, we find that 25 were entirely cured, in 18 the disease was arrested, 3 were improved, 1 advanced, and 24 died. In other words, 33.8 per cent died. It is interesting to note that the cost of this treatment was $38,963, or $549 per patient.[1]

Realization of the gravity of the tuberculosis situation in New York City was the cause of the organization of the Joint Tuberculosis Committee representing the Free Synagogue, the Montefiore Home and the United Hebrew Charities of that city. The careful investigation made by the Committee of 459 cases discharged from the Bedford Sanitarium shows that 55 per cent suffered a relapse within a short time after their discharge. Of the families cared for by the Joint Tuberculosis Committee, only 8 per cent relapsed. Thus the value of the work of the Joint Committee is emphasized: It is producing good results.

It is interesting, however, to mention a study of the physical and home conditions of two hundred and seventy-one families, in which one or both of the parents were suffering with tuberculosis. This study showed that 56 children, out of 692, were suffering

[1] United Jewish Charities of Cincinnati, Annual Report, 1914.

with the disease, and that 105 showed signs which placed them in the category of suspects. This condition is easily explained when we learn from the same investigation that of 274 active consumptives, there were found in these 270 families only 112 that had separate rooms.

While in this country, the Jews have made considerable effort to cope with the tuberculosis situation, still, there is a considerable field which is barely covered, that must receive serious consideration. There is no need to establish specifically Jewish sanitaria, but there is a need for more intensive and continuous effort in after-care of the tubercular patients, for which neither state nor city is as yet adequately provided, and which the private agencies must bear as their legitimate burden. The sooner the Jews realize that sanitarium and medical treatment of tuberculosis represent a minor part of the problem, the easier it will become to appeal to the public for the funds necessary to combat the dreadful ravages of the White Plague, and in this, as in other fields, the Jews can well afford to be the pioneers.

F. Insanity

Another problem that is attracting considerable attention in the field of Jewish philanthropy is that of insanity. The idea is prevalent that the immigrants in general contribute more than their proportion to the population of our insane asylums. It is interesting to mention that Mr. M. D. Waldman made a study of statistical data presented by the New York State Hospital Commission in 1912 and came to the following conclusions: 1. The increase in the number of insane in the state institutions is no greater than the increase of the population. 2. That the proportion of foreign born insane in state hospitals is little, if any, higher than the native born.

Nevertheless, there are quite a large number of families dependent on account of insanity of the breadwinner. As far as custodial care is concerned, the Jews are utilizing the state and municipal institutions, but recently efforts have been made to provide ample care for this particular class of dependents, and also to do preventive work as far as possible. The initiative in this work belongs to the Bureau of Personal Service in Chicago. Similar work is also done in New York through the Free Synagogue Mental Hygiene Department, and also in Baltimore, in connection with the Federation. While no definite methods have been devised in preventing and curing insanity, field nurses, ample relief, and careful consideration of each and every case, are means for the desired end. Much is done in the after treatment of patients discharged from the hospitals, for if the conditions to which they return are unfavorable, their relapse is unavoidable. Here is where social service counts.

G. Convalescents

In the treatment of the sick, the work of the Convalescent Home deserves consideration. The first

Jewish convalescent home was established in New York in 1906, and is known as the Loeb Memorial Convalescent Home, but at present other cities have also organized institutions for the care of the convalescents.

H. Chronic Invalids

The Montefiore Home for Chronic Invalids and Country Sanitarium for Consumptives, organized in New York in 1884, is the foremost institution of its kind in the United States. It has a capacity of over one thousand. The Touro Infirmary in New Orleans and other institutions in different cities accommodate a limited number of chronic patients. On the whole, however, the facilities are not sufficient, and in a large number of cases, municipal institutions are utilized. Sectarian private institutions also care for a limited number of Jewish patients.

Chapter Ten. The Sick

Questions

1. What are the reasons for specifically Jewish medical aid agencies?
2. Discuss the advantages and disadvantages of free medical help.
3. State the need of home treatment.
4. Discuss Jewish infant welfare work.
5. What are the functions of school hygiene agencies?
6. Describe the different classes of defectives, and Jewish agencies dealing with them.
7. What is the origin of Jewish hospitals?
8. What is the probable extent of tuberculosis among Jews in the United States?

9. What are the Jewish National Institutions for the care of consumptives?

10. Discuss home and sanitarium treatment of consumptives.

11. Describe the Cincinnati Method.

12. State the importance of the after-care of consumptives, and the work of the Joint Tuberculosis Committee in New York.

13. Discuss insanity as a problem in Jewish philanthropy.

14. What are the Jewish institutions for convalescents and chronic invalids?

XI

DEPENDENT WOMEN AND CHILDREN

Dependency of women and children, caused by the death of the head of the family, has been taken to be, hitherto, a natura phenomenon and the care of widows and children considered the foremost duty of charitable endeavor. It is only recently that society is beginning to realize the abnormality of the situation and is ready to acknowledge that in the majority of cases the dependency is caused by the premature death of the breadwinner from preventable causes. Thus, in the investigation of a limited number of widows receiving State pensions in Cincinnati, it has been demonstrated that the age of the deceased parent averaged thirty-eight years, and that the principal causes to which deaths have been ascribed are tuberculosis, cancer, and industrial accidents.[1]

It is evident, therefore, that the problem of the orphans and widows could be very materially lessened if more attention were paid to guarding against conditions that are responsible for premature death. As it is, however, the widows and orphans have to be provided for, and the question is merely that of method, rather than that of principle.

[1] Maurice Hexter, "The Survey," December 12, 1914.

A. Congregate Systems

The institutional care of orphans received the approbation of the Jews as early as 1832, when the Hebrew Benevolent and Orphan Asylums were established in New York City. In 1855 the New Orleans Jewish Orphans' Home was established. The Hebrew Sheltering and Guardian Society in New York was founded in 1879. There are similar institutions in different parts of the country, notably, Philadelphia, Cleveland, Brooklyn, Milwaukee, and others, with an approximate capacity of about six thousand.[1]

B. The Placing-Out System

While the results of the institutional treatment were satisfactory, still the general antagonistic attitude against congregate systems of child caring has also spread among the Jews. An institution necessarily lacks home atmosphere,—the most important adjunct in child life,—it neglects individuality and is detrimental to the free development of character. At the Second National Conference of Jewish Charities in Detroit, Dr. Lee Frankel raised the question of the possibility of introducing another method, namely of adopting and placing-out. The attempt to utilize the facilities of the Independent Order of B'nai B'rith for finding suitable private homes for dependent children was not successful, but a joint committee on dependent children was formed in New York in 1904. And in

[1] Lee K. Frankel, "Placing out of Jewish Children." Third Conference of Jewish Charities, 1904.

DEPENDENT WOMEN AND CHILDREN 161

conjunction with the Department of Charities of that city, a special agent was engaged, who was to look for available homes. The results were quite encouraging. Without any special difficulty, a number of families made application for children; three-fourths of them expected to be paid, while one-fourth offered free homes. Only a few of the latter were found to be unsatisfactory, while of the former, half were rejected.

Thus, one objection, namely, that homes could not be procured, was removed. But, granting that there is a possibility of finding private homes for the dependent children, thus making it unnecessary to place them in institutions, the question still remained as to the comparative advantages of the two systems, namely, the congregate and the placing-out methods. Dr. Lee Frankel maintained that while in some instances institutional care of children is necessary, for instance when both parents are living or in the case of semi-orphans, he thought that in the case of full orphans the placement system is more advisable. In this connection the study of Dr. Loewenstein in 1906 is of interest.[1] It shows that of three thousand, one hundred and eighty-two children in institutions, there were only one hundred and three, or thirty-seven per cent full orphans. The most enthusiastic adherent of the placing-out system, and the arch enemy of the congregate system is Dr. Ludwig Bernstein, Superintendent of the Hebrew Sheltering and Guardian Orphan asylum, who is an

[1] "Institutions for Children," Solomon Loewenstein. Proceedings National Conference of Jewish Charities, Philadelphia, 1906.

authority on child-caring work. Dr. Bernstein presented a very interesting report of results in placing-out achieved by the joint committee in 1906, when the number of children handled in this way reached three hundred and thirty-three. It was quite natural that his statements awakened considerable opposition from the adherents of the old institutional system. Dr. S. Wolfenstein, Superintendent of the Cleveland Orphan Asylum, led the opposition. Dr. Wolfenstein had been Superintendent of the Cleveland Orphan Asylum for over thirty-five years. He devoted his life to the upbuilding of this institution. He could speak as an authority on child caring, for he had cared personally for thousands of them, and he certainly knew his children. He kept a definite card record of every child that he had had under his care, and presented, in 1910, a statement of the results obtained.[1] This record covers one thousand, five hundred and thirty-four graduates. The average stay in the institution was between seven and eight years. Six hundred and thirty-nine girls present the following status:

Married and living in their own homes	209
Salesladies and clerks	93
Stenographers, bookkeepers and cashiers	84
Housekeepers, mostly in families of their own folks	58
Milliners	35
Dressmakers	31
Trained nurses	31

[1] Proceedings of the Annual Conference of the Education of Backward, Truant, Delinquent, and Dependent Children, 1910, St. Louis.

DEPENDENT WOMEN AND CHILDREN

Living in families with a view to becoming nurses	18
Continuing studies for professions	18
Teachers	18
Matrons and assistant matrons	3
On the stage	1
Chronically sick and insane	8
Bad records	8
Died	24
Total	639

Of the boys: out of 895, there were

In commercial pursuits	410
Pursuing trades	183
Stenographers and bookkeepers	140
In professions	35
Continuing studies for professions	30
In United States Service, Army, Navy, and P. O.	29
On the stage	6
Chronically sick, and insane	4
Bad records	14
Died	44
Total	295

The placing-out and adoption system has been especially favorably received in Chicago, where, through the enthusiastic and generous support of Mr. Julius Rosenwald, and the co-operation of Miss Minnie Low of the Bureau of Personal Service, a special society was organized, known as the Home Finding Society of Chicago. This organization, besides supporting widows with dependent children, is finding homes for children for adoption. In 1915, this organization cared for one hundred ninety-two widows with five hundred and seventy-six children, besides placing out one hundred eighty children in boarding homes, and succeeded in causing the adoption of eight children.

C. THE COTTAGE SYSTEM

The Hebrew Sheltering Guardian Society has removed its institution from the city of New York to Pleasantville, and is at present presenting the most advanced methods of child-caring agencies among the Jews. This institution is situated among the beautiful rolling hills of Westchester county, and occupies one hundred and seventy acres, upon which are numerous buildings. The children are housed in separate cottages, each accommodating about thirty children. The society maintains its own school along the most modern lines, including manual training and domestic science courses. Each cottage maintains its own household, and the children perform all the household duties, under the management and supervision of the cottage matron. The curriculum of the school, the routine of the management, the religious and moral training, are models of their kind. All in all they have about six hundred children in the institution, but besides this, over three hundred are boarded out by the institution in private homes, under the careful supervision of a special staff. A special department for the after-care of graduates is worth while mentioning.

D. SELF-GOVERNMENT

The other large orphanages in New York, while still retaining the same quarters, have changed considerably in the method of training children, introducing club activities and self-government. These innovations, to a larger or smaller degree, are taking place in almost all the other Jewish orphan asylums in the country. The initiative in this respect should be ascribed to the efforts of Mr. Chester Teller, who in 1910 established a system in the New Orleans Orphan Asylum known as the Golden City, which was enthusiastically received and was popularized among the Jewish social workers.

E. State Subventions

In the case of dependent children, the Jewish institutions and organizations are utilizing in many instances the subventions granted by states and municipalities for this purpose. Thus, in New York, the orphan asylums receive a per capita subvention for each child in their care, and again, in other states, the widows' pension acts relieved the burden on Jewish communities to a great extent. The subvention of widowed mothers is not a new phenomenon in Jewish charity. In many cities the Jewish relief societies granted regular pensions to deserving widows, and at present the state pension is considerably augmented by the allowances of the Jewish private agencies.

F. Orthodox Tendencies

In speaking of institutions for dependent children, mention should be made of a comparatively recent tendency to establish orphan asylums on a strictly orthodox basis. This refers to the Nathan Marks Orphan Asylum in Chicago, where the children are living under a strictly orthodox régime, and receive a large amount of religious training. This tendency is also responsible for the introduction in many orphan asylums, not conducted in accordance with the strict dietary laws, of kosher kitchens. The two great child-caring institutions of New York introduced kosher dietary in 1911. It meant considerable initial outlay and an additional annual expense of not less than six to seven thousand dollars a year. The institutions hoped, however, that this innovation might gain them the financial support of the large numbers of "extremely religious members of the community," who were non-subscribers before.

There is, however, a much deeper argument for *Kashruth* among Jewish child-caring agencies. "No child comes to an institution free from the influence of its surroundings. It has already imbibed the predilections fostered by its environment; it has received a spiritual inheritance, such as it may be. The tenacity of these youthful impressions is expressed in the formula that the first seven years of the child's life fix the religious coloring of its mind irrevocably. But there is more to attach the child to the cast of its early life. This is grooved into its surroundings, and parental teaching and respect, neighborhood opinion, friendly intercourse, are bound up in the rule of life that dominates the little world in which they all have their being. Destroy the world, and he becomes a stranger

DEPENDENT WOMEN AND CHILDREN

to his own blood, incapable of old friendship, impervious to old discipline." [1]

G. CHILD-CARING METHODS

Opinions as to the best child-caring methods are quite at variance. A working set of rules prepared by Dr. Bernstein [2] is quite suggestive. These rules are as follows:

1. If the home of the child be a good one, and can be kept together adequately, it should not be broken up on the death of the breadwinner.
2. The home, on the other hand, if lacking in good influences, should not be kept together on a mere pittance, merely for the sake of so doing.
3. A child should always be taken out of a consumptive's home.
4. As infant mortality in the very best institutions is high, under no circumstances should infants be placed in an institution.
5. A total orphan should be kept out of institutions whenever possible and placed in a carefully chosen home.
6. To avoid human tragedies a child, though legally adopted, should be kept in touch with till its majority.
7. Children of ten or twelve years and over are usually physically better off in institutions.
8. The child-placing man who boasts only of the success of his cases is a man well worth avoiding. It is impossible to detect his failures which must exist.
9. If it be impossible to place children under seven or eight years in cottage homes, it is better to place them with private

---

[1] L. H. Levin, "The Question of Kashruth," "Jewish Charities," 1911, Vol. II, No. 2.
[2] "A Child-Caring Primer," Ludwig B. Bernstein, "Jewish Charities," Vol. II, No. 3, page 7.

families properly supervised, than in congregate institutions where discipline is too rigid for a young child.

10. A child of ten or eleven years who has outgrown the moral and mental influence of its boarding mother should be allowed to leave. Unmanageable children are often merely evincing a healthy desire of entering into healthy competition in work and play with others of their age.

So much for the vital question of what to do with the child that becomes "dependent." And now, what are the salient points in the training of these children, after we have determined upon the course to be pursued with them, whether it be on the family home or on the institution plan?

1. Dependent children, whether in an institution or private home should have frequent physical examinations and the results carefully recorded and compared with previous records.

2. The eyes and teeth of the children should be examined and attended to periodically.

3. The education of a child should not cease at fourteen, but should be continued long enough to allow the child to develop its latent abilities to the fullest degree.

4. The education which the child receives in public school is insufficient and should be supplemented by higher educational work. An institutional school could be easily devised combining both elementary and high school work in from eight to nine years as is done in Europe.

5. Industrial and vocational training is industrial preparation for life and should not be construed to mean menial labor.

6. The child should be given a substantial religious training, which, to be of lasting value, should not be overemphasized.

7. Children should be kept in contact with men and women of education, culture and character.

8. The child in the institution should be allowed freedom and

self-government. Too rigid discipline crushes individuality and kills self-reliance and initiative.

9. The child should have plenty of recreation and spontaneous play in the company of children of his own age.

10. The efficiency of a child institution varies *directly* as the per capita cost.

11. The child should be kept in touch with by a capable, tactful and devoted worker even after employment has been found for it.

H. After-Care of Orphans

It stands to reason that the work with dependent children and especially with orphans, does not cease with the graduation of the latter from the institution. A system of after-care has been devised by the different orphan asylums. In many instances Big Brothers and Big Sisters Organizations are formed. The latter come in contact with the individual child, and after his graduation endeavor to assist him in finding an occupation and adjusting himself to the new environment. The after-care of the Hebrew Sheltering and Guardian Society is conducted through the medium of the Fellowship House, which has somewhat of the character of a settlement. The Fellowship House was organized in 1913. It conducts an employment agency, attends to the social needs of the alumni, holds Friday evening services, maintains classes in stenography, arranges entertainments, etc.

I. Day Nurseries

In speaking of the care of dependent children, mention should be made of the functions of the day nurseries. Day nurseries are primarily designed for the day care of children, who are unable to receive care from their mothers out at work during the day. In New York and other large cities, we find day nurseries either as separate institutions or as parts of other agencies, such as settlements, relief societies, and so forth.

The fact that women are compelled to work away from home and delegate the care of their children to institutions seems to be rather a deplorable situation. The idea has been advanced that the very existence of day nurseries fosters and promotes the need for them. Women who could get along without earnings from shops and factories still prefer it to everyday home duties. In some instances the husbands take advantage of the situation and make their wives work, thus lessening their own burden. As the maintenance of children in day nurseries is quite expensive, it is a question whether a subvention to the mother for the necessary income would not be a better arrangement. However the need is quite urgent, and in many cases the day nurseries prevent considerable want and misery. The admission of children to day nurseries requires definite and careful consideration. The Helen Day Nursery, a constituent society of the Jewish Charities of Chicago, reports in 1915 that the predominant cause of application is desertion and insufficient income. In some cities homes for the temporary care of children are maintained. They usually accommodate children when the mother is getting medical attendance at the hospital, or when the family is temporarily disrupted. Frequently these institutions were utilized as temporary abodes for children that were eventually sent to permanent institutions, or disposed of in some other way.

J. FAMILY DESERTION

1. *Family Desertion as a Problem*

Just as with the death of the head of the family, the wife and children become dependent upon charity assistance, so it also happens when the man deserts his family. The phenomenon of family desertion has been of quite frequent occurrence, and it is generally believed in charity circles that it is on the increase. There are no definite figures to prove this assertion, but it is certain that the dependency caused by wife desertion is receiving greater attention than in former years. It is estimated that in New York City there are eight thousand abandoned children, toward whose maintenance in child-caring institutions the city is paying approximately one million dollars. In addition to this, the institutions are required in many cases to supplement the allowances granted by the city for the children. Moreover, thousands of abandoned children are maintained in their own mothers' homes by private relief agencies.

Among the Jews, family desertion has also been a matter of great concern, and as early as the year 1900 a number of cities took up the problem of family desertion as one of the most perplexing questions of modern

Jewish charities. The giving of relief to deserted women and their children, the placing of these children in institutions, the utilization of day nurseries for this purpose, were the usual means of handling this problem. Unfortunately, this meant no solution to the difficulty, nor did it lead to an abatement in the growing number of wife desertions, until the time came when consideration was given rather to measures that would prevent family desertion than the mere treatment of the results of the lack of responsibility of the man who left his family to the mercy of the community.

2. *Causes of Desertion*

Thus, at the National Conference of Jewish Charities in Chicago in 1900, a Committee on Desertion presented a report in which was outlined the status of the desertion situation at that time, and a résumé of the legislation in the various states directed toward the punishment of desertion. Some general suggestions were also made tending toward the eradication of desertion. Later, attention was called to the immediate causes of family desertion. A study of actual cases treated by the United Hebrew Charities of New York City in 1903, made by Mr. Morris Waldman, showed that a large percentage of desertion was not due, as had been supposed, to lack of work or inability to earn a living, but to various forms of immorality. A similar study of the general situation in Boston in 1901, disclosed the fact that thirty-three per cent were due to drunkenness. Dr. Lee K. Frankel called the attention of the conference in 1906, to the fact that there are in addition to the usual reasons for desertion, specific causes that apply to Jewish desertion.[1] Of particular interest should be mentioned the fact that owing to a forced immigration from European countries, the husbands frequently come to the United States in advance of their families, contract new ties when they arrive here, and are unwilling, for this reason, to maintain responsibilities originally contracted before they left their native places.

3. *Promoting Legislation*

The Jews were very active in promoting legislation tending to punish family deserters. In many states, there were no laws at all making family desertion a crime, and in some it was considered a misdemeanor, under which extradition, in case the deserter was located in another state, was impossible. Again, there were some states where family desertion was deemed a felony, despite which juries would often show considerable leniency, defeating the purpose of the act. Accordingly, a law which was quite novel was passed in New York in 1905, which refers to the abandonment of children and which in part reads as follows: "A parent or other person charged with the care, or custody, for nurture or education of a child under the age of sixteen years, who abandons the child in destitute circumstances and wilfully omits to furnish necessary and

[1] "Desertion," Dr. Lee K. Frankel. Fourth National Conference of Jewish Charities, 1906.

proper food, clothing, and shelter for such a child, is guilty of felony, punishable by a fine not to exceed one thousand dollars, or by imprisonment for not more than two years, or by both."

4. *Publicity as an Aid*

Immediately after the law was passed, the United Hebrew Charities of New York City determined to make a very active campaign for the prosecution of deserters under the new law. Publicity through the daily Jewish press was utilized both for location of the deserter and for the effect that such a method would have for routing desertion that was contemplated. The results from the very beginning were quite encouraging, and the experience of New York and other cities soon followed the more or less sound method—persistent prosecution of the deserters—though in all instances, the main object was to reunite the families wherever it was possible, without punishment by imprisonment or fine. It must be remembered, however, that desertion is not an evil which can be eradicated by legislation alone.

5. *Study of Desertion in New York*

Quite an elaborate paper on the subject of family desertion among the Jews was presented by Mr. Morris D. Waldman, at the National Conference of Jewish Charities in St. Louis, in 1910. In this paper, Mr. Waldman calls attention to the fact that family desertion is not distinctly a Jewish problem. The United Hebrew Charities of New York, during the two years ending September 30, 1908, had desertion in 11.66 per cent of all its cases. Of five thousand cases of the Charity Organization Society of that city, selected at random, 12.12 per cent were such cases. In the Associated Charities of Buffalo, desertion cases formed during the past four years, from ten to thirteen per cent of the total. In that city, desertion among the Jews is hardly known.

Mr. Waldman, however, calls attention to the fact that family desertion among the Jews was already known in the middle ages. The extent of family desertion among the Jews in the United States is indicated by the following figures. In 1909, seven per cent of the applicants in St. Louis were deserted women, in Baltimore sixteen per cent, in Chicago eleven per cent, in New York ten per cent. The number of children of deserted women cared for by child-caring agencies of New York probably exceeds 600, costing annually for their maintenance $70,000. The United Hebrew Charities of New York has in its records for the year 1909, 1,046 deserted women as against 1,655 widows.

In discussing the question of desertion, Mr. Waldman recognizing the complexity of the problem, succeeded in 1902 in tabulating 244 cases according to cause in the following subdivisions. Other women, 65; licentiousness, 10; dissipation, 10; gambling, 7; drink, 6; woman's immorality, 3; laziness, 16; marriage for money solely, 3; incompatibility of temperament, 19; interference of relatives, 12; roving disposition, 3; to seek health, 9; man's insanity, 4; woman's insanity, 1;

woman's sickness, 1; money fever, 1; to seek work, 62; unknown, 12.

In discussing the remedies, Mr. Waldman calls attention to the fact that almost half of the deserters care for what becomes of their children, and therefore believes that stringent measures, as adopted in Cincinnati where the deserted women and children are handled by a different agency like the Humane Society and the relief given is in its form and amount inadequate with subsequent but temporary suffering, might bring back the husband who has left and prevent a number of others from leaving.

However, in other cases, this method, in his opinion, does not achieve the proper results. Consequently, he expresses his belief that the main way of checking desertion, if not eradicating it entirely, is proper laws, together with a strict prosecution of the deserter.

6. *The National Desertion Bureau*

As a result of this paper, it was deemed advisable to form what is known as the National Desertion Bureau, whose purpose is to centralize the treatment of family desertion for all cities, and help prosecution through the medium of publicity. This Bureau publishes weekly in the Jewish daily press, the pictures and descriptions of the deserters and aids in their prosecution whenever necessary. It maintains headquarters and an office force in New York City. The Jewish charitable organizations in the various cities of the United States act as its local agents. If a man deserts a family in St.

Louis and complaint against him is lodged with the St. Louis Charities the organization obtains certain information. This information and the photograph of the deserter are forwarded to the New York office. The office then causes the picture and the information to be printed in several Yiddish newspapers, in what is known as the "Gallery of Missing Husbands," a sort of modern rogues' gallery. These papers, being read all over the United States and Canada, accomplish the desired results. Persons recognizing such deserters, gladly inform the nearest charity office. The arrest is made, and arrangements are made to return the man to the city to which he belongs. In the majority of cases, reconciliation is effected, in other cases, support of the family is arranged. Where the man is obstreperous, his case is pushed to the limits of the law.[1]

In the report presented to the Conference of Jewish Charities in 1914 by the manager of the Bureau, it was evident that desertion had been considerably checked, that the organizations in the different cities had been enabled to locate the deserters, and the recent legislation in the different states had made prosecution more feasible. Up to that time, for a period of seven years, the Wife Desertion Bureau received nearly nine hundred cases and succeeded in locating almost six hundred deserting husbands, or about sixty-six per cent.[2]

[1] "Family Desertion," Oscar Leonard, Missouri Conference of Charities and Corrections, 1913.
[2] "Desertion," Monroe Goldstein. Proceedings National Conference of Jewish Charities, Cleveland, 1912.

The record of Cincinnati in regard to desertion, deserves consideration. In a survey of ten years' activity it showed that the entire number of desertions from 1904 to 1913 were one hundred and nineteen. The entire cost of treatment of these cases was as follows:

No cost	11
$1, to $99	88
$100, to $199	5
$200, to $500	15
Total	119

Of the hundred and nineteen cases treated, sixty-one were aided through the instrumentality of the Ohio Humane Society, sixty-three were settled by means of transportation, only in eight cases were there pensions granted, and the final outcome of the cases is as follows:

Husbands returned to the city	48
Families reunited in other cities	51
Families sent to relatives	6
Families self-supporting in Cincinnati	8
Pending	6
Total	119

7. *Methods of Treatment*

These results, together with the discussion of the subject, indicate the method of proper treatment of desertion cases from the standpoint of charitable organizations, which can be summarized as follows:

a. Desertion is not only a felony and is considered so

by the law, but is a crime which should be prosecuted by the charity organization to its fullest extent.

b. A charity organization should give service reluctantly to the deserted woman and her children, and whenever possible, should refer it to agencies that will render relief on a lower standard than the Jewish organizations usually do. This method prevents the recurrence of the desertion which is committed in order to obtain charity, sometimes with the connivance of the wife. It will prevent desertion of the man who really cares for his children, which in Jewish charity work is almost a general thing.

c. In each and every case, all efforts should be made and no expense spared to locate the husband. The National Desertion Bureau should be utilized, and all other means brought into play. The prosecution of desertion should be as stringent as possible, though in all cases where a reunion can be effected, sentence should be suspended, if possible.

CHAPTER ELEVEN. DEPENDENT WOMEN AND CHILDREN

QUESTIONS

1. What is the modern idea of lessening the burden of dependent children?
2. Describe the two systems of child caring.
3. What are some of the experiences in the placing out of Jewish children?
4. What are the arguments in favor of the congregate system of child caring?
5. Describe the cottage system.

6. What are the new ideas in management of child-caring agencies?
7. Tell of the new "Orthodox" tendency in Jewish orphan asylums.
8. State twelve rules of child-caring work.
9. State the problem of the after-care of orphans.
10. What are the purposes of day nurseries and what are their negative features?
11. What is the problem of family desertion?
12. Discuss the causes of family desertion.
13. Describe the functions of the National Desertion Bureau.
14. What are the principles of desertion treatment?

XII

INSUFFICIENCY OF INCOME

A. Causes of Insufficiency of Income

Under ordinary conditions, the combined incomes of the adult members of the family ought to be sufficient for the necessities of life and save the family from dependency. It frequently happens, however, especially in the experience of Jewish charities, that the family is compelled to apply for relief for no other immediate cause than insufficiency of income. In other words, in this instance, the combined efforts of the breadwinners of the family are not sufficient to meet the necessities of life. An analysis of this particular class of dependency shows two principal subjective conditions responsible for the situation; first, the inefficiency of the breadwinner, or second, the disproportionately large family unit, in which the family consists of one breadwinner, and many children, together with a wife, dependent upon him. In temporary cases, insufficiency of income may be due to scarcity or lack of work.

1. Inefficiency of the Breadwinner

In the majority of cases, inefficiency of the breadwinner is due to the lack of training. It is natural that the immigrants who have come to this country as adults, and who in their early days were not used to hard manual labor should find it difficult to obtain remunerative employment in any of the trades that require skill and practice. Lack of physical endurance prevents their doing hard, manual labor, and willy nilly, they are forced into the ranks of the thousands of workers in the needle trades. But even if they come to this country as mechanics from the old country, they are lacking in speed and dexterity and are not used to the American system of division of labor in the realm of manufacture. A social worker, extending relief in this case, must be aware of the fact that palliative measures, while necessary for a time, will not solve the problem, and in many instances may interfere with the natural and desirable acquisition of resources for independence. In some instances, the teaching of a new trade to the immigrant would serve the purpose, in others, an initial expense for an independent business pursuit may place the family on a self-supporting basis, and only in a few cases should a regular weekly or monthly allowance be granted for a more or less extended period.

2. *Training in Trades*

The question of teaching the immigrant trades was attractive to the workers in Jewish philanthropy during the mass immigration from Russia in the eighties. With this purpose, the Baron De Hirsch Fund established what is known as the Baron De Hirsch Trade School. This institution, in its incipiency, received adult pupils, preferably newly arrived immigrants, without limitations as to age, and granted them a weekly allowance so as to make it possible for them to continue their trade training. Classes in carpentry, plumbing, machine work, and sign painting, were established. During the first year about one thousand pupils entered the school, but almost without exception, they remained in the school only for a short time, and left it at the first opportunity to secure employment on the outside. It was then eventually agreed that the attempt to teach the adult immigrant was a failure, and that the subsidy given to students while they learned a trade was unwise. A reorganization of the school was therefore found necessary. Then the school offered its facilities for the training of the younger generation; the requirements for admission were made to include knowledge of English; the course was definitely set for five and a half months, and the pupils were to supply their own maintenance. This innovation has proven in late years to be a success, and the school, through efficient administration of J. Ernest G. Yalden has proved its usefulness, attracting large numbers of students, and every year graduating from two to three hundred.

Another attempt along this direction was the establishment of a factory by the United Hebrew Charities of New York City, where the immigrants were given an opportunity to learn some very simple operations, such as garment work, and where they were paid for their work while learning. This venture was also found to be inadequate, and created considerable legitimate opposition from the workers in this trade, who claimed that this arrangement clashed with their interests. As a rule, immigrants enter the different shops of the city, joining especially the throng of sweat shop workers, who in the beginning pay for the opportunity of learning the trade, or work gratis, and receive a miserable pittance after they are through with their training. Months sometimes elapse before they can earn a living at a trade. This enterprise is still in operation. Attempts were also made to establish night trade classes, and quite a successful venture was made in this direction in Philadelphia, where the class in cigar-making was especially well patronized.

All these methods of trade training, however, are more or less obsolete at present, as far as the adult immigrant is concerned. It is only in individual cases where the immigrant avails himself of the opportunity offered by the different educational institutions. As a rule he prefers to work out his own salvation by going from shop to shop and getting experience as it comes. With the minute specialization of our industry, the teaching of a trade requires considerable time and application, and is not altogether adapted to the needs of the adult immigrant, who must augment his earning capacity immediately.

3. *Self-Respect Fund*

The United Hebrew Charities of New York, through the thoughtfulness of Jacob H. Schiff, in 1909 organized what is known as the self-respect fund. At that time, Mr. Schiff offered to contribute fifteen thousand dollars to be applied to the temporary relief of families that had never before received assistance from the society, in order to enable them to tide themselves over the period of unemployment. Mr. Warner Van Norden, of New York, supplemented this contribution by a contribution of his own amounting to four thousand dollars. This self-respect fund, as indicated in the report of the United Hebrew Charities for 1914, saved a large number of families from becoming regular recipients of charity from the organization.[1]

4. *Employment Agencies*

But what is more important in cases of dependency on account of lack of work is not the palliative relief, but provision of work for the unemployed. The organization of finding work is only now beginning to receive the serious consideration that it deserves from the Federal, State, and municipal governments. State and city employment agencies have been organized all over the country, but even now there is still need for private effort along this direction.

For years, the Jewish relief societies in the different cities conducted what was known as the employment department. This usually consisted of a paid agent, who made it his business to come in contact with the employers of the different kinds of labor, to find out whenever there was an opening, and to place the appli-

---

[1] "Self-Respect Funds," Dr. Lee K. Frankel. Eighth National Conference of Jewish Charities, Memphis, 1914. "Jewish Charities," August 8, 1914.

cants that he had on hand. In some instances, the employment agent would meet the applicant early in the morning, and together they would start to visit the factories and shops, enquiring for work. The newspaper announcements were utilized, as well as telephone communications. Frequently the applicant was given a letter to a place where there was an opening. On the whole, however, the work was done in a haphazard way, and little attention was paid to the specific qualifications of the applicant.[1] In some cities like Chicago, the employment is under the auspices of the independent order of B'nai B'rith, again, in some cities it was found efficient to employ a lady in the capacity of employment agent. The rise of municipal and state agencies will make it unnecessary for the Jewish agencies to continue this work to the same extent. It is only for the immigrant and the handicapped that private effort will have to supplement the work of the government.

[1] "The Problem of Unemployment," Miss Frances Kellor.

An exception to the general run of employment bureaus is the one conducted in New York City under the auspices of the Kehillah. Subsidized by the United Hebrew Charities of New York, the New York Foundation and the Jewish Protectory, this bureau specializes in procuring work for handicapped persons—applicants for relief, non-English speaking persons, sabbath observers, ex-convicts, discharged soldiers and sailors, juvenile delinquents, cripples, etc. The bureau is very efficiently conducted, handles several thousand cases a year, and, considering its class of applicants, has a high ratio of placements. Moreover, it makes a point of investigating each individual case within thirty days after placement. Twice a year, a similar investigation on a broader scale is made.

B. Establishment in Business

Another method of increasing the income of the family has been found in establishing the given person in a business of his own. It is quite frequent that a person cannot qualify to fill a position in another establishment but is quite capable of working for himself. In this instance he will require his own tools and some investment for materials, a location and equipment for a little store or a shop as the case may be. Thus, a number of shoemakers who have come from the old country where they were plying their trade for themselves, find that they cannot join the large factories in this country, where machinery and division of labor make their specific skill unnecessary. This particular class of mechanics, however, find a livelihood in following the cobbling trade, and by opening a little shop, they may gradually work up into a store of their own. A similar experience is to be had in the case of tailors, who have succeeded in establishing their own business as repairing and cleaning shop-keepers, and eventually in securing their own customers for tailor-made clothing. This is true, practically speaking, for every trade where a small investment equips a person to make a livelihood in his own trade. In such cases, employment for others would mean a hard and difficult road to self-advancement. Then again, there is the case of people who have no special training whatever. Their experience as small tradesmen in their own country does not equip them with earning capacity here. Lacking a knowledge of

English and conditions, they cannot get positions as salesmen, but, with a little capital of their own they are capable of starting into business as peddlers, hucksters, storekeepers and so forth. From the standpoint of a relief agency, assistance given to a person for the purpose of establishing him in business of his own should be considered only to the extent that it saves the family from remaining a burden on charity. In other words, if a family is compelled to apply for relief more or less periodically, and if an investment of a certain amount of money would make the family self-supporting, or would lessen the dependency of the family, then the wisdom of establishing it in business is self-evident. As in every other business venture, however, these investments are uncertain and very frequently result in loss, but in judging of the results of this particular kind of effort, we must take into consideration the increase in earning capacity that resulted rather than the solution of the case in question. An investigation made by the United Jewish Charities of Cincinnati of forty-eight cases established in business indicates that over one-fourth became self-supporting.[1] Adding to this proportion the cases in which the relief agency was compelled to supply less than twenty per cent of the minimum necessary to support the family, only one-fourth were failures. Of the total amount invested in business, fifty-seven per cent remained intact. The average weekly earning capacity was about eight and four-tenths per cent

[1] "Jewish Charities," Vol. 5, No. 8, Maurice B. Hexter.

INSUFFICIENCY OF INCOME 189

for each dollar invested. There is another phase to the situation. A case may become self-supporting and nevertheless earn less per week and per dollar invested than one who did not succeed in covering expenses. This depends upon the amount invested and the size of the family. We find that even in cases where the relief organization has to supply relief, from fifty to ninety per cent of the amount necessary to support the family, the investment still paid from seven-tenths to one per cent a week for each dollar invested. The method of establishing dependent families in business is especially adapted in cases where the breadwinner is handicapped in his earning capacity, for instance in the case of old age, sickness preventing hard manual labor, etc. The character of the business selected depends upon the conditions as well as the individual peculiarities of the person in question.

In connection with the establishment-in-business method, relief societies have recently developed a method of free loans to the poor. This should not be confused, however, with the work of the Gemilath Chesed,—free loan societies where the clientele's credit is guaranteed by endorsement or pledges of some solvent parties.

The largest of these organizations is that established in New York in 1892. In 1914 this organization was reported to have a capital of one hundred and eighty-four thousand dollars and to have distributed during the year six hundred and thirty-two thousand and four hundred and ten dollars in the form of loans. The money is loaned on notes endorsed by responsible people, without charge of interest or expense of any kind, the borrower repaying the loans in small weekly installments. The statistics of the society show that ninety-seven per cent of the loans are repaid by the borrowers themselves, and only two per cent by the endorsers, while there is only about one-half per cent loss.[1] Similar organizations are established in almost every large city. Most of them are conducted as separate agencies, supported largely by the orthodox constituency, though lately a free loan society is becoming an important part of organized philanthropic effort, as shown in Chicago, where the Free Loan Society connected with the Bureau of Personal Service is doing excellent work.

C. Self-Support Funds

The self-support fund of the United Hebrew Charities of New York City was established in 1900 and was made possible through the contribution of the sum of five thousand dollars by Mr. Jacob H. Schiff of New York. In making this grant Mr. Schiff made the condition that the sum was to be loaned to deserving poor whose economic condition had been carefully ascertained, and where there seemed to be some likelihood of enabling the family to become self-supporting, as a result of the grant. It was further understood that where possible, the effort should be made to have the grants returned. In other words, it was understood in

[1] "Free Loans," Julius J. Dukas. Proceedings of the National Conference of Jewish Charities, Memphis, 1914.

making the allowances that the beneficiaries received them as loans rather than as relief granted. The conditions under which the loans were to be repaid were exceptionally easy. No collateral was required of the borrower nor were any endorsements required on the note which he was expected to give. The larger proportion of the loans made during the first year were granted in the hope that the individuals who had received the benefit of sanitarium treatment and who had returned to their families either cured or improved might, as a result, be enabled to establish themselves in some small business enterprise, such as peddling, storekeeping, etc.

Since 1900 Mr. Schiff has generously made additional contributions to the self-support fund. The total results from thirteen years show that one thousand four hundred and eighty loans were made amounting to one hundred four thousand and six hundred seven dollars and forty-nine cents, that fifteen per cent of all the borrowers repaid an amount equal to thirteen per cent of the sum invested, that thirty-four per cent repaid in part about fourteen per cent of the money invested, that fifty-one per cent of the borrowers did not repay at all. Of the latter loans, however, eleven per cent are considered to be collectible. From the standpoint of a free loan society, the proportion of the loans collected is discouraging, but from the relief standpoint the question is not how much was collected, but to what extent did this investment result in diminishing the dependency of a family. In one hundred four of the New York cases selected at random in 1916, it was found that ninety-two had become self-supporting.

D. TEMPORARY DEPENDENCY

Insufficiency of income is frequently due to some temporary condition, and dependency in this case is abated by the savings of the individual, by the credit power that he may possess, or by a temporary reduction in the standard of living. This is the case for instance, when work is slack or when a person is temporarily thrown out of his regular employment. Temporary relief in cases like this becomes necessary and frequently the family is reduced to dependency for no other reason than lack of work. In a time of continuous industrial panic, the problem of finding employment is difficult of solution. Some artificial employment is usually inaugurated to bridge over the hard time. Municipal work established in different cities during the panic of 1914 was utilized to a large extent by Jewish philanthropic agencies. Jewish unemployed participated in the different works established by the cities, but this was not sufficient in many cases. To cope with this, relief agencies in some instances organized their own works, giving employment to those who needed help. The character of the work, however, and the management did not differ in any way from the methods usually employed in private and municipal efforts.

There can be no doubt that the period of industrial depression throws a large number of self-supporting families into the class of dependents, who under normal economic conditions, would require no charity interference. There is always danger that relief granted during bad times may weaken some of the applicants and tempt them to continue their dependency upon charity, when it is not absolutely necessary. During the industrial depression of 1910, the United Jewish Charities of Cincinnati took the situation into consideration and carefully watched each and every case of relief-giving to the unemployed, endeavoring to rehabilitate the family on a self-supporting basis as soon as possible. On the other hand, it was quite careful to continue adequate relief whenever it was necessary and to avoid hardship caused by an abrupt withdrawal of relief, thus giving families an opportunity to regain their independent existence, which had been shattered and dislocated by conditions over which they had no control.

The total number of cases applying for assistance on account of lack of work for the period of thirty months, beginning October, 1913, to February, 1916, was one hundred and eighty-nine. These and their families comprised four hundred and twelve adults and five hundred and forty-one children, making a total of nine hundred and fifty-three individuals. The duration of dependency is expressed as follows:

    18.5 per cent were assisted only for one week.
    22.7 per cent were assisted not more than one month.
    50.2 per cent were assisted not more than six months.
    8.6 per cent were assisted more than six months.

Analyzing the duration and cost of the above cases,

we find that in total, they were assisted on account of lack of work one thousand five hundred and forty-five weeks, at a total cost of ten thousand four hundred ninety-eight dollars and fifty-six cents, or six dollars and seventy-nine cents per case per week, or one dollar and thirty-six cents per person per week.

Of these, forty-one were never before applicants for any charity assistance; these and their families comprised eighty-seven adults and sixty-five children, making a total of one hundred and fifty-two individuals.

> 24.4 per cent were assisted only for one week.
> 36.5 per cent were assisted not more than one month.
> 36.5 per cent were assisted not more than six months.
> 2.6 per cent were assisted more than six months.

Analyzing the duration and cost of the above cases, we find that in total, they were assisted on account of lack of work two hundred and forty-four weeks at a total cost of one thousand four hundred eighteen dollars and eighty-eight cents, or five dollars and eighty-two cents per case per week, or one dollar and fifty-one cents per person per week.

Of the total, there were one hundred and twenty old cases, comprising two hundred and sixty-three adults and three hundred and eighty children, making a total of six hundred and forty-three individuals.

> 17.5 per cent were assisted only for one week.
> 25.0 per cent were assisted not more than one month.
> 46.7 per cent were assisted not more than six months.
> 10.8 per cent were assisted more than six months.

Analyzing the duration and cost of the above cases,

INSUFFICIENCY OF INCOME

we find that in total, they were assisted on account of lack of work one thousand and ninety-three weeks at a total cost of seven thousand seven hundred and five dollars and nineteen cents, or seven dollars and five cents per case per week, or one dollar and thirty-three cents per person per week.

The remaining cases, twenty-eight in number, were those registered in the charity office on previous occasions, but had never received assistance on account of lack of employment. This group comprises sixty-two adults and ninety-six children, making a total of one hundred and fifty-eight individuals.

14.3 per cent were assisted only for one week.
32.2 per cent were assisted not more than one month.
46.3 per cent were assisted not more than six months.
7.2 per cent were assisted more than six months.

Analyzing the duration and cost of the above cases, we find that in total, they were out of work two hundred and eight weeks at a cost of one thousand three hundred and seventy-four dollars and nine cents or six dollars and sixty-one cents per case per week, or one dollar and eighteen cents per person per week.

CHAPTER TWELVE. INSUFFICIENCY OF INCOME
QUESTIONS

1. Enumerate causes of insufficiency of income.
2. What are the means of increasing income?
3. Discuss the differences between self-respect funds and self-support funds.
4. What are the criteria of success in the use of the method of establishing in business?
5. Discuss temporary dependency caused by unemployment.

XIII

STANDARDS OF RELIEF

While the different aspects of the relief problem have been receiving serious consideration and thought by organized Jewish effort and thought, it is strange that in all these years, the question of standards of relief, so vexing a proposition with non-Jewish agencies, was seldom if ever, brought up for discussion. There must be good reason for this omission, as well as some ground why the question should receive our attention at present.

At different times, under different conditions, the standard of relief to the poor, and the corresponding obligation of society to the needy, was differently answered by the Jews. Thus, the ancient Hebrews prescribed that we should feed the hungry, clothe the naked, and provide for the homeless in accordance with their individual usages: if they are accustomed to servants, they should be supplied with them, if used to a higher plane of life, they should not be deprived of it. There was no general uniform standard to be followed. Later, we find the development of a standard leading toward a constructive policy—the highest form of help to the poor is enabling them to help themselves, and again, personal service as the criterion of the efficacy of relief is emphasized. The idea that the poor are entitled to a minimum allowance is of recent origin with the Jews. The problem was formerly considered from the standpoint of the giver; it was a question of how much a person ought to contribute for charity, rather than the extent to which the individual poor should receive assistance.

There can be no doubt that the total charity distributed among the Jews as relief funds by the Jews is on the increase; the generosity of our people is not weakening, but at the same time we observe that in almost all instances there is a lack of funds to meet the demands for adequate relief, and a very marked deviation from the ambitious claim of the Jews that they themselves will take care of their own. They are compelled to utilize the municipal and state agencies to which they are duly entitled, but which they avoided in previous years in handling the poor, and in some instances are willing to accept help from private, non-Jewish sources to meet their own problems.

The new interest in regard to standards of living may be prompted by this general tendency for economy, conditioned by necessity. On the other hand, Jewish endeavors fall short of funds to meet the demands of the relief work, yet they are constantly extending their activities in other fields of philanthropic activity, showing that the capacity for the support of charitable endeavor has not reached its maximum. The probability is that the results of our relief practice are not altogether satisfactory, and that they warrant a study of our methods and an examination into the question whether we did not sin in adopting standards which were either too high or too low. It is still necessary to justify the expenditure of large sums of money for relief and to prove that the money spent serves a good purpose.

Excessive relief would express itself in the demoralization of the poor and spread pauperism, while inefficient relief would spell suffering, degradation, and further wreckage of humanity with all its deplorable sequences. The fear of the demoralizing effects of excessive relief in the field of Jewish endeavor was thoroughly and forcibly dispelled by Dr. Lee K. Frankel at the Detroit Conference in 1902. Two years later, Dr. Lowenstein presented a discussion on the subject of adequacy of relief,—touching on the same subject. He expressed great doubt that there was any reason to suppose that cities like New York had reason to expect demoralization because of excessive relief given by the organizations. A superficial study of persistency of dependency, as expressed in the number and character of the applications for relief for a period of five years was presented at the Philadelphia Conference in 1906, leading to the conclusion that Jewish charity organizations need not be in fear of fostering or promoting pauperism. Thus indications are that the difficulty lies not in excessive relief, but rather in inefficient relief, a low standard that is so flagrant that it requires the attention of the public.

A. DIFFERENT STANDARDS

It is interesting to note the attitude of the different Jewish communities to the relief problem of to-day. For some years, the United Hebrew Charities of New York advanced the idea that the number of persons applying for relief is diminishing. At the same time, they have recognized that the cost of treating their dependents has been considerably increased. The diminishing number of applicants for relief in this organization can be differently interpreted, as was suggested at the New York Conference in 1904. It may mean that poverty is on the decrease in the metropolis; it may indicate that the efficient methods of the organization forced the applicants to greater exertions to become self-supporting; or it may simply point to the fact that those who really need assistance seek it in other quarters and do not apply to the United Hebrew Charities, knowing that they cannot obtain it there. There is, however, no doubt that those who come for relief now, come for graver reasons than in the days when the applicant came for temporary relief only. This condition we meet in all cities. Temporary relief, the problem of helping the individual in a small way to bridge over a short period of embarrassment, be it right after his arrival or during unemployment, slight ailments, and so on, is largely a matter taken care of by neighborly assistance, without great concern to organized efforts.

The applicant of to-day presents a more complicated problem. He is the victim of tuberculosis, away more or less permanently from his natural setting, his family presents a case of prolonged and persistent dependency. He is the person suffering with a chronic or incurable disease and presenting a continuous problem of the care of the family, or it is the widow and her children left without any provision for their independent existence, the large army of deserted women and children, and last, but not least, the man with the large family and insufficient income to meet the necessities of life. These very cases presuppose continuous treatment; they are cumulative in their very nature.

The United Hebrew Charities of New York reports that of three thousand two hundred and ten cases treated during the year 1912-13, one thousand nine hundred and seventy-five required more than twenty-five dollars assistance; that tuberculosis and widowhood, permanent factors of dependency, required 54.3 per cent of the entire amount expended; that 80.2 per cent of all the applicants were residents of the United States for over five years. All these facts indicate the character of the work that the Jewish charities are handling, and the seriousness of the problem with which they are confronted.

The Jewish Aid Society of Brooklyn acknowledges the inadequacy of relief and reports that the average amount granted per case has fallen from $ 23.75 in the year 1910, to $20.97 in the year 1911.

The United Hebrew Charities of Philadelphia ventures the assertion that it is impossible for any chariable organization to assist each and every applicant, however worthy, who may require assistance. The organization, therefore, endeavors to help a few wisely, rather than endeavoring to scatter broadcast the money in its care.

The Hebrew Benevolent Society of Baltimore reports a very small number of cases of dependency, and an exceedingly conservative amount spent for relief. In the report for 1912, it presents also an interesting study of a growing tendency toward incapacity, manifested in Jewish families of a certain group, pointing to the problem of "pauper blood."

Cleveland also mentions pauperism with which they have to cope, while Cincinnati continues to insist upon adequate and generous relief, and increases its budget for the relief department year after year.

Boston acknowledges that it is not doing or giving enough, especially to the sick or disabled.

St. Louis, on the other hand, reports a decrease of expenses, and a considerable increase of per capita allowance for the pensioners, and Detroit finds the number of pensioners increasing.

It is refreshing to read the report of the Jewish Aid Society of Chicago. They are doing great things there, and they spent more money in 1914 than any time before. They are proud that they have a larger staff and a better administration, and they threaten to make it even more efficient and more expensive.

B. Individual Standards

It is neither wise nor expedient to insist upon uniform standards for all cases belonging to different categories. The criterion of proper standards should be, after all, sought in the results, rather than in the course of treatment. Thus, in the care of tubercular cases, economy would be wise and legitimate only with certain limitations. The problem, primarily, would be to save the life of the individual and to enable him to regain his earning capacity, to maintain the unity of the family, and to rehabilitate the entire group to a normal condition of self-support. Relief should be adequate, but not too large to weaken the desire upon the part of the individual to regain his independent standing.

The fear of doing too much for a widow and her children is not justifiable, as long as the treatment does not interfere with the development of the children. It is self-evident, that if the children are provided with necessities, given the opportunity for education and the advantages of proper surroundings, there can result no harm, either to them or to society. If the children are not fortunate enough to be born into families that are endowed with the blessings of plenty, if their natural guardian and provider, the father, was prematurely taken away before they reached maturity, if society is to act in "loco parentis," why should not they be provided with conditions of normal living and an opportunity for a better and fuller life? It is quite different, however, in the treatment of cases, the dependency of which was caused by family desertion. Excessive or even more or less adequate relief will tend to make desertion attractive and prevent the solution of cases that can be solved. It would probably be only an impetus for a man in difficulty to shake off his responsibilities letting the charities take care of his family. Prevention in this case is possible, and more important than the palliative treatment.

The question of granting continuous relief on account of insufficient income, lack of work, and so on, also presents great difficulty. Theoretically, no organization can cope with this problem. Excessive relief in this instance is undoubtedly of questionable value, and still it seems to be impossible to avoid helping families whose income does not permit even the minimum allowance for necessities. It need not be mentioned that this minimum is relative and does not permit of strict definition.

C. Existing Standards of Living

A study in 1913 of the actual expenses for food of fifty-two families of Cincinnati who are either supported in full by the charities or temporarily assisted in time of need has been made the basis for a calculation of a usual standard of living as practiced by the class of our people where the expenditure of every cent has to be carefully considered. This has been taken as a guiding principle in giving relief to families, with the reservation that in case of sickness, the standard is accordingly increased, while under other circumstances, correspondingly decreased. Schedules of daily expenses prepared for this purpose were carefully filled out for a period of three weeks; these were taken as a basis for the study of the expenditures for food, from these an average for a normal family, consisting of man, wife, and three minor children was deduced, which expressed itself in twenty-five cents per unit per day. The differing values of the individuals in the family are taken from the scale adopted by the United States Bureau of Agriculture ("Farmers' Bulletin," No. 142, p. 12), which is as follows:

> An adult woman requires .8 as much as an adult man.
> A boy of 15 to 16 requires .9 " " " " " "
> A boy of 13 to 14 requires .8 " " " " " "
> A boy of 12 to 14 requires .7 " " " " " "
> A boy of 10 to 11 requires .6 " " " " " "
> A girl of 15 to 16 requires .8 " " " " " "
> A girl of 13 to 14 requires .7 " " " " " "
> A girl of 10 to 12 requires .6 " " " " " "
> A child of 6 to 9 requires .5 " " " " " "
> A child from 2 to 5 requires .4 " " " " " "
> A child under 2 requires .3 " " " " " "

A tentative hypothesis was assumed that, a priori, there is a direct relation between the cost of food per unit in the family and the size of the family. By graphic representation of the data, indicating the deviation of the size of the family and the cost per unit from the mean, this was conclusively proved to be so. In order to ascertain the exact relationship of these two variables, the true standard deviation was determined by exact, statistical method, and a graphic representation was obtained, from which curve, by interpolation, the following table of cost per unit in families of diminishing size was obtained. Naturally the number of cases represented in the study was too small to make it accurate, but it is sufficient for practical purposes. The table used is as follows:

Number of Units in Family	Daily Cost per Unit for Food	Weekly Cost per Family				
		Food	Clothing	Fuel and Light	Miscellaneous	Total (exclusive of Rent)
1.5	35.0 cents	$3.67	$1.10	$.50	$1.10	$6.37
1.6	33.7 "	3.77	1.13	.51	1.13	6.54
1.7	32.5 "	3.87	1.16	.52	1.16	6.71
1.8	31.2 "	3.93	1.18	.53	1.18	6.82
1.9	30.0 "	3.99	1.20	.54	1.20	6.93
2.0	28.8 "	4.03	1.21	.55	1.21	7.00
2.1	28.6 "	4.20	1.26	.57	1.26	7.29
2.2	28.4 "	4.37	1.31	.59	1.31	7.58
2.3	28.2 "	4.54	1.36	.61	1.36	7.87
2.4	28.0 "	4.70	1.41	.63	1.41	8.15
2.5	27.8 "	4.87	1.46	.65	1.46	8.44
2.6	27.3 "	4.97	1.49	.67	1.49	8.62
2.7	26.9 "	5.08	1.52	.69	1.52	8.81
2.8	26.4 "	5.17	1.55	.70	1.55	8.97
2.9	25.9 "	5.25	1.58	.71	1.58	9.12
3.0	25.4 "	5.33	1.60	.72	1.60	9.25
3.1	25.2 "	5.47	1.64	.74	1.64	9.79
3.2	25.0 "	5.60	1.68	.76	1.68	9.72
3.3	24.8 "	5.73	1.72	.78	1.72	9.95
3.4	24.6 "	5.85	1.75	.79	1.75	10.14
3.5	24.4 "	5.98	1.79	.81	1.79	10.37
3.6	24.3 "	6.12	1.84	.83	1.84	10.63
3.7	24.2 "	6.25	1.87	.84	1.87	10.83
3.8	24.1 "	6.27	1.88	.85	1.88	10.88
3.9	24.0 "	6.55	1.97	.88	1.97	11.37
4.0	24.0 "	6.72	2.01	.89	2.01	11.63
4.1	23.5 "	6.74	2.02	.91	2.02	11.69

Number of Units in Family	Daily Cost per Unit for Food	Weekly Cost per Family				
		Food	Clothing	Fuel and Light	Miscellaneous	Total (exclusive of Rent)
4.2	23.1 cents	6.79	2.04	.92	2.04	11.79
4.3	22.6 "	6.80	2.04	.92	2.04	11.80
4.4	22.2 "	6.83	2.05	.92	2.05	11.84
4.5	21.7 "	6.84	2.05	.92	2.05	11.86
4.6	21.6 "	6.96	2.09	.94	2.09	11.88
4.7	21.6 "	7.11	2.13	.96	2.13	12.33
4.8	21.5 "	7.22	2.16	.97	2.16	12.51
4.9	21.5 "	7.37	2.21	.99	2.21	12.88
5.0	21.4 "	7.49	2.25	1.01	2.25	13.00
5.1	21.4 "	7.64	2.29	1.03	2.29	13.25
5.2	21.3 "	7.75	2.32	1.05	2.32	13.44
5.3	21.3 "	7.90	2.37	1.07	2.37	13.71
5.4	21.2 "	8.01	2.40	1.08	2.40	13.89
5.5	21.2 "	8.16	2.45	1.10	2.45	14.16
5.6	21.1 "	8.27	2.48	1.12	2.48	14.35
5.7	21.1 "	8.41	2.52	1.13	2.52	14.58
5.8	21.0 "	8.53	2.56	1.15	2.56	14.80
5.9	21.0 "	8.67	2.60	1.17	2.60	15.04
6.0	20.9 "	8.78	2.63	1.18	2.63	15.22
6.1	20.9 "	8.91	2.67	1.20	2.67	15.45
6.2	20.8 "	9.03	2.71	1.22	2.71	15.68
6.3	20.8 "	9.17	2.75	1.24	2.75	15.91
6.4	20.7 "	9.27	2.78	1.25	2.78	16.08
6.5	20.7 "	9.42	2.83	1.27	2.83	16.35
6.6	20.6 "	9.52	2.86	1.29	2.86	16.53
6.7	20.5 "	9.62	2.87	1.30	2.87	16.66
6.8	20.5 "	9.76	2.93	1.32	2.93	16.94
6.9	20.5 "	9.90	2.97	1.34	2.97	17.18

Thus in determining the minimum standards of relief, calculate the number of units in the family, take the corresponding amount showing the total expense exclusive of rent, and add the rent paid by the family per week.

STANDARDS OF RELIEF

In Cincinnati, the monthly rent ranges from three dollars and a half to four dollars a room and the number of rooms to each family is usually conditioned by the number of individuals—usually from two to three individuals to a room. Thus, a family consisting of a man, wife, and three children could be housed in two rooms at the rental of eight dollars a month. Naturally, in cases of tuberculosis or other sickness, requiring separate rooms for the patient, the rental will be correspondingly higher.

The allowance for clothing in dependent familes is less certain, for much is supplemented by secondhand clothing, usually given by the organization. In this respect, however, we are safe to assume that the minimum given by the New York investigation into standards of homes could be taken as a guide. The same probably would be the case in regard to incidental expenses, fuel, light, car fare, and so on. In this way, the necessary average amount required in Cincinnati by a family consisting of a man, wife, and three children below working age would be roughly estimated at one dollar and eighty cents a day, distributed as follows:

	Per cent	Amount
Rent	47.5	$ .854
Food	14.5	.266
Clothing	18.5	.333
Fuel and Light	6.0	.108
Miscellaneous	13.5	.243
Total	100.0	$1.804

There will be considerable variations from this standard, but only in exceptional cases will these variations be great without indicating an abnormal situation.

D. Standards of Relief

No organization can afford to claim that it dispenses adequate relief unless its dependent families live on a standard that the poorest of them would live on if they were independent. The great difficulty with relief societies is the uncertainty as to the other resources that a dependent family may have. How about the income of the breadwinners that the family may occasionally have, or is there any other agency or individual that contributes to the maintenance of the same family? These are perplexing questions, and it stands to reason that the poor are tempted now and then to hide the truth and disguise the real situation. Hence, the relief agency is nolens volens put on guard against imposition, and, as a rule, starts with the assumption that the applicant could get along without the material help from the organization; the burden of the proof lies with the applicant.

The mistrust of the applicant on the part of the organization, and the lack of truthfulness vitiate standards of relief. The problem reduces itself to a mere guessing proposition, not to how much the applicant requires to live on, but how little the organization can afford to give to escape a risk of being imposed upon; this is a question of individual adjustment. It depends upon the agent who distributes the relief as well as upon the persistency of the applicants. In a large measure this situation is responsible for the unkindly attitude of the community to the relief agencies, which are, as a rule, condemned for their inquisitorial policies prompted by necessity.

The only remedy for this unwholesome condition is a more thorough, definite and frequent investigation as to the real setting of the dependent family, a stronger and more systematic connection with agencies liable to duplicate efforts, concentration of the handling of a dependent family entirely by one organization, and the popularization of the work thus conducted, enlisting the co-operation of the entire community and the interest of individuals willing and ready to supply the necessary information as to the status of the family in question.

The spread of the confidential exchange, in the different cities, development of personal service, federation of different charities, making possible a central administration of all kinds of relief, and last, but not least, the broader view that the family compelled to apply for charity should be helped adequately, are all signs of a better solution of the relief problem.

CHAPTER THIRTEEN. STANDARDS OF RELIEF

QUESTIONS

1. Discuss the reasons for obtaining a definite standard for relief.
2. State the variation in standards in different cities.

3. Why can a uniform standard not be applied to all cases?
4. Describe the study of standards of living in Cincinnati.
5. State the difficulties in getting a standard of relief, from the standard of living.
6. State the possible ways to overcome these difficulties.

XIV

EDUCATIONAL AND SOCIAL ORGANIZATIONS

A. The Rise of Jewish Social Organizations

While the Jews of the United States have always shared with the rest of the population political and economic equality, and have had no difficulty in entering into the social atmosphere of the community in general, there seems to be a demand for special social organizations. As early as 1769, a social club was started in New York City, and similar organizations were founded in many other sections of the country. American Jews have also been especially given to the forming of secret orders. The latter have had primarily an educational and charitable purpose, but have also had much social influence and tended powerfully toward the continued association of Jews with one another, when the hold of the synagogue upon them had relaxed. Thus, the Independent Order of B'nai B'rith was organized in 1843 for the purpose of instilling the principles of morality among the followers of the Mosaic faith, inculcating the spirit of charity, benevolence, and brotherly love. A large number of other secret societies were established later, as the Free Sons of Israel, in 1849 and the B'rith Abraham in 1859.

1. Young Men's Hebrew Associations

The spread of Young Men's Christian Associations in the United States, beginning in 1850, which was an outgrowth of a movement in England, and in the beginning strictly limited in its membership to adherents of evangelical churches, gave rise to similar institutions connected with other faiths. In 1874, the first Young Men's Hebrew Association was organized in New York, for the mental, moral, social, and physical development of young men as its aim. This is the parent institution of similar organizations that have been established throughout the United States. In many instances, the Young Men's Hebrew Associations functioned in connection with the various congregations while in others they represented independent activities in most cases very much like those of Y. M. C. A.'s.

With the influx of Russian immigration, the interest in these particular institutions was considerably abated. New conditions arose requiring an intense public devotion to new problems. The Y. M. H. A's in many instances gave way to a new type of an educational agency, primarily introduced to serve the needs of the newly arrived immigrants. Thus, in 1891, the Y. M. H. A. of New York joined a new movement and for a time became a part of a new institution, the Hebrew Institute. Similar transformations took place in other cities, and for a time, the Y. M. H. A. movement was, practically speaking, at a standstill.

In late years, however, the needs of the young

men and women became quite pressing, and a revival of the Y. M. H. A's again sweeps the entire country. In an article entitled, "The Timely Advent of the Y. M. H. A. Movement," Mr. B. Palitz gives the underlying motives of this new awakening.

"The synagogue faintly rings its parish bells for the flock of little ones to come and be formally instructed in the 'ancient' religion, but it has never been so indifferent to the needs of reaching the older boy as it is at the present time; never so utterly stripped of application and authority as it is in this age. It is no longer the nesting place to keep the spiritual life of the young warm and their minds alert against dangers and temptations that lure them from without.

"For such a disintegrated state in the organic structure of our present-day Jewry, what remedies are proposed? What substitutes for the old social guidance and spiritual shelter exist? What other methods are employed to meet the new needs?

"The formation of Young Men's Hebrew Associations throughout the country may be heralded as the coming of a new and practical agency to grapple with these vital questions. The value of the work of these associations in directing good morals, promoting physical health, and infusing a clear social vision into the hearts and minds of the Jewish young men, has caught the eye of our social workers. About one hundred associations, with a membership of about twenty thousand, are in actual existence, and new organizations are formed day by day.

"The time seems to be ripe for the associations to raise a national structure, with a set of uniform and definite principles and aims laid down, and thus increase the strength of every individual association, cause it to emerge from the state of a separate spirit, and cause it to grow into more effectiveness.

"The existing associations, the pioneers, can no longer afford to confine themselves to the shepherding of their own flocks, but must invade the entire camp of American Israel, and free the captive youth from confusion and waste." [1]

In 1913, a National Organization of Young Men's Hebrew and kindred Associations was effected in New York City. Its purpose is to promote the religious, intellectual, physical, and social development and well-being of Jewish young men and women, and to that end to stimulate the organization in the several States and the Dominion of Canada of Young Men's Hebrew Associations, to assist, advise, and encourage such associations when formed; to further the correlation of their activities and the mutual interchange of the advantages which they afford and to co-operate with other corporations or associations conducted under Jewish auspices.

The Young Men's Hebrew Association should not be confused with a settlement or a neighborhood house. It is not intended to attract inhabitants of a certain vicinity only, and, on the other hand, it is supposed

[1] " Timely Advent of Y. M. H. A.," B. Palitz, " Jewish Charities," Vol. II, No. 7.

to appeal to young men primarily. The membership idea of a Young Men's Hebrew Association, excludes the patronizing attitude, so much in vogue in the settlements; it removes it from every suspicion of being an agency of philanthropic endeavor, and the idea of uplifting the constituency through the influences of the better class, is in this case rather negative.

The Young Men's Hebrew Association should be considered as an institution where young men can get educational advantages, be it physical culture, science, literature, and so on, which they want but cannot get elsewhere with the same facility. It should present social advantages which will attract young men and make them feel the advantages of joining the membership. In other words, the Young Men's Hebrew Associations should be both a school and a club house for Jewish young men of the city.

2. *Religious Educational Agencies*

While religious instruction is a matter of private concern and is, in its narrower meaning, not a subject of social service, still, inasmuch as it refers to the masses and answers an existing need, it is a legitimate topic for our consideration. In the beginning of social service activities among the Jews, the Free Congregational School and the Sabbath Schools were the only types of educational institutions where the children of the poor could receive instruction free. Some of the earliest Jewish schools in this country supplied at the same time a secular education. The first Sabbath School in the United States was founded in 1838 in the city of Philadelphia by Rebecca Graetz. This was followed by a number of similar schools, established in different cities. The large influx of Russian Jews with their intense desire to give a thorough Jewish training to their children, made the problem more complicated, not only in extent, but also by the newcomer's introduction of new types of schools and standards of instruction. In Russia, the education of the children was the main duty of the parents, for poor as the Russian Jews were, they seldom considered themselves poor enough to forego the privilege of paying for the religious instruction of their children. "Though you have to secure the means by begging, be sure to provide the instruction of your children in the Torah" is a dying father's admonition to his children. Most of the children paid their tuition to the Cheder,—the private school,—and only the poorest of the poor availed themselves of the free school, the Talmud Torah. With change of environment, the situation received a different aspect. The Russian Jews were compelled by necessity to reduce the standards of religious education. There was neither time nor inclination of the children to spend long hours in the study of the Talmud. It is only the elementary Cheder and the Talmud Torah that could be transplanted to the new surroundings, and even this with considerable modification. It is estimated that there are about one thousand Chederim in this country, half of them in New York City, with an annual budget of six hundred thousand dollars.

The Talmud Torah became the most popular institution. The first Talmud Torah in New York City was founded in the early eighties. Originally it was designed to accommodate the poor children who could not pay, and in a large measure remained a charitable enterprise.

In the analysis of the census of Jewish institutions, published in 1908 in the "American Jewish Year Book," Dr. S. Benderly [1] presents the following facts: There were two hundred and thirty-five sunday schools with one session weekly; ninety-two congregational schools with two, very seldom three, sessions a week, and two hundred and thirty-six daily schools, Talmud Torahs. There are, according to Dr. Benderly, three hundred and sixty thousand Jewish children of school age. The number of boys taught in Cheder (for which no data were available) including those who received private instruction, was computed roughly by Dr. Benderly to be forty thousand. The total number of children who received Jewish religious instruction in 1908 amounted altogether to about one hundred thousand, so that fully two hundred and sixty thousand, among them probably one hundred and seventy thousand girls, were left without any religious instruction.

Since then, considerable progress has been made, not only in promoting the establishment of new schools,

[1] "Jewish Education in America," Dr. S. Benderly. "Jewish Exponent," January 7, 1908.

but also in improving and regulating the instruction. Through the munificence of Mr. Jacob H. Schiff, the Teachers' Institute of the Jewish Theological Seminary and a similar institution under the auspices of the Hebrew Union College were established. In New York, especially laudable effort has been made to help out the situation.

3. *The Bureau of Education of the Jewish Community of New York City*

The Jewish Community of New York (Kehillah) made an investigation in 1909 into the status of religious education of that city. It was found that out of the entire Jewish school population, computed to be one hundred and seventy thousand, only forty-one thousand four hundred and four were taught in some kind of Jewish educational institution. Making allowances for those taught at home privately, two-thirds were left without a knowledge of Judaism and its religious institutions. The Kehillah succeeded in obtaining generous donations for improving and promoting religious primary education in New York City. Dr. S. Benderly, a Jewish pedagogue of Baltimore, was placed at the head of the Bureau of Education, a department of the Kehillah, formally opened in 1910. It is quite interesting to observe that one of the problems of the Bureau is to change the status of the existing Talmud Torahs from charity schools to self-supporting institutions, and the first attempt in this direction is quite interesting. Prior to the advent of the Bureau six of the Talmud Torahs which co-operate with the Bureau, collected twenty thousand one hundred seven dollars and eleven cents in tuition fees during the school year 1910–11. The same institutions in which the number of children had increased only two per cent collected thirty-five thousand nine hundred sixty-two dollars and eighty cents through the medium of the Bureau during the last school year (1912–13), an increase of seventy-nine per cent.

An agreement reached with the Talmud Torahs affiliated with the Bureau of Education of the New York Kehillah contains an interesting clause as to free tuition:

"The Bureau of Education agrees to pay a Talmud Torah affiliated with it, one dollar and twenty-five cents for every child taught in the Talmud Torah for one month free of charge, provided that the number of such children does not exceed one-third of the total attendance. The other two-thirds of the children attending are to be divided into two parts, one-half of the children are to pay the full tuition fee, one dollar and twenty-five cents per month, and the other half pay half of the tuition fee, sixty-five cents per month.[1]

B. Sabbath Schools

In regard to free sabbath schools, considerable improvement has been achieved through the work of the Synagogue and School Extension Department of

[1] "Aims and Activities of the Board of Education of the Jewish Community," by Dr. S. Benderly, New York, 1912.

the Union of American Hebrew Congregations, which, besides granting subventions to schools in the needy neighborhoods, conducts a department for the promotion of modern methods, publishing text-books and guides for teaching. The National Council of Jewish Women and the Jewish Chautauqua are also contributing to the welfare of the Jewish sabbath schools in this country.

While there may be difference in opinion as to the character of religious instruction that the children ought to receive, great effort is made to improve the sanitation and housing conditions of the schools, and also to regulate the hours of instruction and discipline till late one of the neglected phases of Jewish activity. While Reform Jews, under the leadership of their Rabbis are endeavoring to attract the children of the poorer classes to sabbath school, the Orthodox constituency is still anxious to have their children in the Cheders and Talmud Torahs, where they receive instruction more or less similar to that which the parents received in the old country.[1]

1. *Radical National Schools*

Lately a new type of Jewish schools is being developed through the initiative of the Nationalistic wing of the radicals. The latter realizing the danger that comes from widening the breach between the old and the new, and anxious to inculcate in the children

[1] " The Jewish Sunday School Movement in the U. S.," Julian Richman, " Jewish Quarterly Review," July, 1900.

EDUCATIONAL AND SOCIAL ORGANIZATIONS

a feeling of national unity, insists that the Yiddish language should be taught and Jewish national ideals implanted in them at a very early age. Hence, the rise of many Jewish schools in large cities, especially in New York, where Yiddish is the language and where no special religious instruction is included in the curriculum.

2. *Religious Instruction and Social Service Agencies*

While the social worker is relieved from the necessity of deciding which type of school should be encouraged, nevertheless, it is within the realm of his duty to contribute his part in promoting modern methods for the care of the children, utilizing the schools as social factors and combating the low standards of existing schools of different types. This is the reason why in many instances, the charities and other philanthropic institutions provide housing facilities for religious instruction, and frequently maintain within the same walls both Orthodox and Reform type of schools. The widespread tendency among Orthodox Jews for religious instruction suggests the possibility of utilizing the Talmud Torah as a center of different social activities.

Mr. Louis Levin, of Baltimore, as early as 1910, in an article entitled "Suggestions for Jewish Settlement Work" says:

"Given a Talmud Torah, with its Jewish population from one hundred to one thousand, why should it not be possible to make it also the center of the best activities of the settlement house? Has it not graduates and alumni, organizable into clubs or classes for further improvement? Cannot the Jewish year, rich in incident, in story, in pathos, in joy, be used to give point to the teachings of national, religious, and domestic loyalty, which is now being sought in many other ways? Would not parents and teachers find it easy to sympathize with and participate in such settlement work?"

Two years later, Mr. Jacob Billikopf of Kansas City informed the public that as a result of this suggestion he has taken a personal interest in the formation of a Talmud Torah, financed largely by the Russian Jewish element of the community.[1] Realizing that such work forms an integral part of the Jewish settlement, the Board of Directors of the Institute cordially extended to the Talmud Torah the privilege of maintaining a school in its main institute. On the other hand, in many places, the Talmud Torah extends its activities along general settlement lines. In Baltimore, the Talmud Torah conducts a library, and owns a printing press; the children are organized into clubs; entertainments and lectures for adults are given, etc.

3. *Religious Services*

Outside of religious instruction, the general social service agencies, and especially the settlement participate also in providing facilities for religious services in the congested districts. Thus, a cursory survey of the situation in 1912 brought out the following facts:

[1] " Jewish Charities," February, 1912.

It indicated that there is a great demand for religious services in Jewish settlements, especially during the New Year holidays. Buffalo and Pittsburg are the only cities that report adequate provision for *Schules*, and consequently no necessity for conducting services at the Institute. Maxwell Settlement, of Chicago, the Jewish Educational Alliance of Baltimore, and many others regret that they lack facilities for arranging synagogues. The New York Educational Alliance conducts nine synagogues during the Holy Days, accommodating twenty-five thousand persons, and, judging by the applications for seats, it probably could fill two or three times as many more. One of these synagogues, known as the People's Synagogue, which is maintained throughout the year, has a membership of about six hundred, each member contributing from one to three dollars per annum. The purchase of seats in this synagogue for the Holy Days carries with it the privilege of membership for the entire year. The other eight synagogues are special organizations arranged for Rosh Hashona and Yom Kippur only. In 1911 it was decided to charge the nominal sum of ten cents for each ticket issued.

The Emanu-El Brotherhood of New York conducts services for about one hundred and fifty people, does not charge any dues, and as there is no extra expense, the charge is nominal.

The Council Educational Alliance of Cleveland conducts religious services during the Holy Days, accommodating six hundred and fifty people. Its synagogue is under direct supervision of the head worker of the settlement.

The Chicago Hebrew Institute has changed its policy in connection with its People's Synagogue. It is now under the auspices of a recently formed, special organization, subject, however, to the rules and regulations of the Hebrew Institute.

The Educational Alliance of St. Louis rents its hall to a society with which it has an arrangement to charge fifty cents for the majority of the tickets, and one dollar for the most favorable seats. The capacity of the hall is about four hundred.

The Detroit Hebrew Institute also rents its hall for holiday services, for which it receives seventy-five dollars.

The Jewish Educational Alliance of Atlanta, and the Cincinnati Jewish Settlement report similar arrangements.

An interesting situation seems to exist in Kansas City. The superintendent of the Jewish Educational Institute of that city writes that during the past three years, religious services have been conducted in the Institute, under the auspices of a struggling congregation. They have generally rented the auditorium for twenty-five dollars and have been given the privilege to furnish free tickets to such people as, in their judgment, were in poor circumstances. The auditorium accommodates comfortably about three hundred and fifty persons, but they have been obliged in the past to crowd in as many as four hundred and fifty to five hundred men, women, and children. The services have been carried on in a truly orthodox style, and while the decorum has been by no means perfect, it has been far better than that which prevailed in the great majority of similar organizations. During the coming holidays, as in the past, they will have two officers in plain clothes stationed at the front door to maintain discipline and decorum. What appeals to one particularly, in connection with the services in the Kansas City Institute is that the women are given an opportunity to rest, and to give their children proper care. The playground, in particular, is of great service to the little ones. Taking into consideration that this same congregation used to meet for years and years in a hall connected with a notorious beer garden, and that frequent fights resulted there, this particular feature of the work is deemed of considerable importance, even though, thus far, it has been impossible to introduce as good a system as desired.

CHAPTER FOURTEEN. EDUCATIONAL AND SOCIAL ORGANIZATION

QUESTIONS

1. What were the first Jewish social organizations in the United States?
2. Describe the origin and purposes of the Y. M. H. A.
3. What are the various types of Jewish religious schools?
4. Discuss the Talmud Torah situation.
5. What are the institutions for training of rabbi-teachers?
6. What are the functions of the Bureau of Education of the Jewish Community of New York?
7. What are the National Radical Schools?
8. Discuss the attitude of the Jewish social worker toward religious education of the masses.

XV

THE EDUCATION OF IMMIGRANTS

In the beginning of the eighties, American Jewry was considerably disturbed by the large and sudden influx of Jewish immigrants from Russia, who landed and proposed to remain in New York City. While the newcomers were heartily welcomed by their co-religionists, who spared no efforts to lighten their hardships and were only too ready to help them to get a footing in the newly adopted country, still, a serious problem was drawing upon those who were their predecessors, a problem as to the future of this new immigrant group, in number, as well as in general make up, presenting a new experience. The economic motive, the main reason for immigration in general, did not play an important part with these newcomers. These new immigrants came here primarily on account of religious and political persecution which they suffered at home. Uncouth and unpleasant in their appearance though picturesque, foreign in speech and manners, different even in their everyday religious practices, they were complete strangers to those who befriended them. It was natural that they should settle in separate districts, and form congested neighborhoods, which since have become popularly known as the Jewish Ghettos of American cities.

Besides the physical disadvantages, the Ghetto spelled isolation of the immigrant from all the blessings of American life. Here was no urgent need to learn English, no demand for acquiring new customs, no necessity for getting acquainted with the duties of American citizenship. The direct environment, though differing from that in which the immigrant lived in the old country, was anything but American, and while the new conditions were crushing the immigrant, sapping him of all his vital forces, it apparently did not call forth any effort on his part toward a change, towards adaptation to the new conditions in a way that would help him and prepare him for the larger field of American life.

A. The Palace of Immigrants

One of the first institutions established for this purpose was the Hebrew Institute of New York in 1889, which became known as "The Palace of Immigrants." The Hebrew Institute, as stated before, was an outgrowth of the Young Men's Hebrew Association. It also comprised activities of the Baron De Hirsch Fund and the Grace Aguilar Library. The money for the erection of the Hebrew Institute was realized partly from a public fair in 1889. Anti-Sectarianism, as well as reasons affecting the support of the institution, led to the change of the name of the Hebrew Institute into the Educational Alliance in 1893. The scope of the Educational Alliance, as stated in the charter, "shall be of an Americanizing, educational, social and humanizing character—for the moral and intellectual improvement of the inhabitants of the East Side." In the annual report of 1897, Isidor Straus says: "At first blush our work may seem sectarian; it is nothing of that sort. It is educational, humanitarian, philanthropic and patriotic in the broadest sense. It is true that we have reached chiefly Jews, but this is due to the fact that the neighborhood in which the Alliance is situated is inhabited principally by Jews. The library, the reading room, the gymnasium, and the entertainments of every sort, are accessible to any and all who choose to avail themselves of them."

B. Americanization

The keynote of all the activities of the Educational Alliance was the Americanization of the newcomer. In the beginning, when the public schools had practically nothing in their program specially adapted for the immigrants, the Educational Alliance assumed the entire burden.

It was evident that if the immigrant was to become an asset, some strenuous measures had to be taken, with the purpose of coping with the situation and encountering the influences that were fostering and promoting the Ghetto Spirit. Besides providing facilities for teaching the immigrants English, special methods were used for their rapid Americanization. All possible means were utilized to impress the immigrant with the glory of his newly adopted country; he was made to laud the American flag, to sing national songs, demonstratively to celebrate national holidays and to express his allegiance to the land that offered a haven to the persecuted Jews from Russia.

Undoubtedly, these efforts were not in vain, but they did not appeal to the great mass of the immigrants; these external manifestations of American patriotism, artificial, superimposed, and to a certain degree compulsory, did not find a respondent chord in the hearts of many—the Jewish immigrants still clung to their old traditions, language, and ideas. The attempt to exclude the Yiddish language from the institutions where Americanization was the keynote, did not contribute to the popularity of these educational agencies. Futile also were the endeavors to teach the foreigners manners and etiquette through the medium of printed signs and oral instructions. The Ghetto continued its own course.

C. Ghetto Forces

The Jewish press and the Jewish theater were called into existence. In New York City a large Socialist group was formed; Yiddish speaking trade unions were organized, Hebrew schools, congregations, and benevolent societies were started in great numbers. The Ghetto was now a fact, a living organism.

The American Jewry could not help seeing that the Russian immigrant was not a "tabula rasa"; he brought with him a deep-rooted potential possibility of his own culture which could not be ignored, could not be stifled nor killed. The Yiddish language was the expression of his soul—he lived in it and would not give it up without a struggle.

Be it said to the credit of the institutions of the American Jewry, as soon as the observation was made its methods were immediately changed. Now the Yiddish language became the vehicle of Americanization; Jewish papers and books were introduced in the libraries and reading rooms, lectures in Yiddish were now given, Jewish speaking societies were permitted to meet within the walls of the institutions, where only a few years ago they were considered dangerous to the welfare of their own constituency. It became a recognized fact that the Ghetto itself had an interest and certain legitimate rights in the planning of the education it was to receive. The activities of the educational institutions began to be planned accordingly.

The Educational Alliance rapidly grew, and little by little became the center of the East Side community. It beamed with activity and reflected the real life of the Ghetto. The radical groups, invading every avenue of social contact, became quite evident within the walls of the institution; the intensity with which the intellectuals availed themselves of the opportunities was interpreted as misdirected influence. The institution was intended for the masses, and a certain restraint of higher ideals and ambitions was to be encouraged.

D. A Change of Policy

The directors felt that while the Educational Alliance was actively engaged from early morning until late at night, the East Side as a whole did not show tangible results in the direction that the influence of the Alliance was supposed to work. The problem became complicated, it was now a question of not only how to provide the immigrant with proper educational and social facilities, but also how to protect the masses from new influences that seemed to permeate the entire Ghetto,—influences that were supposed to be entirely opposed to those for which the Educational Alliance was called into existence. Socialism, the spread of the Yiddish language, a disregard for the basic standards of American life, an aggressive labor movement, and thousands of other manifestations of the new situation produced rather an uneasy feeling among those who were in the lead of the Educational Alliance.

E. David Blaustein

In 1898, David Blaustein assumed the superintendency of the institution. David Blaustein was a Russian immigrant. Born in 1866, he came to America in 1886 and landed in Boston, where he opened a modern Hebrew school. From the very beginning he took an active part in communal affairs. Later he entered Harvard as a special student in Semitics, and received his Bachelor of Arts degree in 1893. From 1892 to 1898 he was rabbi of the Congregation of the Sons of Israel and David, in Providence, Rhode Island.

The Educational Alliance to which he came to assume the duties of head worker was at that time a living institution. The East Side population was earnestly and intensely interested in its different activities. The Alliance was the real educational and social center—no one could deny its influence; some thought it was for the good, others for the bad, but all agreed that the work of the Alliance counted in the life of the Ghetto, and therefore should be watched and guarded, not so much as to its efficiency but as to its policy and tendencies.

The change of administration was rather sudden and uncalled for—the resignation of a man that New York loved, knew and trusted, as Isaac Spectorsky the predecessor of Blaustein was, and the appointment of the latter, who was an entire stranger, and whose previous experience had been more that of a rabbi than that of a social worker, created considerable criticism among the leaders of the East Side. The disgruntled intellectuals decided to assert themselves by blocking the progress of the institution and preventing the success of the newcomer who was brought to New York, as it was thought, to undo, rather than to develop, all the previous efforts of the Alliance and change the policy of an institution with which the Ghetto had so much concern.

Within a short time, Blaustein became a figure on the East Side. He joined different organizations, participated in the different movements, was present at every social function of the neighborhood. This idea of utilizing the existing movements and tendencies in shaping the policies of an educational institution was

THE EDUCATION OF IMMIGRANTS 233

original and unique. Blaustein did not fall into a routine, so common among social workers; he did not copy blindly the methods of similar institutions; he did not imitate the non-Jewish agencies, but, on the contrary, endeavored to study the existing needs and tried to adjust the activities of the Alliance to the actual demands that were pressing. He formulated the problem first, and only then tried to solve it accordingly. From the very first, he undertook a survey of the neighborhood. Since then this has become a popular method, but with him it was new, and, in fact, never received due consideration by his supporters.

F. New Conceptions

He soon realized that the East Side is not a homogeneous body, and he also learned, to his great concern, that the leaders of the East Side were, practically speaking, indifferent to the matters pertaining to their immediate neighbors. They were busy with higher ideals; they were engaged in the strife of world-wide movements; they were combating each other; they were divided into factions, groups, constantly fighting, constantly quarreling.

In the midst of this discord, he grappled with the problem of unity. He proposed to find a ground where people with different views and tendencies could meet—he proposed to make the Alliance the melting pot of ideals—he wanted the orthodox to come nearer to the reformers, the socialists to come in contact with the Zionists, the radicals to mingle with the conservatives. He saw in all of these factions a potential possibility for the betterment of the Ghetto; he believed in its own reclamation. "In combating the evil, we must utilize the good, this is my problem," he used to say. He did not, therefore, prescribe a panacea for all these evils; he did not claim that Americanization or Zionism was the only remedy, he did not make the Alliance stand for one or the other specific tendency, but tried to introduce educational and social features that would exert a wholesome influence and in their sum, reach every possible group of the entire East Side.

G. Opposition

The Educational Alliance of New York is a prototype of a large number of similar institutions that have sprung up all over the country, and are designated by different names; Jewish settlements, neighborhood houses, and so on.

It seems, however, that as a rule these institutions did not strike a responsive note among the constituency whom they were supposed to serve. In 1904, A. H. Fromenson, in an address before the Conference of Jewish Charities in New York, severely arraigned the policies of the Educational Alliance, and stated that this institution is regarded by a very large number of East Siders with absolute antipathy, and by another with mistrust. These institutions have contributed practically nothing toward the solution of the graver problems. Jewish delinquency spread on the East Side with great rapidity; it was evident that some-

THE EDUCATION OF IMMIGRANTS 235

thing must be done to save the situation. Now, religious instruction, Jewishness became the keynote of Jewish educational effort. "The Salvation of the Jew in the past was his religion, and whenever he has been lacking in religion, he has deteriorated." [1]

On the other hand, the radical element in the East Side objected to the Educational Alliance on different grounds. In 1901, a new institution was formed, known as the Educational League. Its purpose was to give an absolutely free platform, permitting the teaching of science, without any restraint, without censorship. It was boldly stated that the organization was effected as a protest against the "retrogressive" policy of the Educational Alliance. The opposition had gained considerable strength, when the president of the Educational Alliance gave public utterance to the fear that the East Side was threatening to become a menace to the Jews of the country at large, and that special effort should be made to control the negative tendencies of the Jewish Ghetto.[2]

Blaustein himself felt that the problem now was quite different from the one he had expected to find. It was not a question of mere Americanization. It was a problem of how to breach over the gulf between the parents and their children. "Reverence for parents used to be looked upon as the foundation for

[1] Proceedings Third National Conference of Jewish Charities, New York, 1904.
[2] "Eastern and Western Education," Professor Morris Loeb, "American Hebrew," September, 1904.

social life, and a thousand pities it is to see the children of immigrants losing it through getting hold of American ideas in the wrong way." The patronizing attitude of the Educational Alliance was especially repulsive to the neighborhood, and when Blaustein left his post, in 1908, the Educational Alliance, while still very popular among a limited group, had lost its direct contact with the great issues affecting the East Side, and since then did not play the same rôle as it had in the social movements of the New York Ghetto.

H. Program of the Educational Alliance

The scope of the activities of the Educational Alliance as given for the year 1913 is interesting:

School of Domestic Art, 32 Classes. Number taught, 1,349.
School of Domestic Science, 15 Classes. Number taught, 623.
School of Physical Culture, 8 Classes. Number taught, 931.
Day Classes in English for Adult Immigrants, 4 Classes. Number taught, 538.
Civil Service Classes, 3 Classes. Number taught, 117.
Reading Room, Days open, 360. Average daily attendance, 882.
Lectures on American History and Civics, in Yiddish, every Saturday evening. Average attendance, 700.
Lectures on American History and Civics, in English, every Sunday evening. Average attendance, 300.
Telegraphy Class. Number taught, 256.
Legal Aid and Desertion Bureau. Consultations, 32,857.
School of Religious Work, 72 Classes. Number taught, 6,609.
People's Synagogue. Average attendance, 700.
Special services for Holy Days, 8 synagogues. Attendance, 2,054.

Sabbath Afternoon Services. Average attendance, 650.
Young People's Synagogue. Average attendance, 200.
Lectures on Moral Topics of the Day, 45. Average attendance, 700.
Entertainments, moving pictures, lectures and concerts, 291 events. Attendance, 200,000.
Branch B. (Thomas Davidson Society) number in classes, 290; number in clubs, 490.
Roof Garden. Average daily attendance, 4,039.
Eighty-three Clubs. Total enrollment, 1,756.
Camp (Junior Division). Number accommodated, 483.
Girl's Summer Home. Number accommodated, 289.
Indoor Playgrounds.
Outdoor Club activities in Parks and Playgrounds.
Social Rooms for Women, Girls, Men, and Boys.
Information Bureau.
Naturalization Bureau.
Classes in Ethics.
Penny Provident Fund Station.
Parents' Meetings.
Free Baths, etc.
The Expenses were $118,068.

I. Experiences in Other Cities

The experiences of the Educational Alliance are repeated in similar institutions in other cities. In Cleveland, the Council Educational Alliance, under the leadership of Isaac Spectorsky, former Superintendent of the Educational Alliance in New York, reached the height of popularity during the years 1900 to 1904. In 1906, during the Garment Strike of that city, the attitude of the Alliance caused bitter feelings among the workingmen. Great opposition was demonstrated, the institution was boycotted, and while, later, the matter was adjusted, the Alliance never recovered from this incident, and does not attract the large working masses that were once wont to be frequenters of the institution.

J. A New Departure

In Chicago, the Hebrew Institute is a representative type of an institution of somewhat different principle from those of the Educational Alliance. Its motto is "Self-Help." It asserts that the establishment of charitable institutions by patronizing lodges or societies in the midst of the Russian Jewish community is a detriment to the people whom it is introduced for, rather than a blessing. The Chicago Hebrew Institute was organized in 1903 by Dr. R. L. H. Halpern. Its beginning was rather modest. The amount of money collected at the organization was only two hundred and fifty dollars. But it did not take long to get under way. The institute first rented a small house in the congested neighborhood, acquired considerable property of its own, and gradually erected a new building in its present location. This is undoubtedly the largest plant devoted to Jewish educational activities.

Its leaflet announcing the activities in 1913 is rather interesting. The cover lauds the fact that this is the busiest institution per square foot of floor space of any undertaking,—commercial, social, or philanthropic, in the city of Chicago. One-fifth of the Jewish population of the West and Northwest sides of Chicago is registered in the Educational, Athletic, and Cultural activities of this institution. Here is the description:

Six acres of ground in the heart of the congested district are devoted to open-air education, athletics, and play. One of the cardinal principles of the institute is that it is not charity. Everybody pays. Children pay for the game rooms and the playgrounds. The English students pay, the Art and Music Classes pay; every club pays. Every theatrical performance charges admission. It is, of course, true that no person is denied the privileges of the institute because of his or her inability to pay the charges, but instances are few where payment is not made.

How far this fact accounts for the institute's popularity and its prevailing air of cheerfulness and freedom it is difficult to say. One-third of the expenses of the institute, including the cost of administration and overhead, is actually received from the students and those who use the institute. This is a larger percentage of internal revenue than is expected of any University.

What is the institute? It is not a settlement. It is not a school. It is not a social center. It is not a club. It is not a charitable institution. It is—Unique.

It cannot be readily classified because it is the spontaneous outgrowth of the demand of the Jewish community of two-thirds of Chicago. It has become a great communal force. It stands for education, refinement, and decorum. That an organization meets at the institute guarantees its respectability. It serves all movements, educational, philanthropic, civic, social, cultural, athletic, and religious. It serves all ages—babes in the crèche, kindergarten tots and those of school age, young men and women, matured adults. It serves equally the immigrant and the native-born. It is frankly Jewish, staunchly American. What is the institute? Well—it is just "*The* Institute."

It would seem reasonable to assume, that this institution is free from the possibility of antagonism and attack from those who are using the facilities. Experience, however, proves the contrary. The Chicago Hebrew Institute was boycotted in 1915 by all the Jewish radical and workingmen's organizations of the city. Five hundred students of the night classes of the institute left it in a body, and refused to return. To make this boycott still more effective, every activity of the Chicago Hebrew Institute was duplicated.[1] The boycott was the result of a misunderstanding concerning a meeting arranged by the radicals, and which the president of the institute called off rather inadvisedly.

Similar difficulties were experienced in this institution before. Dr. David Blaustein, who was superintendent of the Hebrew Institute from 1908 to 1910, had considerable difficulty in adjusting matters. At one time the situation was as follows: Blaustein had made some remarks concerning Christmas Carols in the Public Schools. The Jewish press took advantage of it and declared him to be the enemy of the people. He

[1] "The Truth About the Boycott of the Chicago Hebrew Institute," Julius Wolffert, Chicago, Ill., 1915.

THE EDUCATION OF IMMIGRANTS 241

prohibited the speaking of Emma Goldman, and the Radicals boycotted the institute. He organized a modern Orthodox congregation, and the representatives of the Reform element found fault with him. Thus the experiment of the Chicago Hebrew Institute to make the institution self-supporting, did not result in a friendly attitude of the constituency as it was supposed to do.

K. NEIGHBORHOOD SELF-ACTIVITY

The self-activity of the masses has lately received expression in institutions administering to certain groups only and having a definite program of propaganda. Thus, in a number of cities, we find Radical Centers, Zion Institutes, Labor Lyceums, and so forth. All these institutions are still in the experimental stage, and have great difficulty in raising sufficient funds. The management is rather crude. It is difficult to predict their future.

L. TECHNICAL EDUCATION

Among the educational efforts on the part of the American Jews to help the newly arrived immigrants, the subject of promoting manual training received serious consideration from the very beginning. As early as 1880, a technical school for girls was founded in New York City. At present the Hebrew Technical Institute for Girls is operating a large plant, comprising industrial as well as commercial classes. The Hebrew Technical Institute for Boys was established in 1883.

The leading spirit of the institution as well as the founder was Dr. L. M. Leipziger, a renowned pedagogue, who has devoted his life to the education of the masses. The institute offers a three years' course in technical and general education to boys fourteen to seventeen years of age who have completed the seventh grade of public school. It is interesting to notice that over seventy-five per cent of all the graduates are following mechanical pursuits. The Baron De Hirsch Trade School is a school for adults.[1] The Clara De Hirsch Home for Girls, in New York, was established in 1905. It was primarily intended as a home for the Jewish working girl of the metropolis,—a home where she might have an opportunity of living comfortably at a small cost and upon return from work meet girls of her own age in a congenial atmosphere. From the very start, however, classes in sewing and domestic science were introduced. At least part of the girls living at the home were not working on the outside, but were given a practical course in some trade. At present there are classes in hand sewing, machine operating, underwear making, millinery and so on. The Jewish Training School in Chicago was a forerunner of the different forms of manual training found at present in the public schools of that city. Manual training classes have also become an ingredient part of every Jewish settlement, and almost every large city has some provision, in addition to the general facilities, for teaching manual training to Jewish children. The Jewish Kitchen Gar-

[1] See page 182.

den and Trade School for Girls in Cincinnati was established in 1892. Here the pupils do actual work, fill orders in dressmaking, embroidery, etc., and receive pay while following the course. Similar arrangements are found in Cleveland, Detroit, and other cities.

CHAPTER FIFTEEN. THE EDUCATION OF IMMIGRANTS

QUESTIONS

1. Explain the origin of the American Ghetto.
2. What were the purposes of the Educational Alliance of New York?
3. What was the attitude of the masses toward Americanizing influences?
4. Discuss the part the Yiddish language played in the work of the Educational Alliance.
5. What were the reasons for changing the administration?
6. State the policy of David Blaustein in regard to the Educational Alliance.
7. State the reasons for the opposition of different groups to the Educational Alliance.
8. Give the experience of the Council Educational Alliance of Cleveland.
9. Describe the Hebrew Institute of Chicago.
10. What were the difficulties in the management of the Chicago Hebrew Institute?
11. Name the institutions founded by the people of the neighborhood themselves.
12. Discuss the institutions for technical education among Jews.

XVI

JEWISH SETTLEMENTS AND NEIGHBORHOOD WORK

It is quite interesting to observe a new controversy as to the tendencies in Jewish institutions. This is especially striking in regard to the so-called Jewish settlements. The first Jewish settlement was probably established in Chicago in 1893. "The Handbook of Settlements" issued by the Russell Sage Foundation in 1911 reports only fourteen Jewish settlements. In the preface of the handbook it is hinted that a typical settlement "under American conditions is one which provides neutral territory, traversing all the lines of social and religious cleavage." In this respect, the rise of specifically Jewish settlements is a deviation from the regular course, and is not typical of the general situation.

Mr. Walter Solomon, head worker of the Jewish Council Educational Alliance in Cleveland, takes the standpoint that the Jewish settlement is a misnomer. A settlement, according to him, can be neither Jewish nor Christian, Mohammedan nor Buddhist. A Jewish settlement conceived of as a racial or national group is an anomaly.[1] On the other hand, at the National Conference of Jewish Charities at Memphis, 1914, the feeling was strong that a Jewish settlement must be

[1] "Jewish Charities," Vol. V, page 190.

Jewish. "Our duty," said Cyrus B. Sulzberger, in his address on the Problems of American Jewry, "is to teach the newcomer the ways of American life without losing his contact with Judaism. The social settlements and their success are to be measured by their ability to reach parent as well as child and prevent the breach which is so frequent between the product of the Old World environment and that of the New." [1]

A. THE SETTLEMENT AS A SOCIAL SERVICE AGENCY

The essential purpose of a settlement is social service. Social service, in its final analysis, is designed for the elimination or reduction of the waste of society. Poverty, as such, is not a new phenomenon. The significance, however, of poverty, in its broader sense, has never before been recognized as it is to-day. To feed the hungry, to clothe the naked, and to shelter the homeless, form only a small part of modern philanthropy. The world has come to realize that poverty carries with it a multitude of other scourges of society, that it is crushing humanity, that it affects character, that it spells misery, sickness, deprivation, corruption and degeneration.

How to prevent these attributes of poverty, how to strike at the very cause of it, how to ameliorate the condition of the poor, these are the problems confronting the modern social worker, and agitating the thinking, feeling part of civilized humanity.

[1] Proceedings National Conference Jewish Charities, Memphis, 1914.

1. *Origin of Social Settlements*

General Booth, probably, was the first to call attention, outside of fiction, to the existing conditions of what he called the underworld. It is quite interesting to mention the experiences of Count Leo N. Tolstoi, when, in the capacity of director of the census, he discovered that the slum, besides possessing digestive organs, has also a heart and a mind, sometimes corrupted, polluted, and vicious, and again, highly sensitive, moral, elevating, and strictly honest. He soon realized that this neglected part of humanity is neither better nor worse, on the whole, than the rest; that human nature asserts itself there as in any other quarters. He realized, however, that he was a stranger to this world, and that if he wanted to live for it he must live with it. This intensive knowledge of the people among whom the social worker is to work is the basis of efficient settlement work. The same experiences we find in England, as expressed in the establishment of the first settlement, Toynbee Hall. In the United States, Miss Jane Addams is considered the pioneer in this movement.

2. *Definition*

A settlement is a center, radiating the collective efforts of individuals, acting as a part of a given neighborhood or community group, and working for the benefit of the latter.

This is the basic principle of settlement work. In its practical application, a social settlement, like every other social service agency, is dynamic in its character, and permits of modification in accordance with changing circumstances.

3. *Residents in Settlements*

Thus in many settlements, we find what is known as the residential quarters, where the workers actually live within the walls of the settlement building, on the supposition that this is the only way in which they can learn the needs of the community and become an integral part thereof. In Jewish settlement work, the residential feature is frequently eliminated, for in this case the personal contact with the community is not necessarily connected with residence in the neighborhood. The Jewish social worker, without residing in the community, may know the latter more intimately, and exert his influence more effectively than the stranger who happens to choose to live among these people. The example of the individual life of the social worker is of little value in the Jewish Ghetto. The Ghetto has enough potential forces for higher ideals within itself, and the function of the settlement is mainly to organize these forces, to protect the community from negative influences, and to present opportunities for educational and social advancement.

4. *Charity in Settlements*

Charity, if properly conducted, must be a neighborhood activity, and no settlement can do efficient work without entering into the different phases of charitable enterprize. Unfortunately, relief agencies are conducted in such a manner that as a rule the neglected neighborhood not only avoids dealings with them, but hates everyone connected. The remedy does not lie in assuming the name of a new concern. True charity ought to comprise a complete organization of all social service agencies.

Thus the residential feature in settlements, and the separation from general charity organizations are not essential features of Jewish settlements. With all this, however, the Jewish settlement is an actual reality, and has specific functions to perform which other agencies cannot fulfill. Inasmuch as the community needs are not answered by general effort, the Jewish settlement assumes the responsibility, though these activities may have no specific Jewish character. Thus, legal aid, teaching English to foreigners, libraries, classes and lectures on general subjects, manual training and physical culture, infant welfare work, playground activities, and a thousand and one other interests are legitimate items in the program of a Jewish settlement. But these activities can be also conducted by other agencies, and ultimately should become the functions of municipal enterprize.

5. *The Specific Problem*

A social worker, coming into close contact with the life of the Jewish immigrant, cannot help deploring the widening of the gap between the old and the young,—the parent and the child. The home influence,

JEWISH SETTLEMENTS

which is in a great measure responsible for the integrity of the immigrant family is weakening from year to year. The parents are unable to keep up with the rapid Americanization of the younger generation; their children are rapidly acquiring new tastes and tendencies, and are losing their attachment and respect for their father and mother.

Considerable effort has been made by different agencies to help the older folks adapt themselves to the new conditions. Classes for adult immigrants, mothers' clubs, lectures, and so on, have been organized in order to hasten the Americanization of the parent, and thus bring them closer to their own children, enabling them to speak and understand the language of the latter. Home surroundings have been also attacked in a fashion to make them more American and to the taste of the growing youth. All these attempts have produced, undoubtedly, the desired effect; but the problem has been tackled only on one side. It has been forgotten that besides the advisability of making the parents more modern and putting them, so to say, in a shape lovable to the children, it is also important that the children should be able to realize the strong and positive sides of their parents, not only as much as they have succeeded in modifying themselves in the process of Americanization. Aside from that, children should be able to appreciate the merits of their parents as they are; they should know the sacrifices that their parents have made for the sake of their religion; they should respect and love them because of their devotion to ideals which they consider right; they should know their struggles and tribulations before and after coming to the land of the free. It is only this intimate knowledge of the real worth in the character of parents that makes the child proud of his ancestry, anxious to maintain its reputation, strengthen the attachment and devotion.

A strenuous effort, therefore, is made in different directions to revive the interest toward Jewish ideals; to return to Jewish culture, to develop an interest toward Jewish history, and to strengthen the weakening ties of the Jews of all the world.

6. *Difficulties in Jewish Settlements*

The Jewish settlement meets many difficulties in pursuing its purpose. To begin with, while administering to the Jewish population, it does not deal with a homogeneous group. There are the radicals and the conservatives, the Reformers and the Orthodox, the fanatics of the different ideals and creeds, and the large mass indifferent to any social endeavor. Again, there is the deeply rooted prejudice against settlements, especially among those who are constantly fearing that an attempt is being made to rob them of their independence, impose obligations upon them and give them ideas that will disturb their social prestige. There is also a considerable pressure brought to bear against the settlement by those who are financially or otherwise interested in keeping the neighborhoods away from forces that may counteract the influence of the saloon, moving-picture show, dance hall, political club, and so on.

There is another side to the problem. What do the Jews of to-day represent? Are they a nation, a race, or a religious sect? The Jews themselves cannot agree upon their own social status. In the land of the oppressed, they insist upon their national autonomy, and are craving for the resurrection of the home of Israel in the Holy Land, and then again, in the land of the free, they repudiate any insinuation of their being a separate nation, and insist that religion is the only tie between Jew and Jew. The Reformed and the Orthodox, the pious and the free thinking, seem to be in continual controversy over the conception of the Jews as a people. Whatever the case may be, the Jews present a most wonderful example of stability of a social unit, making the Jews of the world into one people, no matter in which clime and condition they may live. The cry of the suffering Jews in the distant lands strikes a quick, responsive note of sympathy and helpfulness among Jews of other countries. There seems to be a subconscious sense of responsibility existing in the heart of every Jew for the conduct of his co-religionists. Victims of false accusations, persecuted and oppressed, driven along the road to exile, the Jews have succeeded in maintaining a high standard of moral integrity of the home. They are taken as a model of exemplary domestic virtue. At least, such has been the case until recent years, when the contact with the new environments in this country seemed to have produced an unprecedented breakdown of the pillars of the Jewish home. Here lies the importance of Jewish tendencies in settlement work. If this Jewish tendency will contribute toward the preservation of the positive features of Jewish life, maintain the home as the unit,—the most important factor in the development of the strong character of the Jews,—if this tendency absorbs the interest of the youth, helps to diminish the breach between father and child, if it will protect the children of the Ghetto during the period of adaptation from the pernicious influences of contact with a lower strata of society, if this tendency will keep the Jews together in the most crucial period of their existence and help them outlive the shattering effects of slum surroundings, if it will prevent the formation of a permanent Jewish slum, its efforts are well worth while making, without any respect as to whether they are pointing toward the conception of the Jews as a race, nation, religion, or simply a social group. Thus, theoretically, the professional Jewish social workers agree upon Jewish tendencies in settlements. In practice, however, many of the existing Jewish settlements are still emphasizing the non-sectarian features, and prefer to stand for something "broader than Judaism."

B. Jewish Activities in Settlement Work

1. *Jews of Many Lands*

A most striking example in introducing the Jewish element in settlement work is presented in the Exposition of the Jews of Many Lands, held at the Jewish

JEWISH SETTLEMENTS

settlement of Cincinnati in 1913 at the time of the convention of the Union of American Hebrew Congregations. Fifty-one different local Jewish organizations, including temples, lodges, synagogues, fraternal and civic organizations, labor unions, Zionist societies, social and literary clubs, lent their co-operation in fostering this new undertaking. The exposition comprised over four hundred charts and tables, covering the entire history of the Jews of twenty-seven different countries, with statistical data and describing present conditions. A rich collection of different articles of Jewish ceremonial, together with a large number of attributes of Jewish life in the different countries were loaned for the exposition, alike by rich and by poor residents of the city. There was the Torah and adornments, the phylacteries, matzoth covers, menorahs, sabbath lamps, spice boxes, etc.; there also were samovars and dishpans, silver candlesticks and a thousand and one other attributes of the foreign household. A rich exhibit of women's handiwork, embroidery and crocheting, fancy filet work, indicated the innate love of the beautiful.

Twelve national, philanthropic and educational organizations participated in the exposition by sending copious material. These included the Council of Jewish Women, the National Garment Workers Union, the Kehillah, the American Jewish Committee, the Industrial Removal Office, the National Farm School, the Jewish Agricultural Aid Society, the Baron De Hirsch Fund, the Alliance Israelité Universelle, and others. All these exhibits were arranged by countries, beginning with the United States and ending with Abyssinia, where, recently, the Falashas, or Black Jews, attracted considerable attention. The growth and achievements of the Jews in the United States were depicted by comparative statistics, and by tables containing the names and achievements of persons prominent in American Jewry, with a detailed history of the Jews in Cincinnati.

In this, as in all other exhibits, there were living demonstrations of the costumes worn by Jews of the different countries, and in the case of the United States, the uniform of the West Point cadet and the athletic attire of a Vassar maid were taken as characteristics. Quite an interesting booth presented the "Back to the Land" movement among the American Jews. There were interesting exhibits of Jewish colonies, and a detailed description of the work of the two Jewish agricultural schools, as well as the Agricultural Aid Society and the Federation of American Farmers.

The Russian department presented a recital of continuous suffering and oppression. The Orthodox rabbi, the soldier, the political prisoner, the revolutionist, the different types of women, represented by immigrants from Russia, re-enacted actual episodes from Jewish life in Dark Russia, with a background of scenery representing the interior of a Russian *izba*,—soldiers, guard booth, and appropriate music and national dances.

The Zionists made a special effort to present to the public the achievements of the Jews in Palestine, indicating the possibility of the establishment of a legally assured home for Jews in the Holy Land. The work of the Bezalel School of Art established in Jerusalem by Boris Schatz only a few years ago attracted considerable attention, not only on account of the artistic products, but also because this school typifies the revival of Jewish art.

The Turkish Jews living in Cincinnati, who originally came from Spain and are known as Spaniolas, occupied an unique place in the exhibit, their songs and dances expressing mixed features of Spanish, Turkish, Jewish and American influence. The Alliance Israelité Universelle, an international association of Jews of all over the world, showed the wide range of its work, covering every country where Jews were oppressed, concentrating its efforts over the Balkan territory and northern Africa.

The Jewish Mothers' Club of the city maintained a lunch counter of the favorite dishes of the Jews of many lands, and the Hebrew Union College exhibited a rare collection of books and manuscripts of ancient Hebrew lore.

The pageant on the auditorium stage expressed the idea of the exposition, taking as the keynote of the prologue the theme of Zangwill's "Melting Pot," and as a finale the recital of the experiences of the Jews with many nations, including Jewish songs of various countries rendered by a large chorus; a musical program by professional talent of the city, and picturesque tableaux of the Jews of Many Lands were also given.

Each and every club in the settlement not only

lent its assistance in making the exposition a success, but took upon its own responsibility at least one of the entertaining features: thus the Sons and Daughters of Zion took charge of the Palestinian department; the Young Women's Improvement Club reproduced scenes from Shulamith; the Lily Club presented a set of tableaux on "Great Women in Israel"; the Young Women's Hebrew Association gave national dances, and the Young Men's Hebrew Association gave an athletic exhibition. Over four hundred active volunteers participated in the entertainment, and there was no single instance of friction or unpleasantness in the execution of their duties. The most remarkable feature was the attitude of the children of the neighborhood toward this enterprize. Their deportment and appreciation of the entertainment given was so strikingly different from the usual course that nothing in discipline could be better expected than the results achieved. The expenses of this exposition were in the neighborhood of one thousand eight hundred dollars. The largest part of it was covered by the income from admission charges. For months preceding the exposition, the entire work of the settlement was devoted to preparation. The charts and tables were largely prepared by volunteer help. Groups of the neighborhood were organized for the chorus, tableaux, program, and so on. A corps of interpreters was formed into classes to study the material. The supervision and the actual management were also placed in the hands of the constituency of the settlement, and with the exception of a few additional helpers to the staff of the settlement, the entire service was done gratuitously.

The exposition attracted wide attention in the city, and a number of Jewish social workers came from other localities to see this new departure in the realm of Jewish settlement activities. Jewish leaders felt that they had been looking in vain for inspiration in so many other directions, that this return to the treasures of the past was a cause for genuine rejoicing. The exposition succeeded in presenting the salient facts of Jewish history. It succeeded in showing that Jews, different in dress, are alike in soul-complexion; different in manners, are alike in fine heart throbs; it proved that difference does not mean inferiority but emphasizes the brotherhood of Israel.

2. *Children's Clubs*

It is not only on special occasions, but in everyday routine that the Jewish settlement has possibilities for emphasizing the specific purpose for which it exists. In children's clubs, while methods are the same as those generally applied in conducting such activities, the content could be made Jewish.

The popular *Travel Club*, both for boys and girls, will be enriched in its content by including items of Jewish interest. Children on imaginary trips will be delighted to visit settlements in other cities, meet men and women of their own faith living under different conditions, get acquainted with the land of their fathers, know the Pale of Russia and the Ghettos of Europe. Why not give them the privilege of spending a holiday in the Jewish surroundings of Galicia? Why not introduce them to the great men and women of Israel all over the world? This ought to be of more interest to Jewish children than visiting the cathedrals in England and the Vatican in Italy. The Jewish agency, be it a settlement or any other educational institution conducting children's clubs, is the only one that can offer a program of this kind.

This is applicable to any kind of a club. For instance, the *Antiquary Club* can make collections of articles of Jewish life,—ceremonials, religious paraphernalia. They can collect autographs, chiefly of Jewish men and women.

The *Art Club* studies the productions of Jewish painters, pictures of Jewish life, collects art postals of Jewish subjects, reproduces scenes of the home, and so on.

In the *Doll Club*, the children dress the dolls in costumes of the Jews of the different countries of different epochs. Even in the athletic field, Jewish features can be easily introduced.

A Jewish Boys' Brigade, as the one formed in New York as early as 1904, with the emphasis laid upon Jewishness, and with the idea that the boys are not only athletes but Jews, cannot fail to add to the efficiency of this particular activity. All these details appeal to the children's imagination, tie them with group interests, develop sympathy for their own people, their own parents, their home.

3. Jewish Games

In the realm of play, games of a specifically Jewish character can be easily developed. Very little has been done in this direction. Barring a few Purim and Chanukah plays, most of them of mediocre merit, there is little material from which to draw. An attempt in this direction has been made in Cincinnati, where a few games were devised, appropriate for different holidays. The "Chanukah Trendel" is made of cardboard, and by following the directions printed, with the help of a match stick the child produces a toy which is similar to the traditional *Trendel*.[1] The Purim Shadowgraph presents the usual cutting of figures and together with a text of a Purim play, gives the child a chance to have his own theater party.

There has also been devised a folding *Succoth*, and a special Jewish calendar in the form of a bookmark, which is distributed before Rosh Hashona. All these toys, however, are adapted for holidays only. In general, it seems that holiday festivities are observed in most of the Jewish settlements.[2]

4. Activities for Adolescents

If the Jewish interests are properly maintained with the children, there ought to be no difficulty to continue the same tendency in the work with adolescents.

[1] Maurice Hexter, "Activities of Jewish Settlements," "Jewish Charities," Vol. IV, No. 6.

[2] "Activities of Jewish Settlements," Maurice Hexter, "Jewish Charities," January, 1914.

However, experience shows that in this period, the emphasis upon Jewish interest becomes quite difficult. Here main effort should be made to bring nearer the young and the old generation. It is during the adolescent period that the estrangement becomes more marked and more serious. The parents should be given opportunities to join the recreational affairs of the young men and women. Athletic and dramatic entertainments where the young generation participate should attract the older folks. An effort should be made to have the young people anxious to entertain their own people, anxious to please and to gain in their estimation. Naturally, if these gatherings can bear a Jewish character, the more appropriate it would be, and the more effective would be its influence. A public debate should preferably be on Jewish subjects; a play on the stage should deal rather with Jewish themes; a ball should be connected with some Jewish affair. This can be easily arranged, if the purpose be kept clearly in view. In arranging activities for the older folks, the Jewish feature must not be overlooked. Yiddish can be used to advantage, and interest shown to old customs and traditions is highly appreciated by the older generation.

5. *Community Forces*

The Jewish settlement has another function distinctly its own, namely, the interpretation and utilization of specific Jewish forces that are present in a Jewish community. The recently arrived immigrants are social beings; many of them, while strangers in their new surroundings, are not able to acquire the spirit of American institutions immediately, but are easily interested in social problems of their own. They may be ardently Orthodox, Nationalists, or earnest Socialists. In each of these cases they exhibit a desire to associate with their own class and form societies, groups, and congregations. These are active social factors in a community. Their constituency represents the best elements capable of further development. It is the function of the Jewish settlement to do all it possibly can to reconcile differences, to avoid partiality, to break up intolerance, to utilize all possible means to achieve its purpose of throwing light on darkness, shocking inertia, and fostering a healthy and stimulating discontent. It is, therefore, important that the settlement should participate in every movement in which its constituency is interested, the building of a new Talmud Torah, the starting of a radical center, an enterprize in behalf of local charity, a Zionist undertaking, nay, even the affairs of local trade unions,—all these ought to be the concern of an efficient Jewish settlement. It is very unfortunate that the broader purposes of the settlement are often misunderstood by persons who stand as leaders in society and who often venture to criticize the settlement and hamper its natural development without contributing to its welfare. The lesson of absolute tolerance, as far as ideas and beliefs are concerned, is one of the most important functions of a true settlement. The neighborhood may possess a number of tendencies that may be contrary to the ideals that the American Jewry would like to see it possess, the entire atmosphere may be repulsive to one who is an outsider, but—without going into a discussion of the merits, ideals and a criterion of their proper estimation,—the settlement, as such, cannot exclude from its scope the existing realities, and as a true center of the neighborhood, ought to reflect the different movements that are alive in the surroundings. In the opinion of some, the Socialists may not be altogether desirable among the immigrants, for the latter, at the very start, ought to be suffused with gratitude toward this free republic, and be perfectly satisfied with things that satisfy the average American. It is better that the immigrant be a red-hot Socialist than a Republican or Democrat, full of political corruption. But there is some justification in thinking that the immigrant has no right to be anything else but what the Americans want him to be. We have the right to wish so, but in reality, conditions are different. The settlement, as an active social factor, has no right to consider the wishes of one or the other class. If the Zionists exist in the neighborhood, they ought to be welcomed to the settlement. They should be used in their turn as an attracting force to an element that otherwise would become the prey of influences of a very much more negative character. The Socialists, by meeting at the settlement, are given an opportunity to promote their own ideas, at the same time learning something from their opponents. Nothing but free, open, sincere discussion on subjects that interest the persons in question can clarify the situation and lead to the path of truth,—the goal of all true ideals. Restriction, exclusion, negligence, and opposition, can never lead to beneficial influences, and, on the contrary, produce a corresponding repelling power.

Giving full swing to the different factions existing in the neighborhood, the settlement must be careful not to become an exponent of a particular creed, and acquire a predominant feature of a certain tendency. Thus, while Socialists, Zionists, and Orthodox, as well as reformers, should find a place on the platform of the settlement, none of them should monopolize the freedom accorded, and defeat the very purpose of a many-sided view upon the different subjects under discussion.

Lately, the subject of trades unionism has been seriously affecting the settlement situation. The growth of trades unions does not gain in favor on the part of those who in their practical activities would rather prefer to handle the individual workingman than the organized body. The settlement need not be the promoter nor follower of trades unionism, but as a neighborhood center, it must and should take an active part in a movement that affects the neighborhood. The trades union meetings in a settlement are one of the most important features, and those that contribute toward a settlement should learn to look for returns and protection to some other agency. The settlement can do nothing else than watch the interests of the neighborhood, and if it does this well it does its duty.

Immigrants should not be considered as a homogeneous unit,—they usually group in separate classes. Often those coming from one locality, working at the same shop, belonging to the same organization, are already grouped outside of the settlement, and this grouping should be retained by all means. It is advisable to arrange social gatherings, and even periodic affairs that will bring these groups as a group to the settlement. Thus, the different lodges should be invited to spend an evening at the settlement, the Socialists and Zionists should have their evenings, and the representatives of the synagogues should also be remembered.

C. Religion in Settlements

While religion among the Jews plays an integral part in the lives of the people, it has a special significance that it does not have with other peoples. To teach religion, with the Jews, is a purpose in itself; as a method of instilling morality, it never was used successfully. The method of the Salvation Army to cure intemperance and crime through the medium of religious conversion, is strange to the Jewish spirit. While we do attempt as a matter of imitation to practice religious preaching in prisons and corrective institutions, in truth, it was never taken up seriously in the meaning that religion will save the submerged. We naturally want the great mass to be religious; we deplore the fact that religion loses its hold upon the people; we endeavor to modernize religion and adapt it to conditions, so as to make it more attractive to the modern man and woman, but the significance of all this is beyond the practical purpose so often attempted by non-Jewish religions, the saving of the individual. Therefore, while the non-Jewish settlements may lay emphasis upon religious activities, hoping through this medium to reach the individual and help him to conquer his own weaknesses, with the Jewish settlement, the religious activity loses its reformatory character and becomes only the expression of a religious demand on the part of the neighborhood. Hence, it seems to be an unpardonable mistake to introduce religious activity that is not in accord with the religion of the neighborhood. This, as a rule, not only fails to attract the neighborhood, but becomes the cause of making the settlement a very unpopular institution.

The majority of the settlers of the neglected Jewish neighborhoods belong to the so-called orthodox element, and it stands to reason that their views should be considered pre-eminently. The settlement should observe the sabbath, in so far as possible. A synagogue of an orthodox character with a few modifications should find place in the settlement, and while other services may be held in different parts of the building, the settlement, in this as in every other movement, should be as liberal as possible. It should not become too closely associated with any of the existing parties. This principle is especially easy to illustrate in the subject of teaching the young. A modern Cheder on strictly orthodox basis, where the children wear their hats, learn Hebrew, and use the traditional prayer book, could and should be simultaneously conducted with a sabbath school of a modern character. The success of either of these schools will easily determine what is the true demand of the neighborhood. The idea of neglecting the Talmud Torah proposition is one of the most conspicuous contradictions in settlement work. Not at the settlement, it will be somewhere else, and under less favorable conditions. Thus the Jewish settlement offers an open forum for the discussion of specifically Jewish affairs; it gives its platform to speakers that appeal to its constituency, and presents different issues from various standpoints; it utilizes its stage for Yiddish performances and thus raises the standard of the Yiddish dramatic art; it affords opportunity for meeting places for various groups, including lodges, mutual aid societies, and so on, and indirectly instills a higher and better manner of conducting these affairs. Incidentally, the settlement provides facilities for weddings and other family gatherings, and thus emphasizes its place as a real neighborhood house. These are all activities that could hardly be undertaken by any agency other than Jewish.

Besides these specifically Jewish activities, however, the Jewish settlement has the general problem of serving the constituency and doing social service among the neglected neighborhood that needs outside interference for its reclamation.

D. Neglected Neighborhoods

The term neglected neighborhood is not fully appreciated if it conveys the impression of a neighborhood where the streets are narrow and filthy, where the houses are crowded, and are unfit for human habitation, where morality is little guarded, and shiftlessness, lawlessness, and drunkenness are rampant. Closer observation reveals a very complicated situation. The neglected neighborhood, though an adjunct to our complex civilization, presents a complete social unit by itself. It is a state within a state, with its own needs, its own missions, its own problems, and its own psychology.

Economically, the neglected neighborhood is deprived of the blessings, as well as the curses, of inherited wealth. There is practically no capital invested, except labor, and this requires proper application to conditions over which the laborer has no control.

The needs of the neglected neighborhood are urgent. They deal with the daily bread and butter, the mere necessities of life. The neighborhood is kept busy, keeping body and soul together. On the other hand, the inhabitants are free from the anxieties of the rich; they are relieved from the fear of losing what they possess. It would seem terrible for a person who belongs to the so-called "better classes" to be suddenly transferred into the position of the denizen of the neglected neighborhood. Besides the unbearable conditions of actual experience, the lack of room, privacy, sufficient food and clothing, the fears for tomorrow, the strain of working for daily bread only, and the gloomy vision of the same sunken position in the future would drive one into insanity.

Fortunately, however, nature, history, and gradual adaptation have put a safeguard against a poor man's thoughts. He cannot think of the future,—the present completely absorbs his mind. The hard struggle for existence leaves little energy for contemplation. If he is equal to the occasion, he makes the best of it; he works; he suffers; he endures; he submerges his needs; he saves for a rainy day, and eventually succeeds in climbing up the ladder to social achievement. Should he weaken, he succumbs to temptation, sickness, neglect of duty, or the transgression of the strict code of morals. These make him an object of charity or throw him into the valley of sin. There are innumerable reasons for the inhabitant of the neglected neighborhood going wrong. The saloon, the cheap theater, the corner politician, the music hall; these are the organized forces that are at work spreading corruption and degeneracy. There is no wonder that many a home is shattered, many a woman is led to a life of shame, and many a man falls into the depths of sin and crime.

It is nothing short of a miracle that, in spite of all these negative conditions, the neglected neighborhood does possess happy homes, balanced and morally sound men and women, beautiful and loving children, and human character endowed with fortitude.

E. Jewish Neighborhoods

The neglected Jewish neighborhood suffers from no inherited economic individual wealth, but there is an inheritance of a different nature with which we have to cope. There is a whole history behind it which explains its present and shapes its future. The Jewish Ghetto is peculiar in this particular respect. It has a peculiar origin and possesses a number of distinguishing features.

The inhabitants of the Ghetto are immigrants, who have been driven out of their own country by persecution and oppression because of their religion. They have suffered for centuries from restriction, political inequality, and by gradual, and long uninterrupted experience, have become adapted to their exciusive and limited surroundings. But even then, living as they have, under great disadvantages, they have not necessarily represented the neglected neighborhood. On the contrary, in Russia, for instance, the Jews, notwithstanding political restrictions and persecutions, do not represent the lowest strata of society, and while on the whole, poverty among the Jews is appalling, still in the matter of education, art, and morals, the Jews stand very much higher than the peasants and city workers. Transplanted to this country of ours, and acquiring all the blessings of free citizenship, the immigrant, and especially the Jewish immigrant, finds new handicaps in adjusting himself to these new conditions. Relieved of the political and economic fetters that bound him for centuries, he faces an unequal struggle in the fierce strife of economic competition. Having freed himself from suffering in his own country, he comes here full of hope and expectation. He is willing to work and is anxious to settle in his new home. He is industrious and absolutely sober. He is worse off than a man without a country; he is without a language. He is physically unable to apply himself, as other immigrants do, to rough manual occupations. He cannot use his hands to advantage. He finds no field for commercial enterprise, and is compelled to enter the Ghetto, the neglected neighborhood. Here he becomes the prey to the usual deleterious forces of the neglected neighborhood that make it necessary for the influences from above to help him. The immigrant is taken advantage of by the greedy employer, who, on the basis of free contract, makes him work inhuman hours for starvation wages. His wife and children are forced to work so as to make up the deficiency. The congestion of the Ghetto breeds disease, physical as well as moral. The Jewish home, the foundation of social integrity, is going to ruin. The saloon becomes an attraction, and we cannot help but despair as we meet with juvenile delinquency and women's immorality. Sad as these conditions may seem, they are nothing but attributes of a neglected neighborhood. In this case, however, the situation is more promising. The Ghetto is a neglected neighborhood, but it is different in many respects from other neglected neighborhoods.

Intemperance, the cause of a hundred vices, is, practically speaking, unknown among the Jews. There is little inherited degeneracy, and idleness and shiftlessness, very much less than in other neighborhoods.

The Jews have their faults, but they are not as grave or as deeply rooted. It is remarkable with what rapidity Jews leave the Ghetto and enter the so-called higher strata of society. It rarely happens that a Jew goes back to the neglected neighborhood once having left it, hence it is only a question of giving the proper attention and helping the immigrants that they may protect themselves from the crushing influences that are unavoidable in a neglected neighborhood. Because of this hopeful situation, the Jewish Ghetto always attracted the best and the most sincere social workers. There is material worth while working with. There are possibilities that cannot be found anywhere else.

As the Ghetto is largely made up of immigrants, it stands to reason that several service agencies must primarily reach the immigrant and that as soon as possible after his arrival.

F. The Teaching of English

The adult and the children need help, need protection, and if properly directed, the settlement, through its activities, may do the greatest possible good, and in the matter of prevention, avoid many a misery. The question of learning English seems to be the most vital one. In some cities, the municipalities have taken up the subject, and provide evening classes for foreigners. Settlements in such instances have justly given up this particular branch of activity for fear of duplicating effort. While there can be no doubt that the evening schools do an immense amount of good, and do teach a number of foreigners, it is worth while noticing that the percentage of immigrants that avail themselves of this opportunity is comparatively small.

A most striking feature is the difference between the attendance and registration. It is usually less than fifty per cent, indicating that over one-half of those that do intend to learn fail to attend. Closer observation reveals the fact that most of the settlements give up evening classes, not because they are unnecessary but because they are not attended. The subject of teaching English to foreigners has been grossly neglected. Only recently have we begun to have books published for this purpose. We still have no authorities in regard to it. The teachers, if not volunteers, are employed only a part of the time, and what is more striking, the subject is seldom discussed. While everyone has difficulties, on the whole, we seem to be satisfied and feel that nothing more can be done. It is true that thousands of immigrants who do not learn English rapidly, suffer continuously on account of it, and after years of residence in the United States, still need an interpreter. If the settlement were to conduct a model class of teaching English, it would gradually become a subject for consideration, and the methods might have been adopted by the municipality. In this direction settlements can continue the work, without fear of duplicating effort.

G. Employment

The immigrant, on his arrival, must first of all solve the problem of his maintenance; he must find employment; as a rule he is at a loss what to undertake, and is eager to get advice and assistance in this particular respect. Unfortunately, the advice given by his own countrymen is not always good, and is dictated often by ulterior motives. The existing employment agencies, as a rule, are connected with a purely charitable agency, and conduct their work perfunctorily. The settlements, until lately, neglected this most important problem, and while in individual cases immigrants are assisted in getting positions, this usually has been done haphazardly, and without much consideration. In connection with this employment proposition, a vocational guidance bureau should be conducted, where the immigrants might be assisted to gain the positions for which they are best adapted. The problem of making the immigrant efficient would lead to the establishment of educational agencies, as well as to their better use. The question of housing the immigrant is also a direct problem of the Jewish settlement. While the general problem of housing in the neglected neighborhood is too stupendous to be handled by any private agency, still the settlement ought to initiate the movement and do its share in the promotion of proper housing facilities. Thus, homes for girls and hotels for single men, successfully started in many cities by non-Jewish agencies should be attempted by the Jewish settlements. The wrongs and unnecessary inconveniences caused by private boarding are too numerous to be mentioned. Let it suffice to say that there is a demand for such an enterprize and that the settlement would be a proper agency to initiate such a movement. The building of model tenements, as well as the supervision of homes, is also a legitimate function of a settlement.

The health problem, in general, including medical service, is one of the most important activities that a settlement should undertake, especially if the existing agencies fall short of adequacy.[1]

In some instances, the work of a legal aid society has been very popular with the settlements. The subject of legal aid in connection with Jewish agencies was presented at the National Conference of Jewish Charities in St. Louis in 1908. Miss Minnie Low gave a thorough exposition of the intricate legal problems that confront the Jewish social worker.

In Baltimore, a Jewish Court of Arbitration was organized in 1913, dealing with all cases except those in which the law of the state will not permit arbitration.[2]

The subject of social gatherings should be considered. The immigrant, after all, is a human being, and has a very active tendency for social intercourse. Unfortunately, the saloon, the private music hall, the meeting hall, are not always proper places for the immigrant. It is, therefore, absolutely necessary that the settlement should become the gathering place for the adult immi-

---

[1] "The House on Henry Street," Lillian Wald, New York, 1915.
[2] " Jewish Court of Arbitration," " Jewish Charities," May, 1913.

grant. Entertainments, musicales, and dramatic performances must be of a high order in order to compete with the cheap shows so prevalent in a neglected neighborhood. A mistake is often committed in underestimating the æsthetic understanding and artistic sense of the masses,—especially of the Jewish masses. While poor and unsightly in their appearance, the large majority of them have had an opportunity to hear and appreciate good music and highly artistic presentations of dramatic art; a settlement makes a wrong move in assuming that all that the masses want is laughter and light entertainment. Such an attitude discredits the attempt to uplift the masses, and while it may lead to an increased attendance, it will lower the taste, and is therefore negative work and should not be encouraged. The classic concert or the carefully staged dramatic performance may not draw at first as large a crowd as a vulgar vaudeville, but its influence, in the neighborhood, is important, and as a rule, is the pride of even those who do not attend it. Strange as it may seem, the recently arrived immigrant is more appreciative of true art than those who have lived here for some time. Probably this is due to our neglect of art, the substitution wherever possible of classic music by ragtime, drama by vaudeville, and similar "stunts." This loss of the artistic sense on the part of the immigrant is one of the saddest phenomena in the process of Americanization.

H. True Americanization

The practice of teaching Americanism by patriotic exercises and blind enthusiasm is not only futile but is absolutely harmful. The immigrant is naturally disappointed in his hopes of finding paradise in his new country. He cannot help seeing from the very first how the ideal of true democracy is laughed at and ridiculed in reality. The type of the policeman does not suggest to him the ideal of American citizenship. He does not meet Washingtons, Jeffersons, Lincolns, and the like. In his little sphere he sees little justice, and finds an immense amount of deliberate untruth. It is natural that the talk concerning the glorious liberty of this country falls upon his ears as mockery. To get him enthusiastic concerning the American flag, and instill patriotic spirit to the tune of "My Country" is difficult as long as the Stars and Stripes are trampled by unclean feet, and the country's soul sold to grafters. It is easier, however, to get the immigrant to appreciate the true blessings of this country, not by speaking and singing and marching and shooting firecrackers, but by actual facts of true democracy. Give him a chance to make an honest living; pay him a living wage; present to him an opportunity for the so much talked about right of the pursuit of happiness; keep him away from the selfish politician; help him to discriminate between his friend and his enemy; protect him from the evil influences of corrupt democracy; exhibit the American virtues as conspicuously as you exhibit its shortcomings and faults, and it will not be difficult to get an expression of true patriotism, based upon a deep-rooted appreciation of all the blessings that the immigrant can acquire in this country.

The right method, therefore, in this case, as in all other cases, is the "truth" method. The immigrant would be interested in the wrongs that are so vivid to him if his co-operation were solicited for their correction. If you interest him in municipal leagues, in the questions of to-day, without trying to paint them in rosy colors, if you acquaint him with the best efforts of American citizenship, he will become attached to the country and his patriotism will be natural and not forced. Do not expect the immigrant to be better, however, than the average American. This is true not only in his political life but in his private life also, and refers to the manners and customs with which we have so little patience. The immigrant, as a rule, is timid, and does not mean to be impolite. His ways, however, may be quite different from ours, and it takes a little time before he acquires ours by imitation. Unfortunately, the example set is sometimes misleading. Our code of etiquette is getting so complicated that even the born American must take special care on occasion to follow a certain routine which changes with time and place. In the settlement, we are often enforcing an exceptionally high standard of etiquette. Take for instance the question of taking off hats. While the American fellow is permitted to keep his hat on whenever he pleases, we are painfully anxious that the immigrant should have his hat off. The best method of having the immigrant take off his hat is to have a check room, where everyone can deposit hat and coat and save much annoyance.

I. Expansion of Activities

The recently arrived immigrant, within a comparatively short time, becomes imbued with the American spirit, and in his turn, looks with scorn upon the "Greener." In the majority of instances, he does not care to associate with him, and is especially averse to the possibility of being classed in one group with him. Thus, in this stage of development, the immigrant gradually ceases to attend the settlement, though in the beginning, he may have been a frequent visitor. This is a very deplorable condition, and an effort should be made to retain this constituency. The influence of those who have, so to say, graduated from the first stage, is important, as regards the new constituency, and the settlement ought to remain a permanent factor. Naturally, in order to achieve this particular purpose, the settlement should extend and modify the character of its activities. Features that may attract the newly arrived immigrant may have no value for the person who has already gone through the metamorphosis of first adaptation. Lectures by prominent persons, organizations of some definite character,—Socialist, Zionist, and those even of a purely political nature, should find place in the settlement. Entertainments, socials, and musicales, will serve this purpose, but better still, enterprizes presupposing some financial standing should be encouraged. Building loan societies, Gemilath Chesed Associations, local philanthropic societies outside of the organized charities, co-operative ventures, agricultural ventures, and so on, are of inestimable value.

The time comes when the immigrant craves for the association with the American. This, however, is a most precarious step. In the majority of instances, the immigrant is not in a position to make connections with people of a higher class. He usually stoops, and invariably falls to a lower strata of society. It is, therefore, of the utmost importance, that the settlement should offer the opportunity, especially for the younger people, to come together and meet in an American atmosphere. At this stage of the game, dancing, socials, athletic games, pool tables, should be initiated, and clubs of a social character encouraged. Men and women, popular in American life, capable of entertaining as well as instructing, should be recruited into service, and special effort should be made to make the settlement attractive to this class of people. This is sufficient reason for the maintenance of classes, provided there is a demand for them, in cooking, sewing, mechanical and free hand drawing, millinery, singing and music, piano, violin, and mandolin, as well as trade school classes. These activities will attract, also, the second generation, a strictly American population.

J. Children's Work

In the work with the children, the public schools, in a large majority of cases, cover the entire scope of education, and it is only in specific instances that school work must be supplemented. The function of the settlement in the work with the children should be mainly, if not exclusively, directed toward counteracting negative influences of the home and street. The settlement should give ample opportunity for child's play, play to which every child is entitled, and of which he is deprived in a neglected neighborhood. A gymnasium, where the children have the opportunity to play basket ball and indoor baseball, to dance and to romp, is a necessary adjunct of a settlement. Entertainments, musicales, picture shows, are legitimate and very desirable activities for the good of the children. The smaller children should be given a chance to play games, and special playrooms well equipped with toys and apparatus, are helpful. The same purpose should dominate in the clubs, organized for, and by children. In this, as well as in mere play, the children should have instilled in them, indirectly, a number of moral precepts, or rather precepts of conduct, that they may miss otherwise. The child needs somebody to direct him, to lead him; he wants to follow and will follow; he craves companionship and under proper supervision learns to appreciate not only his own interests but the interests of others. The child's instincts, left to nature, would probably, as Rousseau said, make him perfect. Unfortunately, the child of a neglected neighborhood is not left to nature, and it requires powerful agencies to overcome the wrong influences to which every child is subjected.

Notwithstanding the lessons taught at school, the child is in need of an additional factor to instil in him the virtue of cleanliness. In all the departments of the settlement, cleanliness should be the first and the most important lesson taught the children. No child should be permitted to come to the settlement unless it passes a satisfactory standard of cleanliness. The gospel of physical strength should also be a living principle. Physical culture should be strongly emphasized; classes in gymnastics, games, dances, and physical exercises should be encouraged. A child of a neglected neighborhood often needs a friend. The teacher may be too busy to give him proper attention; the mother and father may be too busy to understand the child, and here is where the settlement can be of inestimable value. Each child attending the settlement should have at least one person interested in him, and intimate enough with him that the child may come at any time for advice, help, or just a little chat.

While physical welfare and cleanliness refer to the welfare of the individual, there are other lessons to be impressed upon the child's life. These are his relations to the outer world, his conduct in relation to others, his life with others. Play is a wonderful factor in transmitting these lessons. Make-believe conditions are just as good as reality. The club is a splendid medium. The child, coming together with other children, under the proper leadership, may become less selfish and more considerate of the rights of his fellow playmates. The natural interests of the child should be taken into consideration. A children's club should be distinguished from a class by the fact that it is practically speaking self-governing, and the work is chosen by the children, or at least, with their consent. The less difficulty a leader has in disciplining the children, the better are the results.

K. Specialization

In some settlements, one particular feature has been emphasized and become the central function of the entire activity. Thus, the Henry Street Settlement is known as the Nurses' Settlement. There are special musical settlements. Special notice should be given to the Graphic Sketch Club in Philadelphia, which is an art settlement. This center was founded in 1896 by Mr. Samuel S. Fleisher. He explains its origin as follows: "In 1910 I wandered about the southern section of the city. I became acquainted with the gray aimless life of the boys and girls who toil all day in the shop or factory, where life means work and sleep and again work, where there are no amusements, save the common dance hall and the cheap theater. I felt the horrors of it. I once happened to see classes instructed at the college settlement in the making of shirtwaists, and I asked myself if there was not something better, something more elevating, after the day already spent in drudgery. I decided that an art class would be a worthy experiment. I wanted to try. I wished to see if the mind of the working boy or girl was capable of something better. A brief experience where we had our first quarters assured me that all these boys and girls needed was a chance. They undoubtedly had capacity for culture and the will to develop it." [1]

The home of the Graphic Art Club is capacious. Class, exhibition, and recreation rooms for both sexes, are splendidly equipped. A dozen or more competent instructors, pursuing their professions outside, compose the teaching staff. Instruction is given in painting, sculpture, illustrating, modelling and practically every branch of fine art. The school has about two hundred fifty students of all races and colors. Annually an exhibition of work done by the pupils is given. Prizes and scholarships are then awarded. That the work is often of high merit is attested to by the fact that the Academy of Fine Arts has thus far awarded twenty-six free American scholarships to the students. Eleven of the recipients were later awarded European scholarships.

The club has a social side as well as an educational one. Three clubs among the students exist, each with its own tea and club room. The entire house is tastefully decorated and contains many fine and rare pieces of art, the work of students and others. In order that a taste for the æsthetic be cultivated among the poor

[1] " The Power of Art Revised," " Jewish Charities," October, 1911.

of the neighborhood, visitors to the school are not only welcomed but encouraged. The instruction is free and the entire expense is borne by the founder.

The club is not only a successful venture, but serves as an impetus to promote art through settlements, a departure noticed all over the country.

L. Politics in the Settlement

Besides strictly constructive and educational work, a settlement is constantly counteracting influences of a negative character. The saloon, the questionable dancing hall, the gambling joint, are forces that the properly conducted settlement is openly opposing, fighting, and trying to minimize by offering better and more wholesome attractions. Even the picture shows, as usually conducted, find in the settlement a bitter enemy and a powerful competitor.

In the questions bearing upon political issues, the settlements, as a rule, are very careful, and in a large majority of cases, remain indifferent. It is not a secret, however, that in a neglected neighborhood, the professional politician is rather unscrupulous in getting votes, and for him the influences that wreck and corrupt the neighborhood are just as good, if not better, than those that strengthen it. In the Jewish Ghetto, the situation is especially deplorable. The immigrant, after he is naturalized, in addition to the duties of an American citizen, carries the responsibility of maintaining the reputation of the Jewish foreigner; upon his conduct depends the attitude toward the newcomer;

his individual wrongdoings are usually interpreted as an organic fault of the entire class to which he belongs. It has been repeatedly proved that the native-born Americans have betrayed political freedom; corrupted politics are by no means limited to neighborhoods inhabited by foreign-born citizens, and still the cry that the immigrant is an undesirable citizen is frequently made. The Jewish settlements have rather exaggerated the need for Americanizing the recently arrived immigrant, and have neglected to guard him just at the time when he is receiving the right to vote, and can exercise his power either to the good or detriment of the community.

The Jewish immigrant is eager to learn his new surroundings; he shows a remarkable interest in the intricacies of American government, and takes to heart the issues of the day. The settlements, in this respect, have done commendable work by arranging lectures, debates, and discussions, but little by little, the immigrant becomes the prey of other influences. He begins to be more sceptical as to the possibility of adjusting his theories to practice. The struggle for existence leaves little room for any other serious interest but his own narrow, personal sphere. He becomes indifferent to social conditions. This is the time when the settlement loses him; he joins lodges, clubs, and so on. The professional politician takes hold of him. His political standing as a voter now counts. The settlement fails to take part in this important issue, and the newly made citizen is not only left to himself, but still worse, he is open to interests that are utilizing him for selfish purposes, and often as a means to his own degradation. His political freedom is gone.

Only lately, with the new law of naturalization in force, have classes in citizenship been organized in the different Jewish educational agencies. New York, Cleveland, Chicago, Baltimore, Boston, and Cincinnati report very successful attempts in this direction. Usually, however, these classes deal with general civics only, and the instruction is limited to the formal preparation for the examination conducted by the United States Court. In Cleveland, an effort has been made to overthrow a political boss in the Jewish neighborhood, the proprietor of a local saloon. Credit should be given to Judge Emanuel Levine who initiated this movement and brought it to a successful issue; but even there the question has been raised whether the settlement has the right to meddle with local politics.

An indirect attempt to combat local political agencies of a questionable character was made in Chicago by Dr. David Blaustein. The results were, however, less successful. In other cities, the settlements and educational centers are trying to avoid political issues. This indifference on the part of the settlement is largely due to the fact that their contributors and supporters do not belong to the same party, and consequently the settlement is unable to take a position without creating opposition among its own subscribers. There is still another more valid reason for the attitude of settlements to local politics, and that is the fear of antagonizing the neighborhood and thus losing its patronage.

A Jewish settlement in particular should be careful in taking up a political issue, for it, as a rule, represents not only a neighborhood, but, in a certain degree, the Jewish interests of the city, and in this respect it carries additional responsibilities. There is not and should not be a compact Jewish vote, and no matter what side the settlement takes, it does not represent the true situation, invariably creating misunderstandings. This being true in regard to a Jewish settlement is also true in regard to any effort to organize a Jewish political group. Unfortunately, the politicians do not worry about ultimate outcome, and as a rule are organizing Jewish political clubs with a definite party feature. Their unscrupulous methods are often responsible for a number of evil conditions in the neighborhood. Their influence can be fought only at the polls; their power can be taken only by an active agitation, and no arguments but the ballot can do this.

The time has come when something will have to be done in protecting the Jewish neglected neighborhoods from corrupting, organized political agencies.

In 1902, the Jewish Educational Alliance of St. Louis offered its auditorium to political discussion. Various political parties were invited to send speakers to present the issues from their standpoints. Four separate evenings were arranged, accommodating the four parties. These meetings, outside of the one arranged by the Socialists, were poorly attended. The administration, however, did not consider this venture a failure.[1]

M. Co-operation

It seems that the most difficult part of the task is to get the co-operation of the neighborhood, especially in matters of practical, local, civic importance. A successful experiment of this kind was attempted in Baltimore, where the Jewish Educational Alliance undertook to fight the existence of disorderly houses that for twenty years had been permitted to flourish in the very midst of respectable East Baltimore, the downtown Jewish section. This could not be done without the co-operation of the entire community. A mass meeting was called, and a petition, signed by one hundred persons, was presented to the court, but the result was still unsatisfactory. A publicity campaign was started. The synagogues, the clubs, the lodges, and the Jewish press were utilized. Then another mass meeting was called, and a petition, got up and endorsed by different organizations, was prepared. The non-Jewish constituency joined the movement for a clean neighborhood. A non-sectarian gathering, representing every element in the community,—members of the gospel, the rabbis, the citizens, Jew and non-Jew,—all formed a compact group, and had no difficulty in bringing this issue to a successful conclusion.[2]

[1] "Politics in the Settlement," Oscar Leonard, " Jewish Charities," November, 1912.

[2] " Neighborhood Co-operation in Baltimore," Max Carton, " Jewish Charities," October, 1912.

N. Difficulties of a Jewish Settlement

The settlement must be careful not to duplicate undertakings of other agencies, and must not interfere with the activities of a relief society. It must be on guard not to duplicate the activities of public schools, and so on. There is an idea in vogue that the main function of a settlement is to be merely the herald of new movements, and that as soon as the latter are taken up by other agencies, and especially by municipal institutions, the settlement must cease its participation in that particular field, considering its mission fulfilled. This has been the case in many cities, with kindergartens which had been deemed a part and parcel of the settlement; in some places the libraries were given up as soon as the municipalities had made ample provision in the particular neighborhood.

Lately, since the public schools have begun to conduct classes in English for foreigners, this has become an unnecessary adjunct of a settlement. With the introduction of public dance halls, and the spread of the wider use of our public school plants, other activities will have to be transferred. Thus the character of activities in the settlement is constantly changing.

O. Juvenile Delinquency

Juvenile delinquency among Jews is a new phenomenon. The idea that the immigrant child or the child born of foreign parents constitutes a large percentage among the juvenile delinquents is not always correct.

Investigation reveals that the Jews do not show a larger number of criminals, proportionally, than any other social group. In Manhattan, in which, according to the last Census 23.5 per cent of the population is Jewish, of the seven thousand eight hundred and twenty-one boys arraigned in the children's court, only one thousand five hundred and fifty-eight or 19.9 per cent were Jews.[1] Jewish communities, however, are quite concerned with this new situation. As far as the punitive and correctional measures are concerned, general agencies like the juvenile court and the reform schools are utilized. However, additional effort is exerted in providing specifically Jewish factors capable of coping with the growth of this negative feature of Jewish life. There is only one Jewish reformatory for boys in the country, the Jewish Protectory, established in Hawthorne, New York, in 1907.

The question is still open as to the need of specific Jewish institutions for Jewish juvenile delinquents. In 1908, at the National Conference of Jewish Charities, Rabbi George Zepin advocated the establishment of an intermunicipal institution for Jewish delinquent children. Judge Julian W. Mack vigorously objected to this plan, and insisted that the state institutions ought to handle this problem.

In 1911, Miss Minnie Low expressed her disbelief in the need of a Jewish reformatory for girls. Outside of institutional care, a great deal of work is done with children paroled by the courts and those that require

[1] " Jewish Charities," Vol. VI, No. 7, p. 109.

special supervision. There are a number of juvenile court protective associations under Jewish auspices. The Council of Jewish Women does considerable work in this direction. The Philadelphia Juvenile Aid Society places a number of children in the Jewish colonies in New Jersey.

The most comprehensive program dealing with juvenile delinquency is presented in the work done by the Personal Service Bureau of Chicago. For the year 1915, seven hundred and seventy-six cases of juvenile delinquency were handled through this organization. The manner in which they handle delinquency among girls is quite impressive. Miss Low described their activities as follows:

"We directed special attention to the so-called incorrigible type. Insolence, disobedience, defiance of parental authority, bad language, late hours, are all forerunners of delinquency, culminating in the one fatal step from which we would fain save every girl. We interested some of our good women in the 'borderline' cases. By giving such girls a chance under better environment, taking them away from homes of grinding poverty, where the parents have lost control over them, and providing new interests for them, it has been possible to reduce the number in our city and state training schools more than seventy-five per cent. Friendly supervision, guiding influence, firmness and discipline were the doses prescribed in new homes with improved living conditions. In place of turning incorrigible girls back to homes where friction, discord, discontent, and often grinding poverty made life intolerable, results have been most satisfactory. Very few failures have attended our efforts.

"Three agents were employed as outlets for the plans indicated. First, the sympathy of kindly women was enlisted. These women represented, principally, the directorates of our small boarding clubs. When it was necessary to remove from her surroundings a girl who was fast traveling the downward path, one who was still a saving proposition—we stated our troubles to these good women. They entered fully into the spirit of things, and made it possible for us to place some of our high-strung, emotional, unmanageable girls in their well-equipped and well-regulated homes. The Ruth Club deserves special mention, because its policies and methods are slightly different from those of the ordinary boarding clubs for girls. A searching study is made of the peculiar needs of each individual girl by the superintendent, Mrs. Clara Reiss. Her marvelous personal influence and big-hearted sisterly interest have helped many a girl to keep morally strong, and grow up into useful womanhood. The Board of Directors provides a personal friend for each girl. This friend makes it possible for the girl to get the necessary vocational guidance and training that will equip her for self-support. When she earns from twelve dollars to twenty dollars a week, as some of them do after a few years, a first-class boarding place is found for her. The Ruth Club retains its interest indefinitely. Its doors are wide open to the boarders living elsewhere, who delight in spending several evenings a week at the club with their old companions.

"When the small boarding clubs, housing from twenty-five to thirty girls, had relieved us of as many as they could accommodate, our Home for Jewish Friendless opened its doors, and took in about a dozen girls, from the ages of thirteen to sixteen years. More than half this number are attending the Lucy Flower Technical High School and are making good in the full sense of the word.

"The third outlet has been to place the more depraved girls, that seemed to fit in nowhere else, with a non-Jewish woman, in charge of a small club, accommodating about a dozen girls. She has made a specialty of the girl problem, and has succeeded in instilling better principles, and greater obedience to the laws of order and decency than anyone else whom we have known. When our Jewish resources failed, and it was necessary to choose between the State training school and this club, we naturally chose the latter. Had it not been for this woman, with the shelter she offered our girls in her splendidly equipped home, and had not her influence been such an important factor in the reformation process, we would have had to send a few more behind locked doors, during the course of the year. It is the exception, and not the rule, when workers feel called upon to recommend that delinquent girls be sent to institutions."

P. Crime Among the Jews

It is only lately that the question of social work with adult criminals has begun to receive special attention from Jewish agencies. The Personal Service Bureau of Chicago has a special department for this purpose. In Baltimore, a special agent is in the field, and in other cities, religious influences are brought into play. The Independent Order of B'nai B'rith is endeavoring to organize the after care of discharged prisoners through a special committee. The engagement of a special director by the Order will undoubtedly help towards the realization of this plan, but so far it is only in its inception.

Chapter Sixteen. Settlements and Neighborhood Work

Questions

1. Give the definition of a settlement as a social service center.
2. Describe the specific problem of Jewish settlements.
3. Give a program of Jewish children's club work.
4. What is the function of a settlement in regard to the adolescents?
5. Describe community forces in their relation to the settlement.
6. Discuss religion in settlements.
7. What are the differences between the slum and the "Ghetto"?
8. Give a general program for a Jewish settlement.
9. Give the true method of Americanization.
10. Describe specialization in settlements.

XVII

ORGANIZATION AND ADMINISTRATION

As in every other field of human endeavor, so in the realm of social service, the simple methods of yesterday have given way to a complicated system, adequate for the requirements of modern life. Organization is a matter of constant evolution. While some agencies achieve a high grade of efficiency, others just begin their existence. The general forms of organization are common and more or less permanent, the details and combinations permit of considerable modification.

A. Leadership

In social service, the idea of organization originated in the endeavor of individuals to solve a given need by collective effort. The idea finds realization through propaganda, be it written or oral. Sometimes a preliminary meeting marks the starting point of the undertaking. It is natural that the initiators of the movement are the logical heads of the newly born organization. In some instances, however, the leadership is turned over to persons who, though not the originators of the movement, possess merit or means to carry out the plans successfully, secure co-operation, and add to the prestige of the organization.

Thus in Jewish social service, certain individuals are

usually sought after in a new organization. Their participation is absolutely necessary in order to obtain the good will of the community. Different groups may have their own leaders, but the same persons are invariably at the head of almost every organization of the same character. Usually these leaders possess the necessary qualifications, but again, some are simply elevated to their position because of their personal generous support or because of their ambitions, often satisfied by unscrupulous means. It is understood that the position of a head of an organization carries with it, besides responsibilities, privileges, honors, and social standing, which in themselves are an inducement for many a person to exert effort in order to achieve their personal ends. Ambition for leadership with ulterior motives is quite common among the Jews, and is quite frequently responsible for the birth of new organizations. It is important, therefore, that in launching a new movement, the selection of sincere and qualified leaders should receive proper consideration.

B. The Selection of Leaders

As a rule, a written constitution provides for the methods of electing the officers, and the directors of the given organization. The contributing public is supposed to have a final say in the matter. However, in practice, this matter is frequently referred to a nominating committee, appointed by the presiding officer, which in its turn receives certain instructions. Unless there is some personal strife, the report is usually accepted without much ado. At times, different factions are in the field and then more than one ticket is to be considered, but in each case, it is only a matter of one or the other group of leaders, and very seldom the concern of the entire body of contributors or members. It is an open question whether in its present state of development, social service can be properly handled through representatives elected by the majority, who may have no standards as to the qualifications of their candidates. However, in Jewish social service, the principle of democracy in this particular sphere is gaining considerable ground. This new tendency received expression in a number of instances when new organizations were started, presumably for no other reason than as protest against the oligarchical management of the more advanced institutions of American Jewry.

The New York Jewish Community or Kehillah is managed on this newer democratic basis. Every affiliated organization is given representation on the governing body, and the affairs of the community are adjudged by it, without special powers or privileges being given to a few individuals. This question of proper representation in governing bodies is especially difficult in connection with organizations like settlements, Y. M. H. A.'s and Y. W. H. A.'s, where the constituency utilizing the institution demands an adequate part in the matter of administration and where self-government is becoming a desirable adjunct of efficient management.

In practical application, these theoretical principles

must receive proper attention, but in each case proper precautions should be taken not to sacrifice the expediency of the situation to a consideration of principle which may, in the given instance, play havoc with the organization. All depends upon local conditions, and upon consideration of the different methods as to which will produce better results in selecting the proper managers of the organization in question.

C. Persistency in Office Holding

It has become quite a custom in social service practice for the same person to retain the office of leadership from term to term. This persistency in office holding, has created a situation that retards the development of an organization. In many instances, the heads of the organization, though very active and useful in their activities, reach a stage where they are unable to cope with new situations or to adapt themselves to new, progressive measures, and become rather dictatorial in their policies. The communities in such cases have to bear their burden silently and wait for nature to take its course. This prevents new forces from entering the field and contributing their share of useful activities. The work suffers. At the second National Conference of Jewish Charities at Detroit, Mr. Max Senior, in his presidential message, expressed the following sentiments, which undoubtedly produced effective results all over the country. He said: "I believe that one of the greatest evils in Jewish charity work is the persistence of the officers of our institutions for many years. We need, in the conduct of our institutions, new blood and new ideas. This is a principle largely recognized in business matters and equally applicable to our affairs. I am a firm believer in rotation of these offices. Long incumbency in office produces a feeling of ownership, which is often disastrous to the best interests of the community." [1]

There are still a number of long timers who have not learned this truth as yet. In adopting this theory of rotation in office, care should be taken that this term of each incumbent should be of sufficient duration to permit of the realization of plans that he may have had for the benefit of the organization.

D. Qualifications of Leadership

It is difficult to enumerate or to define the various qualifications that a leader should possess. It is, after all, a matter of personality and standards. A leader, popular under certain circumstances, may be an absolute failure under other conditions; and again, a strong personality may carry a situation when conditions may seem unfavorable and popular support lacking. In selecting a leader in Jewish social service, consideration is usually given to his financial and social standing, to his generosity in supporting different agencies, to his ability to give his time and energy to the particular cause and to his achievements in the past. At times, initiative, enthusiasm, and devotion,

[1] Proceedings National Conference of Jewish Charities, Detroit, Michigan, 1902.

success in some other line, ability as a speaker, and last, but not least, special talent in getting the co-operation of different classes are reasons why a person is selected as a president of an organization. With the modern advance in social service, a new feature must be added; a leader must possess a broad view of the situation; he must be capable of appreciating the new tendencies and he must be willing to adjust his particular activities to the demands of the times, with a scientific interpretation of facts and a desire to reach the highest possible efficiency. The proper leader of to-day is not a dictator, he does not seek to impress his authority by sheer force. He is open to conviction, and does not demand continual approval of his actions. He is anxious to get the co-operation of his co-workers and the community at large, but he does not pose as a martyr, nor does he become irritated when his efforts are not fully appreciated. He realizes the importance of collective effort and does not undertake to do everything by himself, leaving no field for the endeavors of others.

E. The Board of Directors

The Board of Directors, known under different names in different organizations, are supposed to be the choice of the public and the trustees of the public's funds. They are instrumental in making ample provision for the material support of the different activities and are responsible for the entire workings of the organization. They are the controlling media and it is their duty and privilege to examine into every detail of the different transactions and to know the actual results. Differences of opinions in the Board of Directors is often a sign of a wholesome interest and leads to a better and more thorough consideration of existing issues. It is unfortunate, however, that in many instances, the Board comprises different factions, continually working at cross purposes, and frequently jeopardizing the progress of the organization. This is especially deplorable when the differences are based upon personal reasons, having nothing in common with the good of the institutions which the directors are supposed to serve.

There has been considerable evil done to a number of social service agencies by the fact that their Boards of Directors comprised a large proportion of members known as "dead-wood," people who have neither time, nor interest, nor ability to perform the services that are required of them. No person should accept an office nor be permitted to accept any office in any organization unless he is in a position to give the time and attention that are required. In some instances, in order to retain the names of some persons on the Board who are not able to give their actual participation, a special class of honorary members of the Board is instituted.

F. Meetings

Usually, the Board convenes at certain stated periods, where the activities of the organization are reported and discussed, and where further action and policies are determined. Besides this, special committees attend to specific problems encountered by the organization. The work of these committees is of great value, as they give an opportunity to the different members of the Board to take a real and more or less intensive interest in at least some part of the life of the organization. Great care should be taken that these committees should really do the actual work, instead of serving, as in many organizations, simply a perfunctory arrangement. A member of the Board, who limits his activities to attending the meetings and not taking any other active interest is not doing his full duty.

G. The Paid Worker

The office of paid worker is a matter of a recent origin. In the beginning, the employment of a social worker is rather a compromise; it is only through necessity that an organization is willing to spend money for management, and even then, there are always some persons who consider the expenses for management not a legitimate item in connection with a philanthropic activity. In many instances, the introduction of a paid worker is gradual; often a person giving his services for a considerable time gratis, is given a small compensation. The latter is seldom sufficient to justify the employment of his entire time, and as a rule, is considered as a side issue. Again, in other communities, the new field opens an opportunity to help a poor but unfortunate man or woman, who is placed in a position where he can, presumably, earn a livelihood. To engage a social worker in this case, is a double charity. While this is true historically, it is also applicable to present conditions, and each and every community, if not as a whole, in part retains the old views and considers a social worker as a charitable adjunct, rather than as a real necessity. Anyone who has had the experience of advertising for a social worker, knows from the character of the persons aspiring to get the position, how little uniformity there is in the supposed qualifications. Men of high social standing in the community will recommend their friends, sometimes even their relatives, whose only qualifications are the close relationship with the given person. Again, pressure is usually brought to get in some deserving member of the community, who cannot do anything else and probably for this very reason will be able to do social work. You get applications from people without any experience, bold enough to say that they believe that they can learn the tricks of the profession very readily, and from others without any education, claiming that they think that education, after all, is not altogether necessary. Again you may get candidates thoroughly qualified, but who take it for granted that if they do not get the appointment, it is not because they come short of requirements, but because they do not carry sufficient pull, or were prevented from getting the position by the interference of someone interested in behalf of another person. In this connection, it is worth while mentioning that the position of a social worker is peculiar in the respect that he has little chance for promotion.

H. Qualifications of a Social Worker

The development of social activities and the specialization according to the character of the work, makes the term of social worker too general. The qualifications of a superintendent of an institution, those of a relief agent, or head worker of a settlement, are, and should be, of a different character. Still there is one underlying principle and this is the general adaptation for social service. The management of our institutions, especially the orphan asylums and hospitals, has lately been considerably improved. The responsibilities connected with these offices became apparent, and the necessity of a qualified person in charge, became imperative. Our Homes for the Aged are still following the old régime. The conditions that are found in our relief agencies are especially instructive.

The office of the Superintendent carries a different meaning in different communities; in some places the Superintendent is nothing but an office boy, a janitor, a clerk; again in others, he is the executive officer with little power and no authority; it is only in a few instances where the Superintendent is considered a leader of the community, where he is directing the work, and is applying plans and policies as to the different philanthropic plans and activities. Unfortunately, professional efficiency is not a general rule among Superintendents of relief agencies. The requirements for the office are still indefinite, and while communities are beginning to recognize the importance of a qualified Superintendent, they are, as a matter of fact, compelled to make their selection from among people without any professional training. Hence, the Superintendent enters the community not as a leader, but as servant, ready to execute orders and follow directions. Imagine a condition in medicine where the physician would be told "we pay you and consequently you have to do whatever we say, but not command us to do what your science directs," and still who can blame a community that is unwilling to trust the care of dependents in the hands of an inexperienced and untrained worker?

On the other hand, in the selection of a Superintendent, different communities are guided by different standards. In some instances, the office is bestowed as a pension upon a person whose services could not be employed otherwise, in others it is purely a matter of connection, something similar to political pull. Lately, the requirements have become more positive. The appearance, the general bearing, the moral tone and disposition, eloquence and refinement are taken into consideration. It is only in the exceptional cases that professional efficiency is sought. How many communities care whether their Superintendent possesses knowledge of sociology, political economy, psychology, and so on; how many of the Jewish communities dealing with immigrants mainly demand that their Superintendent know the language of the immigrants, their past, their peculiarities, their tendencies, their merits or their shortcomings? And these theoretical preparations are only a part of the qualifications of a Superintendent, who is destined to become a leader in modern philanthropy.

In our settlement work, the conditions are still less satisfactory. The requirements of a settlement worker are unreasonable; the work in its character is indefinite; the accomplishments of an efficient settlement worker are too manifold to be found in one person. Besides, the bulk of the work is done by volunteers, and selection of the latter is a difficult matter, and as a rule, the head worker has little choice in the matter. As a result of all these conditions, the qualifications of a settlement worker are measured by the degree he or she is pleasing to the volunteers. Here the charming personality, the smooth talker and an effective smile, a jollier and a favorite of some selected circles, what is called a good soul, has better chances than the efficient communal worker, a man or woman of ideas, sincere and well meaning, but not possessing external pleasantries.

I. New Positions

A social worker, assuming a new position and engaged by a new organization, finds that one of the first, if not the most difficult tasks is to secure the confidence of the Board of Managers and to gain a hold upon the community that will establish proper relationships between him and his organization. If the record of his previous achievements is of some value, it will help him to start with a reputation that has been made already; he will be accordingly introduced, and will have to live up to the expectations which his previous record promises. But even then, his first impression, manners, voice, conversation, tendencies, views that he confesses, sociability, and so on, will be critically scrutinized, and will mean a great deal in assuring him a strong foothold in his new position. Should he, however, be a person who has already been known to the community, and has been chosen for some other reason than on the strength of his former experiences as a social worker, his road towards success is still more difficult. The entire attitude toward him will depend upon how successful he may be at the very beginning.

In this case, he meets a critical attitude, a lack of confidence, and a somewhat anxious expectation on the part even of those who have engaged him. For even they have had doubts as to his ability to cope with the situation and naturally are willing to change their views after a reasonable trial. Often the relations of the social worker and his organization are aggravated from the very start by the interference of a third party, directly or indirectly, personally interested in causing trouble, to see him fail and make place for somebody else. As a rule, however, a social worker, when engaged for a new position, finds that he is met with open arms, and is shown a great deal of consideration in the beginning. But often his first experiences are not lasting. The trouble frequently begins from an insignificant episode, a mistake. Unnecessary friction that could be easily avoided and overlooked causes anxiety and is sufficient to overthrow the entire equilibrium, producing a storm, in what promised to be an ideal atmosphere.

Under these circumstances, it is quite natural that a social worker has to be careful from the very start, and this leads us to the consideration of a peculiar psychological feature, namely, the social worker's fear of his organization. Notwithstanding the growing demand for social workers, each and every one of them is in constant fear of losing his position, for he knows and his friends do not fail to tell him, that to lose a position is, after all, a great deal easier than to get another one. This fear on the part of the social worker makes him very sensitive to the opinions of his superiors. He cannot stand any criticism coming from them, exaggerating its importance, taking too seriously every word uttered by any of his directors, a condition which is responsible for a peculiar ambition, characteristic of almost everyone connected with social service. Realizing this ambition, the organizations are very generous in giving praise to their paid workers, though very careful in advancing their salaries, making public acknowledgments of the wonderful achievements and willing to mention them in every report issued by the organization.

J. Difficulties of a Social Worker

The relations that a social worker encounters are often of a subjective character. This is due to personality and the methods employed. The most frequent cause for friction between the social worker and his organization is the difference of opinion as to methods and tendencies of the work itself.

In the relief agency, the worker may be accused of being too lenient or too severe, as the case may be; in the institution the question of discipline may cause considerable trouble; in settlement work, the lack of restraint and the character of the activities may not meet with the approval of the Board. This is a legitimate and natural controversy, and it is the duty of the worker, if he is given a chance, to bring about a uniformity of ideas. Unfortunately, the worker often sacrifices his own personality in attempting to compromise difficulties; he becomes a champion of a cause in which he himself does not believe; he changes methods, not because he considers them wrong, but because the Board will be better pleased with others. By doing so he does not emphasize the fact that he is not responsible for the new way. On the contrary, he praises the things that he hates and downs those that he internally believes to be good.

The tendency on the part of the members of the Board to apply a business criterion to philanthropic activities is often the cause of considerable friction between the organization and the social worker. The social worker is often made responsible for raising of funds, and is kept busy in inventing schemes or in executing the schemes of his Board for the purpose of obtaining money for different activities. In some organizations, an unreasonable economy is enforced, and the recent fad to get returns from the constituency itself leads to a most unsatisfactory rôle the social worker is made to assume.

In institutions, hospitals, asylums, schools, etc., the importance attached to the sometimes very insignificant income is usually exaggerated. Meanwhile, the social worker is compelled to show results in dollars and cents, and if he fails in this particular respect, he loses his standing; he realizes the falsity of his position, and naturally protests against this unfair measure of his achievements, which creates a feeling of discontent on the part of the organization.

In settlement work, the lack of appreciation of special paid assistance and the idea of getting along with volunteer service exclusively is responsible for the physical breakdown of many a social worker and for the unavoidable failure, producing friction and unpleasantness in the relations of a social worker and his Board. The social worker who fails to recognize, however, the rights of the members of the Boards, who fails to appreciate the importance of the views of a large number of contributors to his cause, and who ignores public opinion, is partly responsible himself if he does not find satisfactory relations between himself and his organization.

K. Attitude Towards the Board of Managers

A social worker must never forget that the Board of Managers are supposed to be the choice of the public. They are the trustees of public funds; they are instrumental in making ample provision for the material support of different activities, and are responsible for the entire workings of the organization. They are the controlling media, and it is their duty and privilege to examine and approve or disapprove his actions. They are entitled to know all the details of the different transactions, and must be put in position to watch results. The social worker who succeeds in being left alone, be it because the members of the Board are indifferent to their duty or are too busy with their own affairs, or because they have full confidence in him and do not want to interfere with his prerogative, may find himself in a predicament when he awakens to the fact that his Board did not keep pace with the progress made, and is unable to give him the co-operation which he may want. The same is true with the worker who is attempting to keep his Board in ignorance of the true status of the situation, who misrepresents reality and substitutes it with results pleasing to the Board. While different Boards are partly responsible for this situation by encouraging social workers to report nothing but what they want reported, still social workers are to be blamed considerably for such deceitful practice towards their organization. This tendency is especially evident in the official statements, and even in the statistical data given by different organizations. Everything is calculated to produce the impression of a perfect situation, and no allowance is made for weak and negative features that are met with in almost every department of social service. In fact, it is hard to say what would happen to a social worker if he should dare to bring before the public his doubts as to the real merits of the work in which he is engaged. It is no wonder that often the social worker is too ambitious in his actions and still more in his utterances as a result of which he gets in more trouble than if he would do otherwise.

The Board is responsible for the social worker, and consequently has the right to employ or discharge him. It is a misfortune to have a social worker who is a fixture, who keeps his office on the strength of his past achievements, or through some occult influence, or as a matter of charity. On the other hand, the social worker, not merely by virtue of his office, but through efficiency, should assert himself as a leader, and under no conditions be willing to serve as a slave acting against his convictions for fear of losing his position. The efficient social worker is not the one who does just exactly what the Board of Managers wants him to do, but the one who is instrumental in making the Board demand what he himself thinks ought to be done. All this is true, however, in a general way. In individual cases, the social worker, in his relations to the Board of Managers encounters innumerable difficulties. The Board, as a rule, is not a homogeneous body. Human beings differ, especially when they are members of a philanthropic organization. The position of a social worker is exceedingly difficult when his organization is divided into factions. These differences are hard to reconcile. Both parties, if there are only two, may be at fault; the entire animosity may be of a personal origin, or based upon petty ambitions and rivalries. The social worker is placed in the position of a politician,—he watches the market and observes each movement of the pendulum of social achievement of one part, or the fall of the other. Woe be to the social worker who is obliged to flatter, gossip, to lead intrigue, and to take advantages of the weaknesses of the individual members of the Board. The zeal with which the social worker tries to get on the good side of the Board makes him forget at times that the Board is, after all, only a part of the public, and that the contributors are also deserving of serious consideration. The favorite of the Board is not always the favorite of the public. His position may be quite secure for a time, but he is liable to get into some difficulty, and with no co-operation on the part of the community at large, will have to stand on his own merits, independent of what the Board may think of him. In settlement work especially, the opinion of the large corps of volunteer workers and so-called sympathizers requires careful handling. Here, as everywhere else, tact and patience are necessary. A little politeness is always in place. A certain duty devolves upon the social worker in regard to the supporters and contributors, as the work depends upon their interest. It is therefore very important that he should do all that he possibly can to acquaint the public with the manifold activities, their workings, and should excite sympathy, enthusiasm and belief, not only in the methods but in the people, for whose benefit the institutions exist.

The tendency on the part of the charity worker to emphasize the faults of the poor, to speak of their deceitful natures, of their depravity, and of their dire ingratitude is wrong means to get the proper co-operation from the organization. An organization based upon hatred and distrust of the people who are its beneficiaries, even if thoroughly organized, does not deserve the name of charity. The charity worker who considers every applicant as a thief and liar is unable to do justice even to the deserving individual. The charity worker who thinks that his sole duty is to protect the community from impostors, is laboring under a false conception of true charity. With him the problem seems to be "how to refuse," not "how to help." The Board of Managers may be curious to know the peculiar and at times, very morbid experiences with the undeserving poor. This is a weakness similar to the love for detective stories, but this will never serve the cause of charity. The social worker should use all possible opportunities to present the true condition under which "the other half" lives, and explain the causes of poverty that are beyond the control of the individual. He should endeavor to get the sympathy for the suffering and excite the desire to be helpful to the unfortunate; he should cite examples of definite results achieved through adequate relief and, in general, act as an enthusiastic advocate in behalf of the poor. In doing so he may encounter a good deal of opposition and criticism, but as long as there is no question as to his sincerity, he is bound to achieve his purpose.

In institutional work the most dangerous tendency is the method of showing off through exhibitions, receptions, etc., during which the social worker is compelled to follow the accepted customs, notwithstanding the wrong involved. For weeks and months, the orphans go through exercises and prepared programs for the entertainment of the patrons. The visit of the Board of Managers to the institution is the cause of an enforced, unnecessary discipline, recompensed, sometimes, by an extra allowance in the diet of the inmates. It is seldom that the institution can be shown to the directors in its usual everyday routine.

In settlement work, the directors are treated by the social workers to affairs that can be shown off in numbers, for which the real, good work is sacrificed. Activities are instituted, not because of a real demand that they meet, but because some particular director may have this hobby that the social worker has to put into operation. In other words, the social worker, in every department, deems it his duty to sacrifice his own personal views to the views of his superiors, and this, carried to an extreme, makes the social worker a tool of others instead of an independent leader.

L. THE ATTITUDE OF THE SOCIAL WORKER TO THE COMMUNITY

This brings us to the final and most important consideration,—that is the relation between the social worker and the beneficiaries, the applicants for charity, the inmates of the institution, and the constituency of the settlements. The idea that a social worker is always misjudged by the people among whom he is working is a most dangerous point of view. Many a Board doubts the efficiency of its workers because the latter are on too intimate terms with their charges. Often the hatred shown to the social worker is taken as an indication of his wonderful achievements. No matter how important it is to get friendly relations from the Board of Managers and the large list of contributors, the social worker must never forget that his mission is among the poor and the needy, the ignorant and the lowly, those that need his assistance, his just and kind attitude.

In relief work, the social worker must never forget that he is a paid agent, that he is placed for the purpose of ameliorating the conditions of the poor, that he is called upon primarily to serve the needy, and should never permit himself to play the rôle of a benefactor; he must give a chance to every applicant to explain to him fully his needs and desires; he must never shirk his responsibility and avoid meeting an applicant whom he cannot or does not want to help. In granting assistance or refusing to do anything for an applicant, he should act in a business capacity. His personal likes and dislikes should find no place in the matter of distributing relief. All applicants should be treated with courtesy, friendliness and sincerity. Kind and forgiving, the social worker should, however, be definite in his actions, decisive and straightforward. Nothing annoys the poor more than the double-faced policy; the social worker need not rehearse a smiling countenance in a mirror. The poor will not believe him, nor will it be of any purpose to put on a mask of dignity, unnecessary sagacity, or stern character. The poor are not easily deceived. The social worker who is really interested in the welfare of his beneficiaries, the social worker who gives thought to each and every case with a view to doing the very best, the social worker who knows what is needed by the community and is frank and fearless in putting his ideas into practice, the social worker who sympathizes with the suffering and never goes back on his promises will have no trouble in adjusting his relations with the people for whom he works.

CHAPTER SEVENTEEN. ORGANIZATION AND ADMINISTRATION

QUESTIONS

1. Discuss the different methods of selecting leaders.
2. What is the new tendency in the administration of social service organizations?
3. What is meant by persistency in office, and what are its negative features?
4. Enumerate the qualifications of a proper social service leader.
5. What are the functions of the Board of Directors of an organization?
6. Describe the different methods of selecting paid workers.
7. Describe the difficulties of a paid worker in a new position.
8. State the reasons for friction of the social worker and his Board and discuss the proper attitude of the social worker.
9. Discuss the proper attitude of the social worker to the constituency which he serves.

XVIII

VOLUNTEER SERVICE

In the beginning of Jewish social service, the work was done exclusively by volunteers, but even later, when paid workers were put in the field, volunteers still remained active adjuncts of the different organizations. In connection with religious work, ladies, formed in committees, visited the dependent families, made investigations, administered aid, gave personal service and planned for rehabilitation. Under these circumstances, no uniformity could be expected; all depended upon the personality of the so-called "Lady Visitor." Some cases were neglected; responsibility was shirked; there was no way to demand definite service. Again, some cases would receive undue consideration. And indiscriminate relief, with all its negative attributes, played havoc with many a family. Blessed and thanked when ample relief was given, the lady visitor was cursed and despised as soon as she withdrew her further generosity, and the poor showed considerable hatred to the lady visitors, who became a bugaboo in the poor neighborhoods.

A. Friendly Visitors as Adjuncts of Relief Societies

In the light of this rather unpleasant experience, considerable change has been introduced in the functions of lady visitors. While ladies were still retained as volunteer agents of relief societies,—now only as investigators,—the function of relief giving was taken away from them. They were to advise the poor,—to find out actual condition. But it was up to the relief society to decide upon the amount of relief to be given, and the administration of the latter was placed in the hands of a paid agent. While this arrangement was to a certain extent an improvement upon the former, inasmuch as there was now a possibility of introducing a more or less uniform scale of relief and inasmuch as the ladies were relieved of unpleasant duties involved in refusing such relief, still the poor continued to look upon the lady visitors as agents of the relief societies, objected to their interference, blamed them for cutting off allowances, and in general considered them spies and detectives,—enemies rather than friends.

Nor were the lady visitors a pleasant arrangement for the paid staff of the relief agency. The friendly visitors could not help expressing their views as to the needs of their families, their requests were frequently unreasonable, nor could their demands be easily ignored, for this led, as a rule, to the loss of their co-operation and financial support.

In Jewish work particularly, the lady visitors often waged war against organized, well-planned effort, often seceded from the organization and tried to give from their personal purses where the relief societies refused to grant allowances. The abolition of the lady visitors altogether as a social service group, as was tried in some individual cities, did not prove a wise step. While the lady visitors were responsible for a number of difficulties in handling the relief problem, still there was another side to the issue. The lady visitors were the only remaining link between the poor and the rich. They interpreted to the wealthy how the other half lived. In some instances they performed good personal service, and were instrumental in keeping the relief agency from becoming a purely mechanical organization. A change, however, in the very functions of this available force was necessary.

B. Modern Conceptions of Lady Visitors

Miss Minnie Low of Chicago was probably the first in Jewish circles to realize the possibility of utilizing the good services of the lady visitors in making them an agency of more personal service, not only as an adjunct of the relief agency, but in a broader sense, covering every phase of social service as applied to a given individual family. Her address on Friendly Visiting, presented before the first Conference of Jewish Charities in Chicago, 1900, was a masterpiece, and has given a new direction to the efforts of lady visitors, whom she designated as "Friendly Visitors."

The friendly visitor now is primarily concerned with the welfare of a given family. She assumes a neighborly attitude,—the attitude of a sister, a friend; she is here now to help and not to command, to assist and not to criticize, to learn and not to betray; she wants the poor family to go ahead, she does not expect thanks nor gratitude; she makes no show of misery; she forgives; she encourages; she sympathizes and helps wherever she can with no other motive than an expression of her love for humanity. It is evident that this conception of a friendly visitor does not necessarily imply direct connection with a relief agency. In Chicago it resulted in the formation of what is known as the Personal Service Bureau, which, since its organization in the city, extended its activities in different directions and wielded influence over almost every effort in the field of Jewish philanthropy.

No matter how noble and deep the motive of personal service may be, with the complexity of modern life a definite plan of action is necessary to avoid the negative results that may accrue from inexperienced interference with the needs of the poor on the part of persons who may be well meaning and still at a loss as to what is best under given circumstances.

The number of persons desiring to serve the community is growing. This is a hopeful sign of to-day. This awakening must be properly directed, and the friendly visitor is one of those functions that require definite direction.

It makes little difference what is the source of contact of the friendly visitor; it may be a relief society, juvenile court, settlement, or just a private meeting. The person intending to help the given family must be careful to gain its friendship. It must be acquired along democratic lines. The family must feel that there is no ulterior motive, that it is love and interest in the family that counts. A person that sees no bright attractive sides to the family cannot be an effective factor, she lacks the capacity of a friendly visitor. Pity alone will not do.

C. THE PROBLEMS OF FRIENDLY VISITING

Now, in what way can a friendly visitor render service? Because of advantages of economic conditions, education, etc., the friendly visitor ought to be able to orient herself in the circumstances of the family and find a way out of the difficulty much better than the family could itself. It is therefore important that the friendly visitor place herself in the position of the family, and try to answer the question: what would she have done in their position? Detailed and careful consideration will help the friendly visitor to meet the different phases of the problem, and prepare her for efficient advice and co-operation. The following is an outline of inquiry which is suggested as a helpful guide to the thoughtful visitor.

1. *The Health of the Poor*

The health of the poor is their greatest asset. The problem, therefore, can be summarized in the attitude of the friendly visitor. How would she, put in the position of the family and with no other resources than it possesses preserve the health of its members? She will ascertain, therefore, the exact state of health of each member of the family. In case of some illness or physical deficiency, she will endeavor to obtain the earliest diagnosis and procure the best medical treatment. She will endeavor to eliminate the causes of preventable disease. She will pay special attention to those members of the family who are handicapped. She will be sure to avoid the different home cures. She will not listen to the advice given by ignorant neighbors. She certainly will not use patent medicines. She will guard against contagious diseases, and she will utilize the private doctor, nurse, and hospital only when she is certain that she gets the proper services. She will make it her business to know what free agencies she can apply to. She will know what she can expect from the district physician, the clinic, and the hospital. She will not miss the agencies that provide treatment for convalescents, and will avail herself of the Fresh Air Treatment offered to the needy. In other words, she will intelligently survey the situation and intelligently cope with it.

2. *Infant Welfare*

If there is a baby in the family, the friendly visitor will put herself in the place of the mother. She will get all the necessary information as to the care of the baby and will share it with the mother. She will undoubtedly see that the mother gets efficient obstetrical assistance; she will take care that the mother conserves her strength so that when the baby does arrive, she will be able to nurse it. She will arrange for proper sanitation and feeding and will make sure that the baby gets prompt and proper medical attendance when it needs it. She therefore will acquaint herself with the literature intended for mothers; she will get into contact with the proper obstetrician; she will avoid the ignorant midwife; she will know how to utilize the Infant Welfare Stations; she will apply to the proper authorities for maternity help; she will get into contact with the Visiting Nurse Association, etc.

3. *Protection of the Health of the Children of the Poor*

The friendly visitor will apply herself to the task of protecting the health of the children of the family, just as if she were a part of it. She will learn of the School Medical Inspections and be interested in the findings of the physician. She will pay attention to the physical defects detected; she will watch out for contagious diseases. She will give her time and effort to the problem of providing the children with proper food, clothing, housing and sanitation; she will see that the children get physical exercise, play, and fresh air.

4. *Tuberculosis, the Scourge of the Poor*

If the friendly visitor happens to minister to a family where tuberculosis is doing its deadly work, she will put herself in the position of the family; she will get a definite, early diagnosis; she will encourage and help the patient to bear his fate; she will get and utilize sanitarium treatment; she will give the patient a chance to learn what is necessary for a victim of tuberculosis to know. She will not forget after-care, and will attend to the process of rehabilitation. She will take precautions for the safety of the rest of the family. She will get a medical examination of each member. She will promote the education that is required in such cases. She will utilize all possible preventive forces.

5. *Indiscriminate Charity*

Indiscriminate charity spells demoralization and leads to pauperism. It stands to reason that the friendly visitor, assuming the part of the family, will endeavor to avoid charity interference. She will ascertain the income of the family. She will find the minimum standard on which the family can live. She will exhaust all possibilities trying to increase its income, and if she finds that the minimum standard is not attained, then, and only then, will she apply for assistance to a philanthropic agency. Under these circumstances, there ought not to be any difficulty in getting proper assistance; there will be no demoralization, and the stigma of charity will be reduced to a minimum.

6. *Proper Housing*

The friendly visitor will realize the importance of proper housing facilities. She will determine the minimum amount of rent that the family can afford to pay. She will demand the conditions that are guaranteed by the existing laws; she will select the location; she will demand that the house be safe as far as fire protection is concerned; she will pay attention to its sanitary appointments. She will make an effort for proper cleaning. When the rooms are already rented, she will arrange proper sleeping facilities and the proper use of the rooms in the daytime. She will try to find proper places for the furniture, kitchen utensils, as well as work out the different details of everyday routine life, coping with conditions as they are.

7. *Sufficient Feeding, an Index to Normal Life*

The friendly visitor will not neglect the proper feeding of the family. She will undoubtedly keep a record of food expenses. She will determine the minimum necessary. She will try to improve the diet, all this as she would have done if she were in the position of the family. Her intelligent study of the situation, her interest and her actual help in solving the perplexing problem will in time succeed in securing the sympathetic appreciation and co-operation on the part of the family itself. This is especially true in regard to food values.

8. *Apportionment of Work Day*

Proper use of time and energy is an everyday asset in the life of the poor. It is undoubtedly a difficult problem for the poor to find sufficient time to attend to the different tasks that must be accomplished from day to day. The friendly visitor will acquaint herself with the entire field. She will know how much and what is to be done. She will make an inventory of the different tasks and the time they require. Then she will try to assign each task to a certain time; she will utilize definitely the help of all the members of the family, she will work out a definite program of routine work, and make housekeeping a pleasant occupation instead of drudgery.

9. *Proper Clothing*

Proper clothing gives courage to the poor. Probably no subject requires more attention than this; it is difficult to limit the amounts required for proper apparel. There are so many conditions, actual needs, conventions, seasons, and what not, that must be taken into account. The friendly visitor will help in studying the solution; she will determine what is the minimum to be allowed; she will provide for proper buying; she will avoid the custom of buying on the installment plan; she will see that the family is properly dressed on all occasions,—during work and on holidays. She will avoid waste, but provide for comfort as well as appearance. Here, more than anywhere else it is important that the friendly visitor should put herself in the position of the family, for the social standing of a particular group makes certain demands upon it that cannot be neglected.

10. *The Career of the Children of the Poor*

The potential career of the children is the hope of the poor. There is undoubtedly great difference in the possible development of individuals. Not everybody is endowed with equal capacities. But the success of the children of the poor is frequently hampered by environment. They are not protected by the material and social wealth of their parents; the struggle is hard, and depends upon a thousand and one factors over which they have no control. How will the lady visitor utilize opportunities for the best possible development of the children of the given family? She will definitely ascertain their natural abilities, she will give them the best chance for their education, adapting the latter to their particular need; she will watch their progress in the schools; she will remain in close contact with the teachers; she will follow their standing and help them in their difficulties. As in the question of their health, she will consult experts when the problem becomes complicated. If they display exceptional abilities or talents, she will not let them remain dormant. She will watch their moral atmosphere; she will know their friends, their conduct and their ideals. She will not neglect their religious training; she will endeavor to strengthen their attachment to their homes, their love of their parents, friends, all humanity. When the time comes for them to leave school and start their earning career, she will try to place them so that they can advance in their vocations, and not remain wanderers in the blind alleys of our modern industry. She will know their employers, and the kind of employment they are engaged in. And because of her sincere, kindly and intelligent interest, the children will learn to love her and look upon her as their big sister, will come to her for advice, and for the encouragement so much wanted in the life of the young generation among the poor.

11. *The Struggle for Existence*

The struggle for existence saps the vitality of the poor. The poor depend upon their own ability to earn a living. The Jewish poor, especially, because of lack of preparation, or ignorance of new industrial conditions to which they are not yet adapted, or because they frequently lack knowledge of English, must struggle hard and incessantly before they are able to gain a footing and earn even a modest wage. The friendly visitor should be able to contribute to the solution of this particular problem. She will know the existing opportunities for the application of labor. She ought to be able to make necessary connections between the employer and employé. She will analyze advantages and disadvantages of a given occupation, she will utilize her friendship and intelligence in securing proper employment; she will be able to encourage the breadwinner and put him in a position to increase his efficiency and earning capacity.

12. *Recreation and Amusement*

The power of recreation and amusement lessens the unbearable strain of stern reality. It is hardly necessary to emphasize the importance of recreation in the case of the dreary life of the poor. The question that confronts the friendly visitor, is how would she, under the circumstances, provide for this particular need. She would undoubtedly draw upon home resources first. She would utilize the home talent for dancing, music, and home gatherings; she would miss no opportunity to celebrate a holiday, a bright spot in a poor man's life. Then the synagogue, especially in the case of the man, could be of great service, and she would encourage the man in his active participation in synagogue activities. She would also see that the social side of different organizations, lodges, mutual aid societies, and so on, should be taken advantage of for recreational facilities.

She will take care of the nets spread by commercialized amusement enterprizes. She will protect the members of the family from the saloon, pool room, dance hall, and candy store. She will know also to what extent the families patronize moving pictures and the Jewish theaters of the neighborhood. She will utilize all possible agencies offering wholesome amusement such as the settlements and social centers. In short, she will give serious consideration to the subject of recreation.

Such are, in general, the different possibilities of useful application of the work of the friendly visitors. A pretentious program, it will require not only the motive for doing good and a sympathetic attitude, but intelligent working out, continuous effort, energy, and persistence. The time has passed when any kindly disposed lady in comfortable circumstances could impose herself upon the poor as their adviser.

Miss Minnie Low said: "A woman who would not willingly send a dress to an unskilled dressmaker for fear that a piece of cloth might be ruined, goes without hesitancy, without any idea how to treat a case of poverty, and by her philanthropic intentions, often jeopardizes the future of an entire family. No one ought to be encouraged to force herself on the poor in a personal way unless she is in training and under the guidance of a professional worker." [1]

D. VOLUNTEER SETTLEMENT WORKERS

This term implies men and women volunteering their services in connection with settlement work in the activities of different clubs and classes, where the work deals with a collective group rather than with the individual. The idea of volunteer service in connection with settlement work seems to be one of the first principles of this modern idea of personal service. The subject, however, referring to the qualifications of the volunteers, is of the greatest importance. That the rich should share with the poor, that the educated should instruct the ignorant, that the volunteers should serve as examples to the wicked, are primary concepts of social service. In settlement work, however, this adjustment is often ignored, and almost purposely violated. Settlement workers, as a rule, take for granted that anyone not coming from the neglected neighborhood can contribute his services to the neglected neighborhood. For Jews, this is quite a new departure.

In the past, even as near as a generation or two ago, the rich, while giving generously to the poor, never expected to teach them. On the contrary, the poor

[1] "Friendly Visitors." National Conference of Jewish Charities, Miss Minnie Low, Chicago, 1900.

"schnorrer" was supposed to pay for the worldly goods he received by a contribution of knowledge and the teaching of moral lessons. The "schnorrer" was brought into the home of his benefactor, was given an honorary place at the table, and after the meal was over, delivered his oration (Droshe) for the good of the host and hostess and especially for the benefit of the children. While enjoying comfort and appreciating their economic supremacy, the rich never failed to pay honor to the learned and the virtuous, though poor and needy. Conditions have changed; the poor of to-day, because they are poor, and especially because they have lived in a neglected neighborhood, are considered to be in need, not only of material assistance, but of education and moral training, and the so-called better half of society takes upon itself to provide them with all their needs, forgetting that only yesterday, the part they played was quite different from the one they now undertake. Consequently, they may not be altogether prepared, or fit to fulfill it properly. Thus the selection of volunteers in settlement work becomes a delicate matter. The fact that a person happens to be in possession of money does not qualify him or her for settlement work; the desire to do personal service is commendable; the motive of this service could be easily overlooked; but efficiency and positive quality must determine the eligibility for entering settlement work. The following tests may be suggested in determining the merits of a candidate for settlement, personal service:

1. What particular subject can the person teach the neighborhood which will benefit the latter?

2. What is there in the character of the person in question that the neighborhood should take for an example?

3. Is the person willing to recognize the necessity of his or her own improvement, and is he or she willing to learn and accept influences from contact with the neglected neighborhood?

4. Can the person appreciate the strong and healthy features existing in the neglected neighborhood alongside of the faults and shortcomings?

These are the fundamental conditions of a settlement worker; next comes the selection of the proper field of activity. It is rather a waste of energy to place a musician to teach bookkeeping, an athlete to instruct domestic science, a person interested in law to conduct public dances. Still, this is the arrangement in almost every settlement, and the results are very discouraging. There are some persons who can be usefully applied to almost every activity of the settlement, but these are exceptions, and cannot be taken as examples of the average settlement worker.

E. THE BIG BROTHERS AND BIG SISTERS MOVEMENT

The Big Brothers and Big Sisters organizations have recently entered this field. The Jewish Big Brothers Association in New York was organized in 1910, and now numbers about two hundred active members. The method, which is adopted with a fair measure of success, consists in having each youngster, who shows a tendency to commit crime, approached by a Big Brother, whose example, experience, and guidance will enable the boy to regain his normal place in the family and in the community in which he lives. The organization has representatives at the courts, and in many cases succeeds in getting cases settled without a court trial. This is the function of the special department, known as the Bureau of Prevention, Investigation, and Advice. Incidentally, the organization provides employment for its charges, temporary shelter to those who need it, recreation and vacation in summer camps, and other services.

The Cincinnati Jewish Big Brothers Association, established in 1911, reports a membership of about four hundred. In the beginning the work was carried on exclusively with boys who were brought before the juvenile court and were placed on probation. It was only a matter of a short time, before it was realized that the so-called bad boy was not the only one who needed a Big Brother, and an effort was made to give as many boys as possible an opportunity to develop under the influence of a Big Brother. The organization now emphasises the fact that it is not an association of probation officers, that it does not deal exclusively with bad boys, that it does not claim the infallible reclamation of a boy who is on the wrong path, but that it is an organization which endeavors through close contact with boys in a congested district to prevent delinquency, and to save them from influences for evil that are so potent in the neglected neighborhood.[1] In its further growth, however, the

[1] "Jewish Charities," February, 1915.

Big Brothers and Big Sisters are extending their activities, selecting their charges from among the inhabitants of the congested districts. While these organizations have been in existence for only a few years, the results already achieved in the prevention of juvenile delinquency are quite telling.

F. EDUCATION OF JEWISH SOCIAL WORKERS

As early as 1890, scholarships were offered to college graduates who desired to receive training in Jewish social service, and while five young men availed themselves of the opportunity, only two of them followed this vocation. Here and there attempts were made to organize courses on Jewish social service in different cities. Thus in Baltimore, a course of this kind was given in connection with the Federation of Jewish Charities, and in Chicago, in connection with the Hebrew Institute. In 1913, Cincinnati established a school of Jewish Social Service and announced quite a comprehensive program of theoretical and practical instruction. This school was under the auspices of the Jewish Settlement of that city. While it attracted a number of students, residents of Cincinnati, there seemed to be difficulty in getting students from out of town. In 1915, the Jewish Chautauqua Society, in co-operation with the National Association of Jewish Social Workers opened a summer school in New York city for Jewish social workers, and in 1916, a separate organization established what is known as the School for Jewish Communal Workers, under the leadership of Dr. S. Benderly. This school is to follow a very ambitious program and comprises a four years' course, for which credit is given in Columbia University. Thus the long felt want for the proper education of Jewish social workers has been satisfied, at least to the extent that there is already a special institution of learning in this particular line.

CHAPTER EIGHTEEN. VOLUNTEER SERVICE

QUESTIONS

1. Give the history of friendly visiting.
2. What is the modern conception of friendly visiting?
3. Outline a definite program in regard to the work of friendly visiting.
4. What are the necessary qualifications of volunteer settlement workers?
5. Describe the Big Sisters and Big Brothers Movements.

XIX

ADMINISTRATION

A. Budget Making

It is self-evident that the maintenance of an organization, the raising of funds and their proper disposition, form an important item in the routine of an institution, and require serious consideration. Efficient management demands a definite plan and a program of all activities. An organization must know, approximately, the amount of revenue it can expect from resources on hand, at least for the immediate future. It must arrange its activities so as to correspond with the funds available. It has to determine more or less exactly what kind and the extent of the activities it will pursue, hence, the necessity of proper budget making. The proposed budget is an estimate of proposed expenses, based upon past experience. It presupposes the definite knowledge of the actual expenses for the period preceding the one for which the budget is made. These expenses are usually thoroughly scrutinized, possible economies are suggested, and additional appropriations made when necessary. Frequently, in making out budgets, comparisons are drawn with the expenses of similar institutions. Unfortunately, there is very little uniformity in the accounting of the different organizations, and proper comparison is almost impossible. It

is, therefore, important that close attention be paid to proper accounting, and that an attempt be made to introduce uniformity in this respect among the different organizations. It is suggested that a proper budget should include at least the following main divisions:
1. Personal services.
2. Services other than personal.
3. Material relief and maintenance.

Personal service deals with the expense of administration, and includes salaries. The public is exceedingly interested in what proportion of the funds raised for an organization is spent in salaries for administration. It also wishes to know what other expenses besides salaries are to be deducted from the sums given to the organization before the share that the beneficiaries get directly is ascertained. This includes services other than personal, the maintenance of buildings, office expenses, supplies, etc.; last comes the material relief and maintenance, indicating the exact amount that goes directly to the beneficiaries. In Jewish philanthropic efforts especially, it is quite usual to meet a situation where the actual expense is in excess of the income, thus causing a deficit. The latter is usually made up by a special, strenuous campaign for added funds.

B. Analysis of Budgets

It is legitimate to ask how much is spent for the collection of funds. The Jews in this respect can show considerable economy as compared with other agencies. However, some of our national institutions where the employment of traveling agents becomes a necessity, pay sometimes as high as thirty-three to forty per cent for their collections. On the other hand, in large federated organizations, to which most of their income comes unsolicited, such expenses are reduced to as low as one and a half to two and a half per cent of the amount collected.

Generally speaking, from six to ten per cent is a happy medium. In the question of relief distribution, twelve and a half per cent seems to be the amount generally spent for administration, while in child caring and other institutions, the cost of administration is usually fifty per cent; in educational agencies it reaches seventy-five per cent and more. It is evident that much depends upon the character of the work. The public, however, makes little distinction, and often institutions, which from the very nature of their work require large administrative expenses, receive undeserved criticism. It must be remembered that reduced expense is not the criterion of efficiency of an agency. One thing, however, is certain, each organization should be able to give to the public a definite statement as to its actual expenses that will show the exact distribution of funds in regard to the three headings stated before. Then, a per capita allowance can be easily calculated and be taken as a unit of comparison for different organizations. Under the present indefinite accounting, such comparative accounting is impossible. Besides a budget of expenses, a program of activities should be definitely arranged. This is especially important in connection with educational and social activities, where plans require preliminary arrangement, and should not be left to the last minute for adjustment. Usually these programs are arranged for a season in advance. Each organization finds it necessary to issue periodic statements as to its activities, comprising not only a description of its work, but actual figures as to its financial transactions, attendance, cost per capita, quantity of work performed, etc. As the compilation of this data becomes quite a task, a system of recording daily transactions should be introduced in such a way that these public statements can be easily made without any special calculations. In this case, as well as in accounting, a plea should be made for uniformity of work.

Considerable misunderstandings frequently take place in the management of the different social service agencies because of a lack of a definite interpretation of the interrelation of the different factors composing the administration. It is very important, therefore, to define clearly the entire scheme of organization, and to ascertain the relationship of the different constituent parts. This is best obtained through a graphic representation of the different agencies, indicating also the functions and actual relationships. A chart of this kind should show the source of authority, the functions that are vested in the different centers, the connections and interrelations of the different groups of activities, and as a whole, should present the complete picture of the entire organization. The following is a sample of an organization chart of the United Jewish Charities of

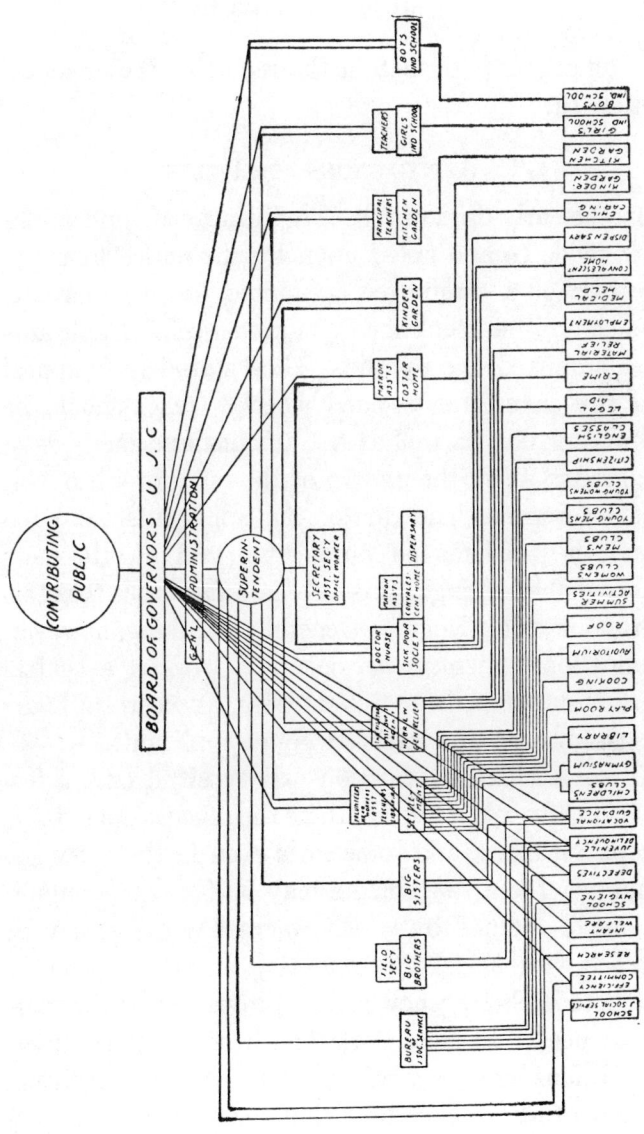

Plate I

Cincinnati, as published in the report of the organization in 1916.

C. Applications for Relief

In the early days of relief organizations, applications were made to and acted upon by the entire Board of Trustees or a committee appointed for this purpose. The committee met once or more a week. Applicants were admitted one by one. They stated their appeal and the committee decided whether relief should be granted or not, as well as the amount and methods of the grant. With the growth of the relief problem, this method became inadequate; the applicants were too many, the problems too complicated, and the interviews rather embarrassing. It is only in a few cities that this method is still in vogue. Generally speaking, however, applications are made to one paid worker, a central office is designated for this purpose, and certain hours are assigned for the interviewing of applicants.

In some cities, applications are received only a few days in the week, while in others the office is open daily, except Saturday, and sometimes even in the evenings. Whatever the arrangements may be for regular applications, a method by which emergency cases may be handled without delay is necessary, and every properly conducted relief agency makes provision for this particular need. In New York, and in many other cities, applications are received by mail and by telephone; while in others it is required that the head of the family make application in person. There can be no doubt that personal applications save at times effort on the part of the organization, but on the other hand, they spell hardship to many an applicant, and are liable to produce rather an unwholesome atmosphere around the office, create congestion and a consequent rush in handling cases. From this standpoint, applications in writing are more advisable. The reception of applicants for relief is arranged differently in different cities. In some it is very formal, almost institutional, in others it is homelike, and often without any special provisions.

D. ADMINISTRATION FACILITIES

Experience suggests that certain accommodations should be provided. The reception room for applicants should be a large, light, well-ventilated room; it should have ample sitting capacity, chairs rather than benches, and should be furnished in a simple but cheerful way. A few pictures, a table, a few odd chairs, some periodicals, make it more attractive than long wooden benches and a row of files and closets. Wherever possible, a classification of the applicants should be made, and two or more rooms be given over as reception rooms. The applications should be made privately, in a separate room, where the applicant and the interviewer may talk over the proposition without being disturbed or overheard by outsiders. The room where the interview is taking place does not need to be too large, but it should not remind one of a cell. It should be cozily furnished, and outside of the desk, record case and a few chairs, should also include a few pictures, books, and so on, to make the room comfortable. The interview room, in addition to an entrance from the reception room, should have an exit door, from which the applicant may leave the building after the interview is over without being compelled to pass the reception room again and come in contact with the applicants awaiting their turn. Another door leading to the office is quite an accommodation, for whatever the interviewer wishes to communicate to the office, he may do it without

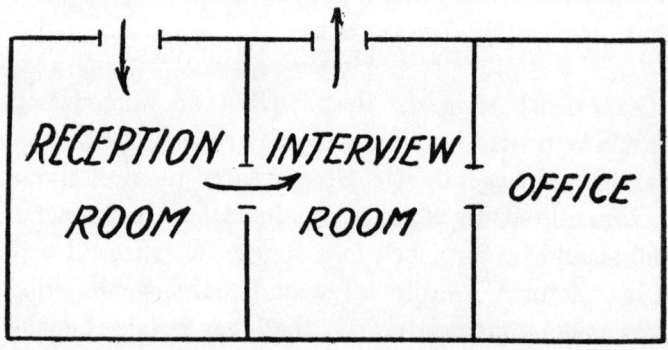

passing into the reception room. The above diagram illustrates the arrangement of rooms required by efficiently conducted relief societies.

Naturally, the plan permits of many modifications, but it indicates the main requirements of comfortable quarters and privacy.

E. Interviewing the Applicant

Efforts should be made to avoid unnecessary waiting on the part of the applicant, so often complained of in different cities. When the numbers are great, applicants should be taken in rotation. In some instances women should be given the preference. Too formal a treatment of the applicant in the reception room should also be avoided. As a rule, if the reception room is properly fitted out, the applicants need very little supervision.

The interviewer, as all charity workers, should be a person of tact and of even temperament. The applicant should be given an opportunity to present his case, and the interview should be conducted in a low voice. The facts, as presented, should be immediately put in writing, and outside of emergency relief, no final action should be taken until proper and thorough investigation is made. The interviewer must avoid verbosity, but should rather devote his attention to obtaining the setting of the application and all the information that may be needed. The interview of the applicant may lead to granting relief, refusing relief, deferring action until investigation is made, or referring the application to another agency.

1. *Granting Relief*

In granting relief in the office, it is usually arranged that the applicant sign a receipt of the relief given by check. The transaction should be referred to the office. He may also be given an order, either for food supplies or for other commodities. In all these instances, the granting of relief in the homes of the applicant by the visitor, is preferable to that given in the office. In some cities, almost the entire relief is given by the visitor at the home of the needy, and even regular recipients of charity receive their allowances in their own homes. In large cities like New York and Chicago, the one who receives the application in the office, is not in a position to handle the case as a whole, and the investigation is usually referred to special investigators or visitors. In small communities, the application is received and acted upon, as well as investigated, by the same person.

Whatever the method may be, an effort must be made to make repeated personal applications at the office unnecessary, and if the visit to the home becomes too difficult, the recipient should be given an opportunity to get the granted allowance without extra burden and without the unnecessary delay of the waiting room. Thus, in some cities, a specified time is designated for the regular recipients of relief. When relief is given in kind, be it food or clothing, a separate department should be conducted for this purpose in which are given out things from the office directly. If the relief is given, however, in groceries or stores, this should be handled simultaneously with the cash disbursement.

2. *Refusal to Grant Relief*

In case the result of an interview with an applicant is the refusal of relief, the situation becomes more difficult to handle. The refusal should be based upon definite reasons, and the attitude of the organization should be explained to the applicant as fully as possible. Argument, however, should be avoided, and the interviewer should be careful in showing the applicant that he or she is acting only as an agent of the organization, and consequently is compelled to act as the situation may require. The refusal of relief may be based upon many grounds. First, the applicant, as a non-resident, may not be entitled to relief from given organization; second, the applicant may be referred to another agency handling cases of this specific character; third, the applicant may be given an ultimatum requiring him to accept certain form of relief, without which the organization would refuse to handle the case; and lastly the applicant may be refused assistance because he may have other resources and can get along without charity interference. In the last case, investigation usually reveals discrepancies between the applicant's statement, and the real condition of affairs as reported by the investigator. Unreasonable demands on the part of the applicant are frequently trying to the interviewer, and here it is that the positive, definite, calm attitude of the social worker is of great importance. The same is true when relief granted is not adequate from the standpoint of the applicant, or when the form of relief granted does not meet his approval.

3. *Investigation*

Applications, either by mail or in person, are in themselves rarely sufficient to give enough data to decide upon the real merits of the case, or to justify the working out of a plan of action. Investigation therefore becomes necessary. The information obtained through the personal interview with the applicant is verified by investigation. A written report is made of the condition of the cases as they were found. This, in a general way, contains the name and address of the applicant, the family unit to which the applicant belongs, the length of time the applicant has been in this country, the length of his residence in the city, his age, nativity, occupation and earnings, and a statement of the immediate conditions leading up to the application. Certain clues are also investigated. The landlord, the storekeeper, the employer, the teacher, the neighbor, the society to which the applicant may belong, are usually utilized in getting necessary information, especially if they can throw light upon the condition of the family. The ability to use these clues to advantage, and the careful and tactful way in which this investigation is made is the criterion of the efficiency of the investigator. In making this investigation, great care should be taken not to injure the self-respect of the applicant and the family investigated, and to obtain information without hurting the applicant by making it public property. Because of the difficulty that proper investigation presents, this investigation should be made by a professional worker, and should not be entrusted, as is done in many cities, to volunteer, inexperienced persons, who often impose upon the private life of the applicant, assume the rôle of detective and are responsible for the enmity that exists between the recipients of charity and the agents of relief societies. While the personal impression of the investigator is of great moment in deciding the merit of the cases, great care should be taken in basing the conclusions of the investigation upon actual facts rather than subjective likes or dislikes.

After registering all the facts pertaining to the case, and formulating the application as well as the actual needs of the case, the course of action must be determined. In some cases, palliative relief is granted at once,—for that matter, sometimes even before the thorough examination,—but in the majority of cases this is only a temporary arrangement. Continuous relief is granted only in such cases where all other resources are exhausted. This should be ascertained through following up all the clues: Does the person possess any assets of his own? Is he entitled to allowances from societies and lodges to which he may belong? Are there any relatives who are capable of helping the family? Is there a way by which the income of the family may be augmented? Is the budget of the family reduced to the desired minimum? What organizations or agencies should be brought into play to work out the problem? What are the conditions that ought to be remedied and changed? All of these should be definitely ascertained, and a definite plan of action determined upon. Naturally, there, as in other plans in handling human factors, we find that the plans as previously arranged, are not always realized in practice. Necessity may dictate certain changes and modifications, but the handling of the case must indicate that a definite plan and method pursued by the agency exists. For this reason, repeated visits by the investigator may become necessary, not only for investigation, but also for advice, instruction, and supervision. Thus, in well-organized charities, the visiting nurse and the visiting housekeeper become an integral part of the organization.

F. Record Keeping

Without a definite system of records, it is difficult to keep track of the applicant, to know his standing, to recollect what has been previously granted, and a myriad of other necessary details. It will not do to trust to momentary impressions of memory experiences. Without a system of records, the efficient administration of relief to the needy, protection against fraud, is an utter impossibility. In addition to the aforesaid, the modern interpretation of adequate relief to the deserving, presupposes not only the giving of material assistance, but also the handling of the entire family group and the use of all possible agencies and resources for the rehabilitation of the individual applicant as well as the entire family unit of which he is a part. Hence, the necessity of a full account and a full description of the families handled by relief agencies. This leads to the introduction of the record system in relief work.

1. *The Record Book*

The primitive method was very simple—merely a book wherein each application, the judgment, and the disposition of the case were recorded. This entry usually dealt only with the applicant, seldom gave information of the composition of the family, and rarely presented sufficient data for continuous, logical, and constructive policy. Moreover, subsequent applications were recorded chronologically and, as a result, it was difficult to follow the development of a single case without referring to former entries. Frequently an index to the book was made, containing references to pages, on which were to be found references to a single case. Clumsy as this arrangement was it proved workable in small communities, where the number of cases was insignificant, and where the persons treating the case knew the details and remembered them intimately. It is impossible to use this system, however, where the field is extensive. Nor is this method of any value for future reference, when the material may be put to some practical or theoretical use.

2. *Individual Records*

Hence, at present, the system of individual case records is generally in vogue. The importance of case records has been sufficiently emphasized by non-Jewish agencies. Efforts have been made to introduce some uniformity in the records of the different organizations throughout the country. In the case of the Jewish relief agencies, certain minor particulars have to be observed.

and the usual records are modified in accordance with specific requirements. Items of great import, such as intemperance, illegitimacy, etc., are of little consequence in Jewish work. On the other hand, the record of previous residence, immigration, citizenship, and industrial efficiency should receive special attention in the Jewish relief record. Again, Jewish relief agencies usually handle the case as a unit continuously for a long period of years, as opposed to the non-Jewish agencies, which usually refer the case to an institution, and so treat most of their cases temporarily or at best for an exceedingly short period of time. These, in the main, are the primary reasons why Jewish relief agencies are using records adapted to their particular needs rather than using the forms devised by the Russell Sage Foundation for the use of non-Jewish agencies. Jewish relief records usually consist of an envelope or folder, on the face of which information is given for the identification of the case, and such other relevant data to which reference is frequently made. These consist of the name of the applicant, his address, the names of the other members of the family unit, social status, occupation, earnings, length of residence in the country and city, and so forth. Within the envelope are placed different cards and information pertaining to the records. The usual size is four by eight inches, although lately, a tendency has been noticed to make the folder large enough to contain letter size, running case records without a fold. To facilitate handling of records, it is necessary to have the information in some uniform system. Different arrangements are adopted by different organizations. The information desired is noted by titles and sub-titles, suggesting in this way to the person in charge what are the particular items to be inserted. It has been felt for some time that the records lack homogeneity, and in this connection, the following description of an existing record is given, which with some modifications could probably be adapted to other conditions.[1]

As Plate II indicates, the record consists of a folder, one side of which is shorter than the other, so that when the folder is closed, the rear side projects over the cover. On the top of the longer side, the first entry is made of the applicant. The first line of the longer side is divided into forty-three spaces—twelve devoted to the months, and the balance to the days. These spaces are used for an automatic ticket device; metallic flags of different colors—each color denoting some special purpose,—are attached to the certain day of the certain month when special attention must be given the record, such as the medical examination, collection of a loan, report from a friendly visitor, etc. The records are gone over daily, and those needing special attention are removed from the files and the matter attended to. Next, reference is made to the name, the address, the housing conditions, the length of stay in this country and in the city. The outside of the folder is arranged in such a way as to give an opportunity to record changes of residence, housing conditions, and rental.

[1] Form used in the city of Cincinnati, by the U. J. C.

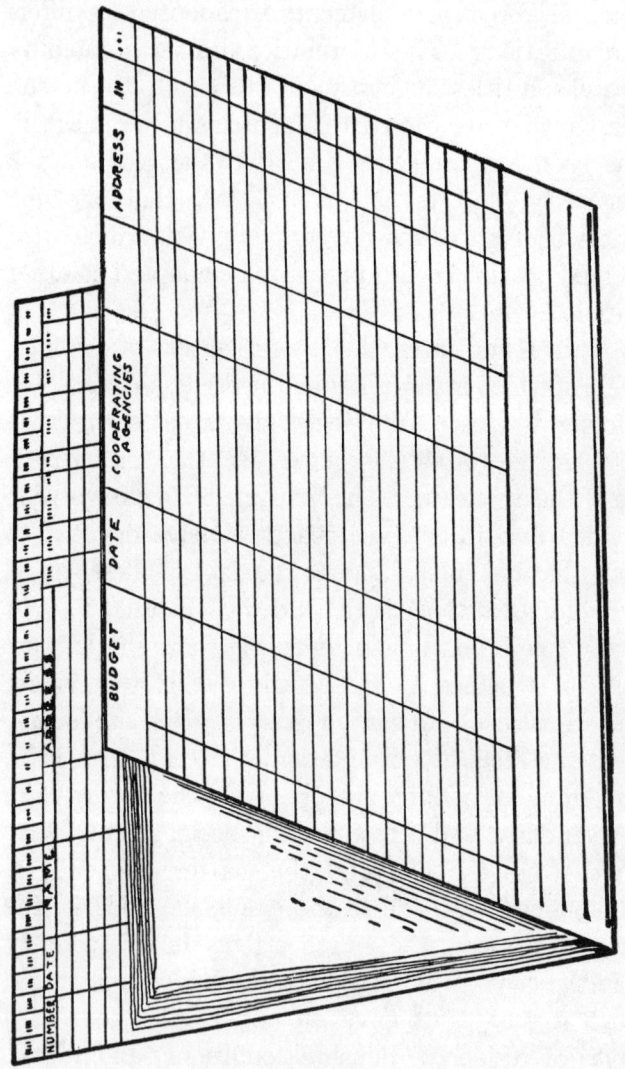

Plate II

Space is left to record the varying budget and income of the family, and also families and agencies interested in the case. The inside of the folder is divided into columns, one being assigned to each member of the family, where his earnings and employer, or his school and grade can be denoted as they change from time to time. On the back of the folder space is provided for a brief summary of the case at the close of the fiscal year. Within the folder, on a special white sheet, called the running case record, are entered the reports of the investigators, and the various entries in the handling of the case, showing the number of visits, interviews, etc. A special sheet, Plate III, presents an opportunity for the entry of the expenses of the case upon a functional basis. Plate IV represents the History Sheet where notation is made of the work, results and observations and a record kept of the visits and character of service performed. Plate V shows a special card used for the record of children where the housing conditions, the health and the school records are indicated. This card is usually renewed every year.

3. *Filing Records*

Records are usually filed numerically, in which case, a special, alphabetically arranged card catalogue is maintained for ready reference. It has been found expedient to separate active or current cases from the dormant cases in order to facilitate the gathering of statistical data. For it is quite evident, that in addition to the direct use of records, they present important data for re-

CASE No. ____________ NAME ______________________________ EXPENSE SHEET No. ____________

DATE	MONTHLY PENSION	WEEKLY PENSION	(a) RENT (b) MOVING	CASH	COAL	(a) GROCERIES (b) MEAT	(a) MILK (b) EGGS	(a) FURNITURE (b) DISHES	(a) CLOTHING (b) BEDDING	(a) SANITARIUM (b) CONVAL-ESCENT HOME	(a) SPECTACLES (b) MEDICAL APPLIANCE	(a) NURSE (b) SERVICE	SHELTER HOME	NOT OTHERWISE SPECIFIED	TOTAL RELIEF	REPAID ACCOUNT RELIEF	LOANS	REPAID LOANS	
TOTAL																			

Plate III

DATA SHEET No.	NAME					ADDRESS			CASE No.			
	January	February	March	April	May	June	July	August	September	October	November	December
Office Call												
Home Visit												
Collateral												
Relief												
Medical												
Investigation												
Family Unit	1	2	3	4	5	6	7	8				

Date	Unit		Agent	Disposition

Plate IV

No.	Name	Sex	Date of Birth	Place of Birth	Began School Age	N. of T. Changed	Grades Repeated	Family in U. S.	Family in City	Name of Parent or Guardian

617-6

Date	Inv. by		Date	Ex. by		Date		Inv. by		
Address			Disease during year			School		Grade		
Adults	Minors					Times Out				
M. Budget	Income					Reason				
Occupation of H. F.			Height	Skin	Orthop.					
T. P. H.–F. R.–R. T.	Floor		Weight	Eyes						
No. of Rooms	Rent		Nutrition	Ears		Subjects—Good in				
			Anemia	Nose						
			En. Glan.	Tonsils		Subjects—Bad in				
General Condition:	G—M—B		Nervous.	Adenoids						
Toilet:	G—M—B		Cardiac.	Pedicul.		Child's Appearance:	G—M—B			
Dark Rooms			Pulmon.			Disposition:	G—M—B			
			Teeth.			Conduct:	G—M—B			
Water Supply in Rooms—Same Floor in Hall—in Yard—						Teacher's Opinion				
			Child Needs Med. Att.			Guardian's Opinion				
Remarks:			Child Needs Country			Recommendations:				
			Remarks:							

Result / Action / Date

Plate V

search work, and consequently the keeping of records should be carefully followed as a means of collecting scientific material. The records are kept either in a wooden or metallic file, although the use of the latter has not become widespread because the intrinsic value of records is not yet universally recognized. A properly filled record of a relief society should show definitely the status of the case at the time of the first application; it should indicate the circumstances leading up to dependency, as well as the different clues which should be followed, either for the sake of further information that may be gained, or for the co-operation and help that can be acquired from the different sources. Thus the relatives and friends and the landlord and the doctor and the teacher and the employer and the lodges and societies all should be indicated. The records should also show to what extent these clues were utilized, what was the actual material help given to the family, what was the amount and character of the social service rendered, what were the subsequent changes that followed, and last, but not least, what was the final outcome of the case when the further interference of the relief agency became superfluous. A record which indicates assistance given without showing the further condition of the family, misses the most important point in constructive philanthropy, and indicates either inefficient treatment or a poor method of recording the actual workings of the relief organization.

The importance of records is not limited to relief agencies only. Every social service organization should have a definite system of records, giving an account of each individual with whom the organization comes in contact. In child-caring agencies, the previous history of the child should be carefully stated; the physical condition, the conduct, the educational progress, should be periodically noted, so that in later years, the entire development of the child can be seen from the individual record of the institutions. While efficient records are not always an index of high standing of an institution, the lack of the former is a true index of inefficiency. This is applicable to any kind of an institution.

In settlement work, however, it is rather difficult to keep a complete individual account of the constituency, and it is even an open question whether it is desirable to insist upon information that cannot be obtained without the jeopardizing of the entire spirit of the institution.

With the multiplicity of social agencies and specialization of their functions, it is evident that one family may be administered to by more than one organization. This frequently leads to overlapping and duplication. In order to get better co-operation between different agencies, and protect the public from imposition, the idea of a central bureau of registration has been devised, and its usefulness demonstrated in almost every large city. Usually the Associated Charities maintain this particular activity, though lately special agencies under different names conduct what is known as a confidential exchange,—a kind of a clearing house for charity recipients. In the Jewish field, this arrange-

NAME		ADDRESS		DATE ARRIVAL		NO.
				IN COUNTRY	IN CITY	

2216 NAME														
RELATION														
SOCIAL STATE														
YEAR BIRTH														
NATIVITY														
OCCUP. OR SCHOOL														

AGENCIES REPORTING	JAN	FEB	MAR	APR	MAY	JUN	JUL	AUG	SEP	OCT	NOV	DEC	JAN	FEB	MAR	APR	MAY	JUN	JUL	AUG	SEP	OCT	NOV	DEC
Dispensary																								
Jewish Conv. Home																								
Jewish Hospital																								
Jewish Shelter Home																								
Jewish Settlement																								
Milk Station																								

Plate VI

ment is of recent origin. In 1912, Miss Cecil B. Wiener brought up this question before the National Conference of Jewish Charities in Cleveland. It seems that simultaneously with this, the Jewish social workers of New Jersey contemplated the establishment of a confidential exchange for Jewish organizations. In 1913, Chicago established the first Jewish confidential exchange, known as the Registration Bureau of the Jewish Charities of Chicago.

In Cincinnati, the Bureau of Jewish Social Service established in 1915 a central registration department. This new departure in keeping track of social service activities undoubtedly leads to better understanding and better co-operation among the existing agencies.

In New York City, the Bureau of Philanthropic Research was established under the auspices of the Council of Jewish Communal Institutions. The Bureau intends to conduct a survey of the needs and resources of the community. In addition to investigating and dispensing information concerning various philanthropic activities, it is expected that it will bring about among them closer co-ordination and co-operation.

Chapter Nineteen. Administration

Questions

1. Explain the meaning and function of a budget.
2. Discuss the relation of administrative expense to the entire amount of the budget.
3. Describe proper room facilities for a relief agency.
4. State the proper attitude for an interviewer for relief.
5. Describe different forms of relief.

XX

THE FEDERATION AND THE SYNAGOGUE

A. Philanthropic Effort in the Synagogue

History repeats itself, and philanthropic effort in the United States indicates stages and settings similar to those of other countries. Here also the cemetery, then the synagogue were the first manifestations of Jewish social activity and when poverty became a problem, the synagogue assumed features of a relief agency. All of our early charitable institutions found their origin within the synagogue; there was instilled the inspiration; there the funds were gathered, and from there were formulated the plans and details of administration. The synagogue of yore was the unifying center of Judaism; it was the one place where all the Jews met as Jews on a common ground.

But times have changed. Though still adhering to the monotheistic conception of the Deity, the Jews of to-day are not altogether unanimous as to their affiliation with the synagogue. Social differences, as well as minor disagreements over the mode of worship, have led to the disintegration of the synagogue. The position of Parnass has become a worldly achievement; competition and strife in acquiring honor and leadership have led to many manipulations and often resulted in secession and the formation of a new congregation.

The cantor and rabbi have lost the monopoly,—by far too many have been endowed with an ambition to get hold,—of the pulpit and gain possession of the flock. Not being able to usurp authority over the existing synagogue, they have been tempted to form their own congregations, separating the Jews, as far as the synagogue is concerned, into fifty-seven varieties, distinguishing themselves in a hundred and one different ways. There are the Reformed and the Ultra-Reformed,—the Orthodox and the Ultra-Orthodox, the Portuguese and the German and the Russian, and the Polish and the Galician disintegrated into as many small groups as there are cities and towns. Great is the variety of the synagogue, great and extensive as the Jewish *Galut*.[1]

When Jewish philanthropy in the United States came face to face with the problem of mass immigration in the eighties, it became apparent that the isolated, uncorrelated agencies for relief, the different groups connected with the synagogue, were unable to cope with the situation. A more efficient organization became a necessity and the idea of co-operation arose.

B. Philanthropic Effort Taken Out of the Synagogue

It was evident that the synagogue was unable to achieve the purpose. A separate movement,—a movement among the Jews for concentrated philanthropic effort,—was started with the result that almost every

[1] Exile.

city in the United States established charity societies, dealing with the poor, and supported by the community at large without any respect to synagogue affiliations.

For some time this arrangement was considered rather favorable, as it was thought that the analogy of separating the State from religion, or the school from the church, holds good in this case. While now and then the synagogue would comment upon the work of the Federation, the representatives of the latter tried to steer apart from anything that might be considered synagogue affiliations. If the synagogue failed to unify the Jews, it was thought that the cause of philanthropy might succeed. Philanthropic effort, based upon efficiency and practical application, avoided the complications that threatened on the injecting of religious and traditional principles in a work of social endeavor, looked upon as a matter requiring a purely business attitude. Other reasons beside a religious motive were assigned for the specifically Jewish philanthropic activities.

C. The Effort to Unite the Synagogue with Charity Endeavor

The synagogue, which willingly gave up its hold upon charity affairs to the relief agency, soon realized its mistake. A vital element now was missing. Jewish religion without applied Judaism became a dead matter. The young generation, especially, was not attracted by oral social service; it required active applications.

Rabbi Stephen Wise should be given credit for being the first in the field to regain the hold upon charity endeavor by the synagogue. His attempt to co-operate with the United Hebrew Charities of New York is worthy of emulation.

A beginning was made at the Conference of Jewish Charities in Richmond, 1906. That was just the time when the principles upon which Jewish charities were based began to be shattered. It was rather questionable whether there was any reason for specifically Jewish activities. If the Jews cannot solve their own problem in its entirety, why should they have any of the activities separated and distinct—why should the Jew contributing to the general cause of philanthropic endeavor not relieve himself of his specific problem? This was the first time that the rabbi was called upon to settle the perplexing problem. The address of Dr. Wise was received in a rather unfriendly way by the professional workers; many things that he said then he probably would not endorse now, but one thing is certain, he did emphasize the new possibility of real co-operation between the synagogue and the Federation and not only in co-operation but in action, a co-operation which meant life to the synagogue and a soul to the charity organization.

D. The Federation and the Synagogue

Enthusiastic over the intricacies of organization, impressed with the complicated details entailed in handling the phenomenon of dependency, the charity

THE FEDERATION AND THE SYNAGOGUE 367

worker could not help over-estimating the significance of the system and objecting to anything that would interfere with well-planned activity. The problem of raising funds was reduced almost to an automatic arrangement; the machinery of handling cases was put under a stereotyped proceeding; it was now annoying to lose time and energy upon unnecessary sentimental features in relief giving. The rich were removed from direct contact with the poor; routine work was delegated to the paid worker; the directors and members of the Boards were now elated over watching the mechanism, and the entire proposition was reduced to a well-regulated, almost mechanical device—"how to cope with poverty." For a time this arrangement seemed to be ideal. The needs, however, have grown, and demands increased. The machinery operated for a time as if by inertia, but with the loss of public participation, the drying up of the varied resources became evident. Public sentiment after getting over the novelty, began to weaken; interest in philanthropic effort lessened; the sceptic began to feel himself on solid ground. The Federation continued its existence but found it difficult to spread or extend its activities. New organizations,—independent,—began to be formed. The strict rule of efficiency could not be maintained; the public began to lose patience and entire organized effort began to feel that it could not continue to neglect the public.

Here is where the synagogue found a possibility to regenerate its function as a social agency. The sisterhoods began to be quite active; different social groups were organized, the synagogue began to take heed of social needs. The Orthodox synagogue became instrumental in the support of institutions and relief agencies with a strictly religious tendency; the Reform synagogue tried to connect its parishioners with actual charitable activity. The sunday school, besides a religious factor, became a point of contact with the needy. The synagogues boldly made collections for purely charitable purposes. In some cities, the synagogue took the initiative in organizing the volunteer workers for the Federation. The synagogue now cries for actual social service application. The Federation is in dire need of inspiration, Jewish—sentimental—if you please. The rabbi comes closer to being a social worker and the latter begins to realize that the rabbi's co-operation is the only thing that will save his cause.

E. The Scope of Social Service in the Synagogue

There is no longer any doubt that the synagogue is again becoming a center of social service—the question is, in what way can the synagogue co-operate with the Federation, satisfy the longing for practical service and, at the same time, feel that it is not duplicating nor interfering with organized effort?

The Federation has demonstrated its efficiency in the way of constructive economic management of philanthropy; it has brought to light the many phases of the intricate problems of dependency, delinquency, and deficiency; it has supplied definite meaning and provided a definite criteria for active social service, but it has realized that it is not making progress unless it is gaining new grounds—it must get the active cooperation of the community—it must enlist the services,—the very sacrifices, of the volunteer forces. Here is where the synagogue can be of active service: it depends upon the synagogue to instill the spirit and enthusiasm for modern public service, and not only to provide the desire for active public work, but also to find, define, supervise and actually perform the task of a philanthropic agency, utilizing the method, the principle, and the facilities of the existing Federation. It is up to the synagogue to see that its numbers adequately provide support to the Federation. The committee of the synagogue, and the entire congregation, should be interested in the extent of contribution of each and every member of the synagogue, not only to the Federation, but to all charitable endeavor.

If certain Jewish clubs have taken upon themselves to reject membership to persons not adequately supporting local charities, does it not behoove the synagogue to take the same attitude? It is the business of the rabbi to see that his congregation as a whole is well represented in the amount contributed by its members to the various charities. If each and every synagogue would do its duty in this respect, it would create, to a certain extent, an impetus to the charity giver. The Federation would soon be relieved of the complaint that it is supported mostly by the few instead of the many. The synagogue, knowing the total amount contributed by its entire membership, would certainly have the interest and the right to ascertan definitely the actual functions of the different charities.

The synagogue, as a whole, or in its special committee, should examine the budgets of the various philanthropic agencies, making an actual test of the comparative standing of the different charitable institutions, so as to be able to direct properly the donations of its parishioners. The synagogue should know the exact status of the Jewish charities, and special committees should be vested with the right and duty of getting the necessary knowledge in regard to local charities. The various synagogues should be actively represented on the different boards of the different philanthropies. The synagogue should be given the benefit of the experience of its delegates and should receive definite reports of their doings. An arrangement like this cannot fail to serve as a great educational factor in the community and would popularize the work of the Federation more than moving pictures and more effectively than the various tricks of commercial advertising recently come into vogue but distasteful to the professional social worker.

The Federation needs competent trained volunteers; the synagogue should know and to a certain extent have a supervisory power over the volunteer service among its members, who are or should be, connected with the active work of the Federation. The synagogue or temple should know who, of its members, serve as friendly visitors for the Federation or relief society.

The synagogue should organize its volunteer forces, make provision for their training, and ascertain their comparative efficiency. An arrangement such as this would relieve the Federation of the unnecessary work of trying to keep the volunteer service together, would do away with the individual handling of the friendly visitors, which produces so much annoyance among the active workers.

Then again, the synagogue should know the needs of the community that the Federation is unable to meet— it should possess the knowledge of the plans of the Federation that remain uneffected because of lack of funds. The synagogue as a unit, should take upon itself the initiative in co-operation with other synagogues in helping the community.

In all these undertakings, the synagogue ventures upon philanthropic fields in co-operation with the Federation—utilizing the Federation, supplying it with new resources, new forces, new interest, and a motive, so much wanted by the organized Jewish charities today.

The synagogue should utilize its contact with the younger generation, instilling in the latter, not only a desire for generous giving but also an enthusiasm for actual participation in the practical endeavors of Jewish social service. The synagogue should provide facilities for training the younger generation along these particular lines; it should give instruction in the principles of modern Jewish philanthropy and should, in co-operation with the Federation, provide practical experience in the active work of the Federation. The Federation cannot do this work on its own responsibility; the funds that the Federation collects do not permit the expenditure for the education of its working forces; its paid employees cannot devote their time in instructing the volunteers, or acquainting the young people especially, with the intricacies of social service. This should be the function of the synagogue; it should see that its members receive the impetus, not only to listen to beautiful and moral doctrines, but to be anxious and fully capable to apply their Judaism in actual, practical life and in answer to actual experiences of the Jewish community.

F. PLAN OF ACTION

The synagogue has an extensive field for philanthropic endeavor; it cannot cover it without the cooperation of organized effort. Departure in this direction should and would be of mutual benefit both to the synagogue and the Federation. There is, however, one difficulty that should not be overlooked. The synagogue must realize that modern conditions have developed a complicated machinery in every line of human endeavor; this is also true in regard to Jewish philanthropic effort. The untrained, or the amateur leader in the philanthropic circle of the synagogue is a pathetic figure and is liable to cause considerable and actual harm. It is necessary that the synagogue should receive the guidance of the professional man or woman who is in a position to direct its social service activities in accordance with the other social agencies existing in the city, and put it on a high plane of efficiency.

In this longing for social activity, many a synagogue is at loss what to undertake; this is especially tantalizing where the Federation is strong or where other synagogues are already in the field. The establishment of study circles, sewing circles, willing and unwilling workers, visiting boards and different committees, raising funds on the sly—is really pathetic and the lack of enthusiasm is appalling. This piecemeal work is not worth the effort; it carries more negative than positive value, both to the synagogue and to the organization—it is detrimental to both.

If the synagogue decides to become an actual factor in social service, it should first of all take an inventory of the forces that it already possesses, and get an account of the actual participation with existing agencies. Should the synagogue survey the participation of its membership in the support of the Federation, it would be an index of existing interest. If the synagogue is sufficiently involved in this enterprise, the study of its workings, the budget of the constituent bodies, the proportion of income spent on administration should be a legitimate field of investigation. Then it is up to the synagogue to start a definite campaign among its members for a more adequate and more balanced distribution of the charity donations of the individual members.

Besides the monetary participation in the philanthropic effort of the community, the synagogue should take account of the personal participation of its members, trying to regulate, direct, and unify their efforts. This is especially important in making connections between efforts of the Federation in the rehabilitation of families and the co-operation of active business men of the community. In all these endeavors, however, a definite conception of the detailed workings of modern charitable endeavor is of paramount importance. While the natural leader in this enterprise should be the rabbi, in cases where the latter is not thoroughly prepared to meet the situation, the leadership should be vested in persons who, besides possessing noble motives, have the necessary knowledge to cope with the situation. In all instances the work should be based upon definite data obtained through painstaking investigation and research which is the only true method of social service to-day.

CHAPTER TWENTY. THE FEDERATION AND THE SYNAGOGUE

QUESTIONS

1. What rôle did the synagogue play in the past as regards philanthropic effort?
2. State the reasons why, in earlier endeavor, an attempt was made to separate charity from the synagogue.
3. Explain the recent change in the tendency.
4. State the importance of professional guidance of synagogue social service.

BIBLIOGRAPHY

Abrahams, Israel. Jewish Life in the Middle Ages. New York, 1897.
Addams, Jane. The Spirit of Youth and the City Streets. New York, 1909.
Addams, Jane. Twenty Years at Hull House. New York, 1910.
Allen, Wm. H. Efficient Democracy. New York, 1907.
Amateau, A. J. The Work with the Jewish Deaf. Jewish Charities, Vol. V, No. 5. December, 1914.
Antin, Mary. Promised Land. New York, 1912.
Aronovici, Carol. The Social Survey. Philadelphia, 1916.
Benjamin, Eugene S. The Baron De Hirsch Fund. Proceedings National Conference Jewish Charities. Philadelphia, 1906.
Berkowitz, William J. Federation of Charities. Proceedings of the Second National Conference of Jewish Charities. Detroit, 1902.
Berlinsky, Garfield A. How to Federate a Smaller Community. Jewish Charities, Vol. V, No. 6. January, 1915.
Bernheimer, Dr. Charles S. Orphans' Guardians Society. Proceedings of the Second National Conference of Jewish Charities. Detroit, 1902.
Bernheimer, Dr. Charles S. The Russian Jew in the United States. Philadelphia, 1905.
Bernheimer, Dr. Charles S. Settlements and the Underworld. Jewish Charities, Vol. III, No. 1. August, 1912.
Bernstein, Ludwig B. A Child Caring Primer. Jewish Charities, Vol. II, No. 3. October, 1911.
Bernstein, Ludwig B. Placing out of Jewish Children. Proceedings National Conference Jewish Charities. Philadelphia, 1906.

Billikopf, Jacob. Advanced Settlement Work. Jewish Charities, Vol. V, No. 7. February, 1915.

Blaustein, David. Preventive Work on the East Side. Proceedings National Conference Jewish Charities. New York, 1904.

Blaustein, Mrs. Miriam U. Memoirs of David Blaustein. New York, 1913.

Bloomfield, Meyer. The Vocational Guidance of Youth. Boston, 1911.

Bogen, Boris D. Extent of Jewish Philanthropy in the United States. Published by section of Superintendents and Social Workers of National Conference Jewish Charities. 1909.

Bogen, Boris D. Jewish Boy Scouts. Jewish Charities, Vol. III, No. 5. December, 1912.

Bogen, Boris D. Persistency of Dependence as Indicated by Relief Statistics. Proceedings National Conference Jewish Charities. Philadelphia, 1906.

Bogen, Boris D. The Relation of Social Worker to his Organization. Proceedings National Conference Jewish Charities. St. Louis, 1910.

Bogen, Boris D. Standards of Relief. Jewish Charities, Vol. V, No. 8. March, 1915.

Bogen, Boris D. Y. M. H. A. Jewish Charities, Vol. II, No. 7. February, 1912.

Bressler, David M. The Removal Work, Including Galveston. Proceedings National Conference Jewish Charities. St. Louis, 1910.

Bressler, David M. The Removal Work. Proceedings National Conference Jewish Charities. New York, 1904.

Cabot, Richard. Social Service and the Art of Healing. New York, 1909.

Cahan, Abraham. The Imported Bridegroom. New York, 1898.

Cahan, Abraham. Yekl. New York, 1896.

Cannon, Ida M. Social Work in Hospitals. New York, 1913.
Davis, Philip. The Field of Social Service. Boston, 1915.
Devine, Edward T. Misery and its Causes. New York, 1909.
Devine, Edward T. Principles of Relief. New York, 1904.
Devine, Edward T. Social Service. New York, 1910.
Devine, Edward T. The Normal Life. New York, 1916.
Devine, Edward T. The Spirit of Social Work. New York, 1912.
Dukas, J. Julius. Free Loans. Jewish Charities, Vol. IV, No. 12. July, 1914.
Eiseman, Chas. Everybody's Business. Cleveland, 1916.
Fishberg, Dr. Maurice. The Jews. New York, 1911.
Fishberg, Dr. Maurice. Tuberculosis and Dependency. Jewish Charities, Vol. V, No. 12. July, 1915.
Folks, Homer. The Care of Destitute, Neglected, and Delinquent Children. New York, 1902.
Fraley, Moses. Federation of Charities. Proceedings of the Second National Conference of Jewish Charities. Detroit, 1902.
Frankel, Dr. Lee K. Placing Out of Jewish Children. Proceedings National Conference of Jewish Charities. New York, 1904.
Frankel, Dr. Lee K. Report of Committee on Dependent Children. Proceedings of the Second National Conference of Jewish Charities. Detroit, 1902.
Frankel, Dr. Lee K. Report of Committee on Desertion. Proceedings National Conference Jewish Charities. Philadelphia, 1906.
Frankel, Dr. Lee K. Self-Respect Fund. Jewish Charities, Vol. V, No. 1. August, 1914.
Fromenson, A. H. East Side Preventive Work. Proceedings National Conference Jewish Charities. New York, 1904.
Gimbel, Jacob. Federation of Charities. Proceedings of the Second National Conference of Jewish Charities. Detroit, 1902.

Goldstein, Monroe M.   Desertion.   Proceedings National Conference Jewish Charities. Cleveland, 1912.
Gottheil, Professor Richard.   Report of Standing Committee on Palestinian Charities. Jewish Charities, Vol. V, No. 2. September, 1914.
Gulick, L. H., & Ayres, L. P.   Medical Inspection in Schools. New York, 1913.
Hapgood, Hutchins.   The Spirit of the Ghetto. New York,1902.
Hart, Hastings.   Cottage and Congregate Institutions. New York, 1914.
Henderson, Charles R.   Modern Methods of Charity. New York, 1904.
Henderson, Charles R.   Social Settlements. New York, 1899.
Herzl, Theodor. The Jewish State. New York, 1904.
Hexter, Maurice B.   The Dawn of a Problem. Jewish Charities, Vol. IV, No. 5. December, 1913.
Hexter, Maurice B.   Real Habilitation. Jewish Charities, Vol. V, No. 8. March, 1915.
Hollander, Professor Jacob H.   The Unification of Jewish Communal Activities. Proceedings National Conference Jewish Charities. Richmond, 1908.
Hourwich, Dr. Isaac A.   Immigration and Labor. New York, 1912.
Jewish Charities.   Monthly Bulletin of the National Conference of Jewish Charities. Baltimore, Maryland.
Joseph, Dr. Samuel.   Jewish Immigration to the United States from 1881 to 1910. New York, 1914.
Kahn, William. Jewish Agricultural and Industrial Aid Society. Proceedings of the Second National Conference of Jewish Charities. Detroit, 1902.
Kohler, Kaufmann.   "Charity" and "Almsgiving" in The Jewish Encyclopaedia. New York, 1904.
Kohler, Kaufmann.   Hebrew Union College Addresses. Pp. 229–252. Cincinnati, O.
Kropotkin, Peter A. Mutual Aid. New York, 1902.

Kuh, Edwin J. The Social Disability of the Jew. Atlantic Monthly. April, 1908.

Leff, Samuel. Relief Versus Self-Support Work in Organized Charity. Jewish Charities, Vol. V, No. 8. March, 1915.

Leroy-Beaulieu, Anatole. Israel Among Nations. New York, 1896.

Levin, Louis H. Social Work as a Profession. Proceedings National Conference Jewish Charities. St. Louis, 1910.

Levin, Louis H. Suggestion for Jewish Settlement Work. Jewish Charities, Vol. I, No. 3. October, 1910.

Levy, A. R. Agriculture, a most Effective Means to Aid Jewish Poor. Proceedings of the Second National Conference of Jewish Charities. Detroit, 1902.

Lewis, Harry Samuel. Liberal Judaism and Social Service. New York, 1915.

Lippmann, Walter. A Preface to Politics. New York, 1915.

Loeb, Professor Morris. Convalescent Homes. Charities. August 1, 1908.

Loeb, Professor Morris. Free Loan Societies. Proceedings of the Second National Conference of Jewish Charities. Detroit, 1902.

Loeb, Professor Morris. State Aid to Sectarian Institutions. Proceedings National Conference Jewish Charities. Philadelphia, 1906.

Low, Miss Minnie. Is There a Need for Reformation for Jewish Girls? Jewish Charities, Vol. II, No. 11. June, 1912.

Low, Miss Minnie. Legal Aid. Proceedings National Conference Jewish Charities. St. Louis, 1910.

Lowenstein, Solomon. Adequacy of Relief. Proceedings National Conference Jewish Charities. New York, 1904.

Lowenstein, Solomon. Institutions for Children. Proceedings National Conference Jewish Charities. Philadelphia, 1906.

Lowenstein, Solomon. A Study of the Problem of Boarding Out Children. Proceedings National Conference Jewish Charities. St. Louis, 1910.

Mack, Julian W. Federation of Charities. Proceedings of the Second National Conference of Jewish Charities. Detroit, 1902.

McLean and O'Connor. San Francisco Relief Survey. New York, 1913.

Magnes, J. Leon. Jewish Community of New York City. New York, 1909.

Marshall, Louis. The Need of a Distinctly Jewish Tendency in the Conduct of Jewish Educational Institutions. Proceedings National Conference Jewish Charities. Richmond, 1908.

Palitz, B. A. Timely Advent of the Y. M. H. A. Jewish Charities, Vol. II, No. 7. February, 1912.

Patten, Simon. The New Basis of Civilization. New York, 1907.

Perry, Arthur. Wider Use of the School Plan. New York.

Philipson, David. Isaac Mayer Wise. Cincinnati, 1900.

Pincus, Joseph W. Jewish Problems in Rural Communities. Jewish Charities, Vol. III, No. 11. June, 1913.

Pool, D. De-Sola. The Immigration of Levantine Jews into the United States. Jewish Charities, Vol. IV, No. 11. June, 1914.

Proceedings of the National Conference Jewish Charities: Chicago, 1900; Detroit, 1902; New York, 1904; Philadelphia, 1906; Richmond, 1908; St. Louis, 1910; Cleveland, 1912; Memphis, 1914; Indianapolis, 1916.

Rabinowitz, Samuel. Transients. Jewish Charities, Vol. II, No. 11. June, 1912.

Reeder, Rudolph R. How Two Hundred Children Live and Learn. New York, 1910.

Richmond, Mary. Friendly Visiting among the Poor, New York, 1899.

Robinson, Leonard G. Agricultural Activities of the Jews in America. American Jewish Year Book, 1912–1913.

Rubinow, I. M. Economic Conditions of the Jews in Russia. Bulletin of the Bureau of Labor, No. 72. September, 1907.

Rubinow, I. M. Social Insurance, with Special Reference to American Conditions. New York, 1913.
Rubinow, I. M. Standards of Health Insurance. New York, 1916.
Ruppin, Arthur. The Jews of To-day. New York, 1913.
Sabsovich, Professor H. L. Jewish Charitable Activities in Russia. Proceedings National Conference Jewish Charities. Richmond, 1908.
Sabsovich, Professor H. L. Retirement Fund for Jewish Social Workers. Proceedings National Conference Jewish Charities. Cleveland, 1912.
Schiff, Jacob H. The Galveston Movement. Jewish Charities, Vol. IV, No. 11. June, 1914.
Senior, Max. Federation of Charities. Proceedings National Conference Jewish Charities. New York, 1904.
Shaler, Nathaniel S. The Neighbor. Boston, 1904.
Solenberger, Alice. 1,000 Homeless Men. New York, 1911.
Solomons, L. Lucian. Immigration and the Panama Canal. Jewish Charities, Vol. V, No. 4. November, 1914.
Sommerfeld, Miss Rose. Homes for Working Girls. Proceedings National Conference Jewish Charities. Philadelphia, 1906.
Steiner, Edward A. On the Trail of the Immigrant. New York, 1906.
Strull, Charles. The Distribution of a $5,000 Annual Budget. Jewish Charities, Vol. V, No. 2. September, 1914.
Sulzberger, Cyrus L. The Problems of American Jewry. Jewish Charities, Vol. IV, No. 10. May, 1914.
Szold, Miss Henrietta. Palestinian Charities Report. Proceedings National Conference Jewish Charities. St. Louis, 1910.
Teller, Chester Jacob. Special Education of Jewish Dependent Children. Proceedings National Conference Jewish Charities. St. Louis, 1910.
Veiller, Lawrence. The Tenement House Problem. New York, 1903.

Veiller, Lawrence. Housing Reform; a Handbook for Practical Use in American Cities. New York, 1910.
Wald, Lillian D. The House on Henry Street. New York, 1915.
Waldman, Morris D. Family Desertion. Proceedings National Conference Jewish Charities. St. Louis, 1910.
Ward, Lester F. Dynamic Sociology. New York, 1883.
Ward, Lester F. Applied Sociology. New York, 1906.
Warner, A. G. American Charities. New York, 1894.
Waters, Ysabella. Visiting Nursing in the United States. New York, 1909.
Wise, Dr. Stephen S. The Function of the Conference of Jewish Charities. Proceedings National Conference Jewish Charities. Richmond, 1908.
Woods, R. A. Americans in Progress. Boston, 1902.
Woods and Kennedy. Handbook of Settlements. New York, 1911.
Zangwill, Israel. Children of the Ghetto. Philadelphia, 1892.
Zepin, George R. Co-operation in Charitable Activities. Proceedings National Conference Jewish Charities. Richmond, 1908.

INDEX

NOTE: Wherever practicable the word "Jewish" has been omitted for obvious reasons. Thus one should look for "Immigrants" and not "Jewish Immigrants."

Addams, Jane, 246
Administration (*See* also Chapters XVII, XIX), facilities of, 343
Agricultural and Colonial Association, 129
Agricultural and Industrial Aid Society, 30, 127, 128, 129, 137, 253, 254
Agricultural banks, 128
Aid Society of Brooklyn, 200
Aid Society of Chicago, 200
Alliance Israelité Universelle, 27, 126, 136, 253, 255
American Hebrew Agricultural Association, 125
Americanization, 5, 228 sq., 249, 276 sq.
American Jewish Committee, 36, 57, 108, 110, 253
American Protective Association, 97
Am Olam, 90, 130
Annual reports, 55
Antiquary Club, 258
Anti-restriction movement, 107
Anti-sectarianism, 227
Applications for relief, 342 (*See* also Relief), granting of, 345; interviewing of applicants, 344; investigation of, 347 sq.; rejection of, 346
Art classes, 239
Art Club, 258 (*See* also Graphic Sketch Club)

Back to the soil movement (see Chapter IX)
Baron De Hirsch, 27, 28
Baron De Hirsch Agricultural School, 133 (*See* also Sabsovich; Woodbine)
Baron De Hirsch Fund, 27, 28, 30, 41, 113, 127, 129, 130, 132, 182, 227, 253
Baron De Hirsch Trade School, 182, 242
Beaulieu, Leroy, 142
Bedford Sanitarium, 154
Begging, direct, 38 (*See* also Tramps)
Bellevue Hospital, 147
Benderly, Dr. S., 217 sq., 336
Benjamin, Eugene, 137
Bernstein, Dr. Ludwig B., 161, 162, 167
Bezalel School, 255
Big Brothers, 169, 333
Big Sisters, 169, 333
Billeten, 60

INDEX

Billikopf, Jacob, 222
Billings, Dr. John, 142
Blaustein, Dr. David, 39, 231 sq., 240, 286
Blind, 144 (*See* also Defectives)
B'nai B'rith, Independent Order of, 33, 41, 57, 108, 114, 120, 147, 160, 211, 294
Boys' Brigade, 258
Bressler, David M., 116
B'rith Abraham, 211
Budgets (*See* also Administration), analysis of, 238; preparing of, 337
Burnett, John L., 108, 110
Burnett-Dillingham Bill, 110 (*See* also Immigration Legislation)

Carton, Max, 288
Central Relief Committee, 37, 57
"Chanukah Trendel," 259
Charity (*See* also Chapter III; United Charities) a duty, 17, 18; indiscriminate, 325; in the middle ages, 23; Mosaic law and, 16, 17; synonymous with justice, 17
Charity box, 21, 39
Charity socials, 42
Charity taxes, 40
Chautauqua, Jewish, 220, 335
"Chazanim," 73
Cheder, 216 sq. (*See* also Religious Instruction; Talmud Torah)
Child-caring, 167 (*See* also Infant Mortality; Infant Welfare)
Children's clubs, 257

Chronic invalids, 157 (*See* also Defectives; Sick)
Cincinnati Jewish Settlement, 224
"Cincinnati Method," 153
Citizenship classes, 286 (*See* also Americanization; Settlements)
Clara De Hirsch Home for Girls, 242
Clothing, 327 (*See* also Standard of Living)
Community forces, 260 sq.
Congregate systems, 160 (*See* also Orphan Asylums)
Congregational Schools, free, 215 sq. (*See* also Cheder)
Consumptives (*See* also Tuberculosis), after-care of, 151; National Hospital for, 78, 148, 149, 152; National institutions for the care of, 34
Consumptives' Relief Society, 34, 149
Convalescents, 156 (*See* also Sick)
Co-operative enterprizes, 128
Council Educational Alliance of Cleveland, 223, 237, 244
Council of Jewish Communal Institutions, 362
Council of Jewish Women, 35, 103, 104, 143, 144, 151, 153, 220, 253, 291
Court of Arbitration, 274
Credit unions, 128
Cremiet, 126
Crime, 294 (*See* also Juvenile Delinquency)

Day nurseries, 169
Deaf, 144 (*See* also Defectives), Society for the Welfare of Jewish, 144
Defectives, 77, 144 (*See* also Blind; Chronic Invalids; Deaf; Sick)
Delinquency, 234 (*See* also Crime; Juvenile Delinquency)
Dependency (*See* also Chapters II, XI; Desertion), causes of, 10; chronic, 12; immigration and, 10; of recent origin, 12; resistance to, 12; temporary, 10, 192
Desertion, 171 sq.
Desertion Bureau, National, 32, 176, 179; Wife, 177
Dillingham, Wm. P., 108, 110
Directors, boards of, 300 sq. (*See* also Administration)
Dispensaries, 138 sq.
Distribution (*See* also Chapter VIII; Galveston Movement; Industrial Removal Office; Removal Work)
Doll Club, 258
Doylestown, Pa., 134
Dukas, Julius J., 190

Educational Alliance, Atlanta, 224; Baltimore, 223, 288; Cleveland, 223, 237, 244; New York, 43, 223, 227 sq.; St. Louis, 224, 287
Educational Institute, Kansas City, 224, 225
Educational League, 35, 235

Educational organizations (*See* also Chapter XIV; Young Men's Hebrew Association)
Emanu-El Brotherhood, 223
Emergency funds, 56 (*See* also Fund Raising)
Employment agencies, 185, 186 (*See* also Kehillah)
English classes, 271
Entrepreneurs, 187 sq.
Environment, 327, 328
Essenes, 18, 19, 20, 21, 25 (*See* also Hasidim)
Esther, Deborah, 39
Exposition of Jews of Many Lands, 252 sq.

Farmers' Association of St. Louis, 130
Farming (*See* also National Farm School), extent of Jewish, 128
Federated Orthodox Jewish Charities, 45
Federation of Jewish Charities, 43 sq. (*See* also Chapter XX; United Charities); Baltimore, 335; Brooklyn, 46, 56; Cleveland, 56; New York, 46
Federation of Jewish Farmers of America, 128, 254
Feeble-minded, 145 (*See* also Defectives)
Fellowship House, 169
Fishberg, Dr. Maurice, 142, 143
Fleisher, Samuel S., 282
Food (*See* also Standard of Living), consumption of, 326

INDEX

Frankel, Dr. Lee K., 160, 161, 172, 173, 185, 198
Free congregational schools (*See* also Cheder), 215 sq.
Free loans, 189 sq.
Free loan societies, 189, 190
Free medical attendance (*See* Dispensaries)
Free Sons of Israel, 211
Free Synagogue, 147, 154, 156
Fresh-air treatment, 323
"Friendly Visitors," 318 sq. (*See* also Settlements; Social Workers; Volunteer Service); modern type of, 320; problems of, 322 sq.
Fromenson, A. H., 234
Fund raising (*See* also Chapter V; Emergency Funds), efficiency tests for, 49; machinery of, 50 sq.; publicity for, 54; subscription method of, 49

Galveston Movement, 111, 122
Games, 259
Gemilath Chesed, 189
Ghetto, 13, 14, 114, 226 sq., 247, 269 sq.
Ghetto forces, 229
"Golden City," 165
Goldman, Julius, 29
Goldstein, Monroe, 177
Goldwater, Dr. S. S., 147
Grace Aguilar Library, 227
Graetz, Rebecca, 216
Grand Island, New York, 86, 125
"Graphic Sketch Club," 282 sq.

Hachnosis Orchim, 36, 71 sq.
Hackenburg, William H., 29
Halpern, Dr. R. L. H., 238
Halukah organizations, 40
Hasidim (*See* Essenes)
Health of the poor, 322, 324
Hebrew, 110
Hebrew Benevolent Society, 86, 201
Hebrew Congregations, Union of American, 109, 219, 220, 253
Hebrew Institute (*See* also "Palace of Immigrants"), Chicago, 224, 238 sq., 335; Detroit, 224; New York, 212, 227
Hebrew Sheltering and Guardian Society, 160, 161, 164, 169, 199, 200
Hebrew Sheltering and Immigrant Aid Society of America, 35, 71, 72, 93, 103 sq.
Hebrew Technical Institute, 43, 241
Hebrew Union College, 255
Heinsheimer, Alfred, 45
Heinsheimer, Louis A., 45
Hekdesh, 25
Helen Day Nursery, 170
Henry Street Settlement, 282
Hexter, Maurice B., 159, 188, 259
Hoffman, James H., 29
Home Finding Society of Chicago, 163
Hospitals, 145 sq.; social service departments in, 147
Hourwich, Dr. Isaac A., 95

INDEX 387

Housing, 325 (*See* also Standard of Living)
"Humane Society," 176, 178

Ida Straus Colony, 130
Immigrants (*See* also Hebrew Sheltering and Immigrant Aid Society of America), aiding, 11, 12, 92; economic status of, 101; education of, see Chapter XV; Portuguese, 84; protection of, 102 sq.
Immigrants' Information Bureau, 111, 122
Immigration, 5, 10, 93 (*See* also Chapter VII; Dependency); early Jewish, 84; from Poland, 89; from Portugal, 84; from Russia, 4, 89, 226; of 1848, 87
Immigration Commission, 90, 107 sq., 128
Immigration funds, 91
Immigration legislation, 91, 96 sq.
Individual standards, 202
Inefficiency, 181
Industrial Removal Office, 31, 67, 76, 113 sq., 253
Infant mortality, 142, 143
Infant welfare, 142 sq., 323, 324
Insanity, 155 (*See* also Defectives)
Insufficiency of income, 181 (*See* also Chapter XII)
Investigation (*See* Applications for Relief)
Isaacs, Meyer S., 29

Jacobs, Dr. Joseph, 48

Jenks, Professor Jeremiah W., 108
"Jewish Charities," 33
Jewish Charity (*See* also Charity; United Charities), beginnings of, in the United States, 85
Jewish Colonization Association, 28, 30, 136
Jewish Community of New York (*See* Kehillah)
"Jewish Farmer," 127
Jewish immigration, 93 sq. (*See* also Immigration); by countries, 93 sq.
Jewish press, 229, 230
Jewish Protectory, 186, 290
Jewish Territorialist Organization, 111, 122
Jewish Theatre, 229
Joint Distribution Committee, 37, 57
Joint Tuberculosis Committee, 154
Joseph, Dr. Samuel, 95
Juvenile Aid Society of Philadelphia, 291
Juvenile delinquency, 289 sq. (*See* also Crime)

Kaftan, Simon, 39
Kashruth, 166
Kehillah, 253, 297, bureau of education of, 218; employment agency of, 186
Kellor, Miss Frances, 186
Kings Park, L. I., 137
Kitchen Garden and Trade School for Girls, Cincinnati, 242

388 INDEX

Know Nothing Movement, 87
Krauskopf, Dr. Joseph, 35, 134

Leadership, 295 sq.
Leonard, Oscar, 177, 288
Leo N. Levi Memorial Hospital, 147
Levi, Leo N., 114
Levin, Louis, 221
Levin, L. H., 166
Levine, Judge Emanuel, 286
Loeb, Dr. Morris, 135, 136, 235
Loeb Memorial Convalescent Home, 157
Loewenstein, Dr. Solomon, 161
Low, Minnie, 163, 274, 290–292, 320, 330, 331
Lucy Flower Technical High School, 293

Mack, Judge Julian W., 109, 290
Maxwell Settlement, 223
Maternity Hospital, 143
Michael Reese Hospital, 141, 142
Modern philanthropy (*See* also Chapter I), Problem of, 1, 6; scope of, 7
Montefiore Agricultural Aid Society, 126
Montefiore Home, 154, 157
Mount Sinai Hospital, 147
Moving Pictures, 56
Music classes, 239

Nathan Marks Orphan Asylum, 165
National Conference of Jewish Charities, 31, 61

National Farm School, 35, 134
National Garment Workers' Union, 253
National Jewish Hospital, 34
National Jewish Immigration Council, 36
National organizations (*See* Chapter IV; Organizations)
National Union of Jewish Sheltering Societies, 36
Neglected Neighborhoods, 14, 266 sq.
Neighborhood Work (*See* Chapter XVI)
New Jersey Colonies, 129
New Odessa, 126
New York Foundation, 186
Noah, Mordecai M., 86
Norden, Warner Van, 185
Nurses' Settlement (*See* Henry Street Settlement)

Office holding, persistence in, 298
Organization (*See* Chapter XVII; Administration)
Organizations, 7, 8; membership of, 8; expenditures of, 8, 9
Organized charity (*See* Charity; Jewish Charity; United Charities)
Orphan asylums, 2, 3, 160 sq. (*See* also Hebrew Sheltering and Guardian Society); Cleveland, 161; New Orleans, 165; Orthodox tendencies in, 165; subventions to, 165
Orphans, after care of, 169
Orthodoxy, 3

INDEX 389

"Palace of Immigrants," 227
Palestine, 254 (*See* also Zionists)
Palitz, B., 213, 214
Passing-on policy, 61
Pauperism, 61, 201
Penny luncheons, 143
People's Relief Committee, 37, 57
People's Synagogue, 223
Personal Service Bureau, 163, 291, 321
Philanthropic Research, Bureau of, 362
Pincus, Joseph, 127
"Placing-out System," 160
Pleasantville, New York, 164
Polish immigration, 89 (*See* also Chapter VII; Immigration)
Portuguese immigrants, 84 (*See* also Immigrants)
Privations in war, 57
Professional beggars (*See* Tramps)
Pushka (*See* Charity Box)

Radical National Schools, 220
Recent arrivals, 83
Record keeping, 350 sq.
Recreation and amusement, 329
Registration bureaus, 362
Reiss, Clara, 292
Relief, agencies of, 2, 120; continuous, 203; principles of, 21-23; standards of, 196 sq. (*See* Chapter XIII)
Religious instruction (*See* also Cheder; Sabbath Schools; Talmud Torah), social service agencies and, 221 sq.

Removal work, 117 sq. (*See* also Distribution; Industrial Removal Office)
Resident-dependents (*See* Chapter X)
Rice, Harry, 29
Robinson, Leonard G., 129
Rosenwald, Julius, 42, 163
Russia (*See* also Chapter VII), immigration from, 4, 89; poverty of Jews in, 11
Ruth Club, 292

Sabbath schools, 215 sq. (*See* also Religious Instruction)
Sabsovich, Professor H. L., 39, 130
Sachs, Dr. Theodore, 148
Sanitarium treatment, 148 sq. (*See* also Tuberculosis)
Schatz, Boris, 255
Schiff, Jacob H., 29, 122, 184, 190, 191
Schnorrer, 38
School for Jewish Communal Workers, 335
School hygiene, 143
School of Jewish Social Service, Cincinnati, 335
Schules, 223 (*See* also Synagogue)
Sectarianism, 2
Self-government, 164 (*See* also Orphan Asylums)
Self-respect funds, 184
Self-support funds, 190
Seligman, Jesse, 29
Senior, Max, 298

Settlements, 221 sq. (*See* Chapter XVI); as social service agency, 245; charity in, 247; children's work in, 280 sq.; co-operation with, 288; employment and, 273; expansion of activities, 278; legal aid in, 274; non-sectarianism in, 252; origin of, 246; politics and, 284 sq.; problems of, 250 sq.; religion in, 264 sq.; resident workers in, 247; specialization in, 282; teaching of English in, 271; volunteer workers in, 331
Shalom, 125
Shearith Israel, 86
Shiftlessness, 12
Shochetim, 74
Sickness, 77, 138 (*See* also Defectives)
Simpson, Sampson, 86
Slums, 13
Social organizations (*See* also Chapter XIV), rise of, 211
Social service (*See* also Hospitals), Bureau of Jewish, Cincinnati, 362
Social workers, 302 sq. (*See* also Superintendents); attitude to board of directors, 310; attitude to community, 315; difficulties of, 308; education of, 335; National Association of Jewish, 335; qualifications of, 304
Socialism, 229, 231 (*See* also Community Forces)

Solenberger, Mrs. Alice, 80
Solomon, Walter, 244
Sons of the Free, 126
Spaniolas, 255
Spectorsky, Isaac, 232, 237
Standard of Living, 203 sq., 325–327
Steinholtz, Elinor, 143
Straus, Ida, 130
Straus, Isidor, 130, 228
Straus, Oscar S., 29
Struggle for existence, 329
Strunsky Survey, 149
Subventions, 53
Sulzberger, Cyrus B., 114, 245
Sulzberger, Meyer, 29
Superintendents, 304 sq.
Synagogue (*See* also Chapter XX), philanthropy and the, 363 sq.; scope of social service in the, 368; volunteer workers and the, 370; younger generation and the, 371

Talmud Torah, 216 sq. (*See* also Religious Instruction)
Technical education, 241 sq.
Teller, Chester, 165
Touro Infirmary, 157
Toynbee Hall, 246
Training School, Chicago, 242
Tramps, 73, 79 sq.
Transients (*See* Chapter VI), temporary dependent, 75
Transportation Rules, 62 sq.; new, 68
Travel Club, 257
Traveling rabbi, 73

INDEX 391

Tuberculosis, 148 sq., 324 (*See* also Consumptives; Sanitarium Treatment); home treatment of, 150

Unemployment, 186
Union of American Hebrew Congregations, 109, 219, 220, 253
United Charities (*See* also Charity; Federation; Jewish Charity); Baltimore, 45; Brooklyn, 46; Chicago, 362; Cincinnati, 77, 152-154, 188, 193; New York, 44, 90, 94, 102, 104, 143, 154, 183-186, 190, 366; Philadelphia, 42, 201
Utah Colonization Fund, 130

Vocational training, 182, 183, 293 (*See* also Baron De Hirsch Trade School)
Volunteer service (*See* Chapter XVIII)

Wald, Lillian, 141, 274
Waldman, Morris D., 46, 155, 172, 174-176

Wanderlust, 61
War, privations of, 57
West Side Dispensary, 141
Widows' pensions, 159
Wiener, Cecile B., 362
Wife Desertion Bureau, 177 (*See* also Desertion)
Wise, Rabbi Stephen J., 366
Wolf, Simon, 109, 114
Wolfenstein, Dr. S., 162
Wolffert, Julius, 240
Woodbine, 130 sq.
Woodbine Land and Improvement Company, 132
Work day, apportionment of, 326
Workingmen's Circle Sanitarium, 149

Yalden, J. E. G., 183
Yiddish, 229 sq., 260
Young Men's Hebrew Association, 212 sq., 227

Zangwill, Israel, 38, 255
Zedakah, 17
Zepin, Rabbi George, 290
Zionists, 110

PATTERSON SMITH REPRINT SERIES IN
CRIMINOLOGY, LAW ENFORCEMENT, AND SOCIAL PROBLEMS

1. Lewis: *The Development of American Prisons and Prison Customs, 1776-1845*
2. Carpenter: *Reformatory Prison Discipline*
3. Brace: *The Dangerous Classes of New York*
4. Dix: *Remarks on Prisons and Prison Discipline in the United States*
5. Bruce et al: *The Workings of the Indeterminate-Sen'ence Law and the Parole System in Illinois*
6. Wickersham Commission: *Complete Reports, Including the Mooney-Billings Report.* 14 Vols.
7. Livingston: *Complete Works on Criminal Jurisprudence.* 2 Vols.
8. Cleveland Foundation: *Criminal Justice in Cleveland*
9. Illinois Association for Criminal Justice: *The Illinois Crime Survey*
10. Missouri Association for Criminal Justice: *The Missouri Crime Survey*
11. Aschaffenburg: *Crime and Its Repression*
12. Garofalo: *Criminology*
13. Gross: *Criminal Psychology*
14. Lombroso: *Crime, Its Causes and Remedies*
15. Saleilles: *The Individualization of Punishment*
16. Tarde: *Penal Philosophy*
17. McKelvey: *American Prisons*
18. Sanders: *Negro Child Welfare in North Carolina*
19. Pike: *A History of Crime in England.* 2 Vols.
20. Herring: *Welfare Work in Mill Villages*
21. Barnes: *The Evolution of Penology in Pennsylvania*
22. Puckett: *Folk Beliefs of the Southern Negro*
23. Fernald et al: *A Study of Women Delinquents in New York State*
24. Wines: *The State of the Prisons and of Child-Saving Institutions*
25. Raper: *The Tragedy of Lynching*
26. Thomas: *The Unadjusted Girl*
27. Jorns: *The Quakers as Pioneers in Social Work*
28. Owings: *Women Police*
29. Woolston: *Prostitution in the United States*
30. Flexner: *Prostitution in Europe*
31. Kelso: *The History of Public Poor Relief in Massachusetts: 1820-1920*
32. Spivak: *Georgia Nigger*
33. Earle: *Curious Punishments of Bygone Days*
34. Bonger: *Race and Crime*
35. Fishman: *Crucibles of Crime*
36. Brearley: *Homicide in the United States*
37. Graper: *American Police Administration*
38. Hichborn: *"The System"*
39. Steiner & Brown: *The North Carolina Chain Gang*
40. Cherrington: *The Evolution of Prohibition in the United States of America*
41. Colquhoun: *A Treatise on the Commerce and Police of the River Thames*
42. Colquhoun: *A Treatise on the Police of the Metropolis*
43. Abrahamsen: *Crime and the Human Mind*
44. Schneider: *The History of Public Welfare in New York State: 1609-1866*
45. Schneider & Deutsch: *The History of Public Welfare in New York State: 1867-1940*
46. Crapsey: *The Nether Side of New York*
47. Young: *Social Treatment in Probation and Delinquency*
48. Quinn: *Gambling and Gambling Devices*
49. McCord & McCord: *Origins of Crime*
50. Worthington & Topping: *Specialized Courts Dealing with Sex Delinquency*

PATTERSON SMITH REPRINT SERIES IN
CRIMINOLOGY, LAW ENFORCEMENT, AND SOCIAL PROBLEMS

51. Asbury: *Sucker's Progress*
52. Kneeland: *Commercialized Prostitution in New York City*
53. Fosdick: *American Police Systems*
54. Fosdick: *European Police Systems*
55. Shay: *Judge Lynch: His First Hundred Years*
56. Barnes: *The Repression of Crime*
57. Cable: *The Silent South*
58. Kammerer: *The Unmarried Mother*
59. Doshay: *The Boy Sex Offender and His Later Career*
60. Spaulding: *An Experimental Study of Psychopathic Delinquent Women*
61. Brockway: *Fifty Years of Prison Service*
62. Lawes: *Man's Judgment of Death*
63. Healy & Healy: *Pathological Lying, Accusation, and Swindling*
64. Smith: *The State Police*
65. Adams: *Interracial Marriage in Hawaii*
66. Halpern: *A Decade of Probation*
67. Tappan: *Delinquent Girls in Court*
68. Alexander & Healy: *Roots of Crime*
69. Healy & Bronner: *Delinquents and Criminals*
70. Cutler: *Lynch-Law*
71. Gillin: *Taming the Criminal*
72. Osborne: *Within Prison Walls*
73. Ashton: *The History of Gambling in England*
74. Whitlock: *On the Enforcement of Law in Cities*
75. Goldberg: *Child Offenders*
76. Cressey: *The Taxi-Dance Hall*
77. Riis: *The Battle with the Slum*
78. Larson et al: *Lying and Its Detection*
79. Comstock: *Frauds Exposed*
80. Carpenter: *Our Convicts.* 2 Vols. in 1
81. Horn: *Invisible Empire: The Story of the Ku Klux Klan, 1866-1871*
82. Faris et al: *Intelligent Philanthropy*
83. Robinson: *History and Organization of Criminal Statistics in the United States*
84. Reckless: *Vice in Chicago*
85. Healy: *The Individual Delinquent*
86. Bogen: *Jewish Philanthropy*
87. Clinard: *The Black Market: A Study of White Collar Crime*
88. Healy: *Mental Conflicts and Misconduct*
89. Citizens' Police Committee: *Chicago Police Problems*
90. Clay: *The Prison Chaplain*
91. Peirce: *A Half Century with Juvenile Delinquents*
92. Richmond: *Friendly Visiting Among the Poor*
93. Brasol: *Elements of Crime*
94. Strong: *Public Welfare Administration in Canada*
95. Beard: *Juvenile Probation*
96. Steinmetz: *The Gaming Table.* 2 Vols.
97. Crawford: *Report on the Penitentiaries of the United States*
98. Kuhlman: *A Guide to Material on Crime and Criminal Justice*
99. Culver: *Bibliography of Crime and Criminal Justice: 1927-1931*
100. Culver: *Bibliography of Crime and Criminal Justice: 1932-1937*